The Treaty of
Guadalupe Hidalgo

The Treaty of Guadalupe Hidalgo

A Legacy of Conflict

By
Richard Griswold del Castillo

University of Oklahoma Press : Norman

Library of Congress Cataloging-in-Publication Data

Griswold del Castillo, Richard.
  The Treaty of Guadalupe Hidalgo: a legacy of conflict/
by Richard Griswold del Castillo.—1st ed.
    p.   cm.
  Includes bibliographical references.
      1. United States—History—War with Mexico, 1845–
1848—Peace. 2. Mexico. Treaties, etc. United States, 1848
Feb. 2. I. Title.
  E408.G75   1990
  973.6'2—dc20   89-38642
  ISBN: 0–8061–2478–4

5   6   7   8   9   10   11   12   13   14   15   16   17

To Mom and Dad,
for the love and support that made this possible

Contents

Illustrations

Maps

Figures

Preface

Within the last few years Americans have become more aware of the importance of studying Mexico and its relationship to the United States. A number of thoughtful books have been written recently that analyze the ways in which Mexico's social and economic problems have affected this country.[1] Mexico has become ever more important to U.S. self-interest and national security as recent controversies over drug smuggling, immigration, foreign debt, oil, border violence, and problems in Central America have heightened national awareness about the importance of good relations with our closest Latin American neighbor. Yet, for the layperson, United States–Mexican relations remain veiled in mystery, partly because of a pervading and profound ignorance of Mexican history on the part of U.S. citizens, but also because the dynamics of the relationship between the two countries have remained the province of specialists. The outlines of this special relationship are revealed to us in the diplomatic and legal histories of both countries. As a shared inheritance, this record provides a common ground for establishing mutual trust and understanding.

This book is about the Treaty of Guadalupe Hidalgo, a document that ended the Mexican War (1846–1848), and that is the oldest treaty still in force between the two countries. This agreement, more than 140 years old, has been important in shaping U.S. domestic and international history. During the Mexican War, U.S. leaders assumed an attitude of moral superiority in their treaty negotiations, viewing the forcible incorporation of almost one-half of Mexico's national territory as an event foreordained by providence, fulfilling the Manifest Destiny of the United States to spread the benefits of democracy to the lesser peoples of the continent. With an arrogance born of superior military, economic, and industrial power, the United States virtually dictated the terms of settlement. The treaty established a pattern of inequality between the two countries, and this lopsided relationship has influenced Mexican-American relations ever since. The Treaty of Guadalupe Hidalgo looms larger in the history of Mexico than in that of the United States. Partially because of the loss of valuable territory, the end of the war in 1848 ensured that Mexico would remain an underdeveloped country well into the twentieth century. Mexican historians and politicians have interpreted for their nation the meaning of the events of 1848. Although their visions of the past have varied according to political philosophy and prevailing opinion, they have generally pointed to the treaty as a bitter lesson in U.S. expansionism. Interpretations of the provisions of the treaty have been important in disputes over international boundaries, water and mineral rights, and, most important, civil and property rights for the descendants of the Mexicans in the ceded territories.[2] Since 1848, Indians and Mexican Americans have struggled to achieve political equality within the United States. In this they have sought to take advantage of the promises made in the Treaty of Guadalupe Hidalgo.

This book analyzes how the treaty has been interpreted by U.S. courts, intellectuals and diplomats in the United States and Mexico, and Chicano activists. The Treaty of Guadalupe Hidalgo has been a rich source of controversy. Its provisions have led to some unforseen confrontations and difficulties between the two countries.

The aim of this book is to provide an overview that can make more understandable some of the complex historical and legal issues surrounding U.S.–Mexican relations and, at the same time, evaluate the way that the treaty has influenced the domestic history of the United States. This is the first book written in English that is devoted exclusively to analyzing the national and international dimensions of the Treaty of Guadalupe Hidalgo. There are excellent in-depth studies of the treaty negotiations in 1847 and 1848,[3] but much of the narrative and descriptive detail in these books is irrelevant to an understanding of the contemporary meaning of the treaty. The Treaty of Guadalupe Hidalgo is part of the common heritage of both Mexico and the United States, and it has had a surprising amount of influence on international issues.

Some of the subject matter I treat in this book, especially in the chapters on the negotiations of the treaty and the Gadsden Purchase, has been written about in greater depth by highly respected scholars. Chapters 5 through 9, however, present new information and arguments relative to the treaty and its interpretation since 1848. In developing these chapters, I was concerned with analyzing the themes most directly linked to the treaty and its interpretation. It would have been possible to expand the topics only touched on in this book by discussing almost all of the conflicts between Mexico and the United States, including clashes between the population of Mexican origin and Anglo-American institutions in the United States. This, I felt, would weaken the focus of the book, that is, the issues directly linked to the treaty and its interpretation.

I owe many people and institutions a debt of thanks and recognition for their assistance with this book. During the research phase of this project I was given a great deal of help by the library staff at San Diego State University, especially the Department of Government Publications; the Huntington Library; the Library of Congress; the National Archives; the Zimmerman Collection of the University of New Mexico; the Archivo de la Secretaría de Relaciones Exteriores in Mexico City; the Colegio de Mexico; the Biblioteca del Universidad Autonoma de Mexico; the Boalt Law School; the Bancroft Library; and the Law Library at the University of San Diego. I also appreciated advice regarding research matters, given freely by Martin Ridge, Senior Research Director at the Huntington Library; David J. Weber, Professor of History at Southern Methodist University; Arnoldo De Leon, Professor of History at Angelo State University; and Gilbert Cruz, formerly of the National Park Service. I received helpful comments of various drafts of chapters from Jorge Vargas, Director of the University of San Diego, Mexico-U.S. Law Institute; Denis Berge, Professor of History at San Diego State University; Josefina Zoriada Vásquez, Professor at El Colegio de Mexico; Armando Rendón, at the U.S. Census Office; Juan Ramón Garcia, Professor of History at the University of Arizona; and Barbara (Sasha) Tenenbaum, author of a very fine history of nineteenth-century finances in Mexico. Helpful advice also came from the members of the Wednesday night history discussion group at San Diego State University. I am especially grateful to John Drayton, of the University of Oklahoma Press, for his detailed editorial suggestions. My work in completing this book was made much easier by grants from the College of Arts and Letters at San Diego State University and especially by an academic exchange with the Colegio de Mexico arranged by the Institute for Regional Studies at San Diego State University in 1987. Finally I want to thank my family for their support and patience.

RICHARD GRISWOLD DEL CASTILLO

San Diego, California

The Treaty of
Guadalupe Hidalgo

CHAPTER I

Background Issues

The American invasion was a question of life and death for Mexico not only because it involved the seizure of its territory but also because Mexicans were reduced to the humiliating state of being strangers in their own land.

GENERAL JOSÉ MARIANO SALAS
IN FRANCISCO DE PAULA DE ARRANGOIZ,
MEXICO DESDE 1808 HASTA 1867

Mexico and the United States share one of the longest international borders in the world. The boundary line separating the two countries was established through centuries of diplomatic and armed conflict, and is an inheritance bequeathed to the New World by the European colonial powers of Spain, England, and France. In the nineteenth century, disputes over the exact location of the old dividing line separating Spanish and English America created many opportunities for people in the United States to move into the western and southern lands and ultimately to claim them for the United States.

Three major issues shaped relations between the United States and Mexico in the 1840s: American expansionist sentiment as reflected in the policies of President James K. Polk, domestic political struggles within Mexico and the United States, and the Texas boundary dispute.

AMERICAN EXPANSIONISM

The Mexican War (1846–1848) and the treaty that ended it were undertaken against the backdrop of Manifest Destiny, the body of ideas and sentiments by which English-speaking Americans justified territorial expansion into lands held, occupied, or claimed by Mexicans and Indians. Disparate groups, from rustic backwoodsmen to sophisticated New England poets, from northern abolitionists to southern slaveholders, fervently believed that God had ordained that U.S. citizens should populate and govern the vast expanse of land west of the Mississippi River.[1]

Expansionism was a pervasive idea in the U.S. culture of the time and was widely promoted in newspapers and political speeches. John O'Sullivan, editor of the *Democratic Review*, created the term "Manifest Destiny" and was a prime mover in shaping opinion of that era. O'Sullivan spoke of the American "destiny to overspread the whole North American continent with an immense democratic population." North Americans were the "pioneers of the continent," who would inevitably spread the benefits of democracy and freedom to the lesser peoples inhabiting the region.[2]

James Gordon Bennett of the *New York Herald*, another spokesman for Manifest Destiny, wrote that "the arms of the republic, it is clear to all men of discernment, must soon embrace the whole hemisphere, from the icy wilderness of the north to the most prolific regions of the smiling and prolific south."[3] Such optimistic predictions of expansion and growth were not limited to journalists but became the province of such nationally known intellectuals as Walt Whitman and Ralph Waldo Emerson and of politicians as diverse as the patrician John Quincy Adams and the populist Andrew Jackson.[4] Ultimately, the popularity of the ideology of Manifest Destiny led the U.S. Congress to a near-unanimous declaration of war against Mexico in May, 1846.

Despite an overwhelming sentiment in favor of the war, there was some opposition. A small group led by northern and southern members of the Whig party opposed the war primarily because they suspected it to be a plot to strengthen the position of slave owners. Over time, antiwar opposition grew and added to the pressures on President James K. Polk to conclude the war and accept a final treaty. Other opposition derived from several concerns. John C. Calhoun, a Democrat, opposed it in the Senate because he feared that the war would lead to increased division over the status of slavery in the territories. Other southerners opposed the war because they feared that the acquisition of a large nonwhite, nonslave (Mexican) population would have an undesirable effect on blacks, encouraging their aspirations for freedom.[5]

President Polk was the most important actor in the drama leading to the Mexican War and the negotiation of the Treaty of Guadalupe Hidalgo. Polk, a Democrat, believed fervently in the westward expansion of the United States, particularly in the acquisition of California.[6] His opponents reviled him as "Polk the Mendacious" and branded him as a proslavery warmonger who used the Mexican War as an opportunity to expand the slavocracy. Historians have been divided over his role in the war. Evidence has been marshaled to support the view that Polk conspired to declare war on Mexico to achieve his own expansionist objectives.[7] Other historians have concluded that Polk acted as a moderating force among the radical proponents of Manifest Destiny within his own party. They argue that he resisted extreme war pressures, but that a bellicose Mexican leadership and events beyond his control finally forced him into the conflict.[8]

Although controversy continues over Polk's responsibility for the Mexican War, there is no doubt that he played an important part in negotiating the peace. It was Polk who decided to send an official peace commissioner to join the army in Mexico; who decided to recall this commissioner once it appeared that the Mexicans were insincere in their negotiations; and who decided to recommend the final version of the treaty to the Senate even though it had been concluded by an unauthorized agent. National politics, particularly the Whig opposition to the war, influenced these decisions. Had there been no pressure on the president to end the costly war, the United States probably would have delayed negotiating a treaty and annexed more Mexican territory than it did.

POLITICS IN MEXICO

In Mexico, one factor in bringing on the war and influencing the treaty was the rise and fall of a war faction. Many Mexican military leaders welcomed war and played on their countrymen's pride to reject offers of peace. They had great confidence in their army's ability to resist and even defeat the Americans. Foreign observers rated the Mexican military highly. The London *Times*, for example, stated in 1845 that the Mexican armies "are superior to those of the United States." French and Spanish observers publicly commented on the superiority of the Mexican forces and geographic situation. The mountainous terrain, deserts and vast expanses, yellow fever in the lowlands, and the Mexican home-ground advantage would conspire to defeat the Americans. During the war, as the Mexican army met defeat after disastrous defeat, the war party's confidence and political credibility eroded. By 1848 it was possible for civilian leaders of the peace faction to negotiate a settlement.[9]

Party politics in Mexico played another role during the course of the war and final drafting of the peace treaty. The struggle between various groups produced chronic presidential instability that in turn made it almost impossible to negotiate a peaceful settlement with the United States. From the end of Mexico's War of Independence in 1821 until the Mexican War, every constitutionally elected president except one, Guadalupe Victoria, had been overthrown by a coup. The unsettled nature of Mexican politics, along with the internal division and distrust it engendered, helped bring on the war, prolong it, and, ironically, compel the leadership to accept a treaty that would end the fighting. Early in 1845, President José Joaquín Herrera, who feared that by seeming to be too conciliatory he would provoke a rebellion, rejected American overtures to negotiate the Texas dispute. This rejection later formed a key incident in Polk's justification for a declaration of war. Mariano Paredes y Arrillaga overthrew Herrera's government, and a faction headed by José Mariano Salas overthrew Paredes. All these changes of administration took place in the months before the American occupation of Mexico City. Prior to the declaration of war, even if the Mexican government had been able to establish a diplomatic dialogue with the United States, any agreement would probably have been renounced by the succeeding government. During the war there were two additional changes of government. General Antonio López de Santa Anna replaced the provisional government of Mariano Salas, and within a few months, following the fall of Mexico City to the Americans in December 1847, Santa Anna resigned the presidency in disgrace and was replaced by the Chief Justice of the Mexican Supreme Court, Manuel Peña y Peña. Competing factions hampered negotiations during the war by refusing to endorse the government's desire for peace or by working behind the scenes to sabotage peace initiatives. In the end some Mexican politicians supported the Treaty of Guadalupe Hidalgo hoping that the end of the war would reunify the country politically.

THE TEXAS BOUNDARY DISPUTE

The precipitating cause of the war, and the key stumbling block in the drafting of the treaty, was the annexation of Texas by the United States in 1845. There was a longstanding difference of opinion over the boundaries of that province. In 1836 the Texans won their independence and established an independent republic. For nine years they maintained that their new country included the territory north and east of the Rio Grande (see map 1). Mexico never recognized Texas claims to independence and territory, but that did not stop annexationists in the United States from pushing for acquisition. In particular, President John Tyler worked tirelessly to circumvent the many political obstacles to annexation. Finally, in March 1845, Congress passed a resolution of annexation, and along with Texas, the United States acquired the controversial claim to the Rio Grande boundary.

The boundary dispute had its origins in Spanish and British colonial rivalries. Imperial Spain claimed the Floridas, which included the present-day state of Louisiana and part of east Texas. When Spain ceded the Louisiana Territory to France in 1800, and when in turn France sold it to the United States in 1803, the exact boundaries separating the Louisiana Territory and Spanish Texas became blurred. The Adams-Onis Treaty was negotiated between the United States and Spain in 1819 to resolve this difficulty. Spain traded the Floridas to the United States in return for both recognition of a boundary line between Texas and Louisiana and monetary compensation (see

Map 1.   Boundaries Relevant to Border Disputes 1803-1846

Map 1. Boundaries Relevant to Border Disputes, 1803–1846. (Map by Bardy Anderson and Ann Brook)

map 1). Because of the wars of independence in Mexico, this treaty was not ratified by the Mexican Republic until 1831, five years before the Texas rebellion—a delay that, in the view of the proponents of Manifest Destiny in the United States, invalidated the Mexican claim to Texas.[10] Thus, one of the first treaties negotiated between the United States and newly independent Mexico was a treaty to demarcate the boundaries of Texas. In these complex discussions, which lasted from 1828 to 1831, the first

American minister to Mexico, Joel Poinsett, presented a draft treaty to the Mexicans. The United States demanded the cession of Texas and the expansion of its boundaries in exchange for cash payment. Mexico refused to agree to the cession, insisting on formal recognition of Mexico's claim to Texas. In 1829 and 1830 the Mexican Congress had difficulty assembling a quorum to ratify a revised boundary treaty, and the U.S. Senate made substantial revisions to its version of the document. This treaty of limits and boundaries was not ratified by both nations until 1831, after the Mexicans had secured the removal of Poinsett and the boundary treaty had been linked with a commercial treaty advantageous to the United States.

Despite the signing of the Treaty of Limits, in 1831, which recognized the sovereignty of Mexico over Texas, serious misunderstandings about the boundaries persisted. The boundaries remained unclear even after the Republic of Texas, formed in 1836, was annexed by the United States. As a result, when a skirmish between American and Mexican troops took place on the north bank of the Rio Grande, in 1846, the president of the United States claimed that the United States had been invaded. This assertion was based on a particular version of the history of the southern boundary of Texas, a version that had little basis in historical fact. In the Spanish period, the boundaries between the various provinces of New Spain had been inexact and the object of frequent conflict, especially during the last century of Spanish rule. In 1718, Spain recognized the Medina and San Antonio rivers as the boundary between Texas and Coahuila. Official maps in 1767 indicated that the Nueces River was the southern boundary of Texas. In the early 1800s, Texas included only the eastern part of the present state and was bounded on the south by the Nueces River.

During the early years of the Mexican Republic, Texas became a department of the state of Coahuila. Mexican land-grant maps drawn by Stephen F. Austin in 1829, 1833, and 1836 indicate that the Nueces River, not the Rio Grande, was the boundary between the department of Texas and the state of Coahuila.[11]

The U.S. claim to the Rio Grande as the boundary sprang from the expansionist ideas of a series of American presidents. Thomas Jefferson, James Madison, James Monroe, John Quincy Adams, and Andrew Jackson maintained that the Louisiana Purchase defined Texas as extending to the Rio Grande. The source of this assertion was a French claim to Texas following eighteenth-century boundary disputes with Spain. Based on this history, the expansionists of 1845 held that by annexing Texas, the U.S. government was simply reclaiming territory unwisely given to Mexico in 1831, when the Treaty of Limits was signed.[12]

Ambassador Poinsett first approached Mexico in 1827 to discuss the Rio Grande boundary. At that time, President Adams authorized him to offer Mexico 1 million dollars in exchange for U.S. sovereignty of Texas, with the Rio Grande as its southwestern boundary. The Mexican government rejected this proposal, but the next year Poinsett was back, this time with an offer of 5 million dollars in exchange for a Texas with a boundary located between the Nueces and the Rio Grande.[13]

Before the Texas Wars of Independence (1835–1836), the U.S. government proposals to purchase Texas claimed the Rio Grande as the legitimate boundary. Following this precedent, the Texans formally adopted the U.S. claim to the Rio Grande as a southwestern boundary for their republic in the Treaty of Velasco, which was signed by a defeated General Santa Anna on May 14, 1836. A secret article in that treaty (Article 4) stated that Texas territory would extend to the Rio Grande. Of course the Mexican congress never approved these new boundaries. When the United States annexed Texas in 1845, the boundaries of the new state were not specified but rather were made an item for future discussions with Mexico. In President Tyler's words, it was "a question purposely left open for the most friendly and pacific arrangements."[14] The Texans were unhappy that the U.S. resolution of annexation did not confirm their boundary on the Rio Grande. Subsequent actions by president Polk, however, served notice that the U.S. government supported the idea of the Rio Grande as the legitimate boundary.

At various times prior to the Mexican War, the Mexican government entered into negotiations over the independence of Texas. Some Mexican politicians realized that Texas could never be reconquered by Mexico and that the best thing for the country would be to turn this loss into the foundation for an alliance with European powers. Both Britain and France were working to oppose annexation by the United States and sought to support Mexico in settling the issue of Texas while that province was still an independent republic. Accordingly, in 1844, Mexico proposed to give up its claim to the territory between the Sabine and Nueces rivers. The proposal contained the proviso that the Republic of Texas pay an indemnity and that Britain and France assure that Texas would never exceed its boundaries. Mexico also asked Britain and France for aid in future boundary disputes with the United States.[15] Britain rejected this proposal as unworkable. In March, 1845, the Texas government proposed that Mexico agree to Texas independence in exchange for an understanding that Texas would not annex itself to any foreign power and that the issue of boundaries would be settled by arbitration. The whole agreement would be guaranteed by Britain.[16] This settlement collapsed, however, when the British were unable to assure Texas that they would support its claims to the Rio Grande.

Polk believed that because both Texas and Mexico had agreed to negotiate, the boundary could be settled peacefully after the annexation of Texas. To accomplish this he sent his emissary, John Slidell, to Mexico. In many ways Slidell's mission, like that of Poinsett before him, was a rehearsal for diplomacy during the Mexican War. The boundary proposals brought by Slidell later became those put forth by the American diplomat Nicholas Trist in the Treaty of Guadalupe Hidalgo. Through the Slidell mission, the president neatly packaged several decades of American territorial ambitions. Slidell was authorized to offer Mexico a series of settlements, each one worth a different amount of indemnity, depending on Mexico's willingness to concede territories. The basic proposal was that the United States would assume its own citizen's claims against Mexico in exchange for recognition of the Rio Grande as the southern boundary of Texas. (Several million dollars in damages and old debts were claimed by U.S. citizens who had been resident in Mexico during the early years of the Mexican republic.) If Mexico agreed to cede New Mexico, 5 million dollars would be paid; if Mexico ceded all territory to the Pacific coast, 25 million dollars would be paid. If in the cession of California and New Mexico (including Arizona) along the southern boundary of New Mexico, could not be agreed upon, Slidell was authorized to offer 20 million dollars for a boundary that would include the San Francisco Bay. As would be true during the discussions leading up to the 1848 treaty, the credentials or appointment papers of the American diplomat became an issue. The Mexican government, fearing adverse political reactions, refused to recognize Slidell as a regular diplomatic agent. They preferred that he be a "commissioner with full powers to adjust all questions in the dispute," meaning the dispute over the boundary. The semantic difference between a commissioner and an envoy seems a small one, but to the Mexicans it meant the difference between official recognition of the U.S. annexation of Texas and an agreement to negotiate the issue during a state of ruptured diplomatic relations and undeclared war.[17]

Having failed to settle the dispute through the offices of Slidell, Polk turned to military pressure to secure the U.S. claim to Texas. He ordered General Zachary Taylor to advance to the Rio Grande to "possess" the territory for the United States. It was not long before Mexican and U.S. troops exchanged shots and joined in battle, thereby giving President Polk his rationale for a declaration of war. Judging from the votes in the U.S. Congress, there was little disagreement over the correctness of the Texas boundaries: the House of Representatives voted 174 to 14 in favor, the Senate 40 to 2.

The general public believed in the moral justness of the nation's inexorable expansion westward. Like most wars, the war between Mexico and the United States grew out of two conflicting interpretations of history. The events that led to the war also led to a particular kind of peace treaty, one that would legitimize a long-standing presidential policy for the acquisition of California and other Mexican territories. By annexing Texas, the United States inherited a civil war between that state and the Mexican Federal Republic as well as a highly debatable claim to boundaries. The volatility of Mexican politics defeated moves to negotiate a settlement of the dispute.

CHAPTER 2

The War and Secret Diplomacy

*"The United States could have secured the peace by
ceasing to assail the Mexicans who were fighting only in
self-defense. . . . [T]he so much desired peace they were
resolved to secure by war . . . was nothing better than
barefaced robbery."*

HUBERT HOWE BANCROFT
THE HISTORY OF MEXICO, 1821–1861

Chou En-lai, the Chinese master strategist, is supposed
to have defined diplomacy as an extension of warfare.
The opposite has often been true as well. One of the char-
acteristics of modern warfare is that diplomatic negotiations often occur simultaneously with and as a part of the
armed conflict. We tend to think of peace negotiations as
taking place after the end of a war, but many times in our
own era peace discussions have coincided with armed
struggle. This is true, for example, of recent U.S. wars in
Korea and Vietnam. Today, peace or disarmament talks
between the Soviet Union and the United States lurch
forward during the sporadic brushfire wars between cli-
ent states of the two superpowers.

Modern policymakers tend to view warfare as part of a
bargaining process in the international arena. The actual
signing of the peace is the final striking of a bargain.[1] The

coordination of warfare and diplomacy has always been an important consideration for winners as well as losers. Each side has often used the threat of military escalation to gain concessions at the bargaining table. The weaker side negotiates in an effort to limit political damages arising from the conclusion of the war. During the Mexican War, U.S. policymakers used warfare as a conscious instrument of diplomacy to achieve their goals of territorial expansion and a favorable boundary settlement.[2]

The negotiation of the Treaty of Guadalupe Hidalgo can be interpreted within the context of bargaining theory. The need to end the war created a bargaining situation, defined as a condition "in which the ability of one participant to gain his ends is dependent to an important degree on choices or decisions that the other participant will make."[3] The Mexican War presented both sides with the necessity of bargaining. Both belligerents saw an agreement to end the conflict as increasingly profitable, but they reached an agreement only when both countries recognized that they could improve their position solely by striking a bargain.[4]

Four stages characterized the development of the peace settlement: secret diplomacy, secret and open negotiations, striking the bargain, and treaty ratification. Diplomacy, negotiation, and bargaining were directly related to military strategy during the war. The military situation influenced the kinds of proposals, concessions, and resolutions offered at each stage.

SECRET DIPLOMACY

The first stage in treaty negotiation lasted from the initial declaration of war on May 13, 1846, to the appointment of Nicholas Trist as the U.S. peace commissioner in April 1847. During those eleven months, President

Polk secretly sought out various political factions within Mexico in an effort to reach an agreement that would achieve his territorial objectives, namely recognition of the boundaries of Texas and the acquisition of California and New Mexico. The activities of special agents Moses Beach and Alexander MacKenzie and communications through the Mexican secret agent Alexander Atocha coincided with the rapid American conquest of New Mexico and California and the invasion and occupation of Veracruz Llave. During this initial negotiation there was a good deal of uncertainty on both sides regarding intentions, objectives, and acceptable proposals.

The military successes of the U.S. army made acquisition of New Mexico and California a fait accompli and consequently made the proposals to acquire these territories nonnegotiable, at least from the American point of view. The continued expense of the war created pressure on the administration to demand even more territory to "pay" the costs. During this first stage, Mexico had little to gain by entering into peace discussions. The United States, on the other hand, stood to gain a great deal. Consequently, the U.S. government was most aggressive in pursuing a negotiated settlement.

The first peace initiatives grew out of an amazing series of communications between Alexander J. Atocha (representing General Santa Anna, former president of Mexico then in exile in Havana), President Polk, and his Secretary of State, James Buchanan. Atocha was a Spanish-American citizen of the United States who had become a confidant of Santa Anna during a number of speculative enterprises in Mexico. On February 13 and 16, 1846, three months before the declaration of war, Atocha met with Polk to communicate a secret message from Santa Anna. Santa Anna proposed a settlement of boundaries that would give the United States the port of

San Francisco and northern California along with the Rio Grande as the southwestern boundary of Texas. This would be in exchange for 30 million dollars. Santa Anna, through Atocha, suggested that this offer would stand a better chance of being accepted by the Mexican people and their Congress if it appeared that the nation had been pressured into the agreement through threatening military maneuvers on the part of the United States. Accordingly, Santa Anna offered advice to the American president regarding the correct military strategy to be followed to create the proper environment for the acceptance of a peace treaty.[5] Polk and Buchanan discounted this overture, because the U.S. government was pursuing a settlement through the diplomacy of Slidell and had no desire to become enmeshed in a fantastic scheme that might compromise the mission of their diplomats.

A year later, on January 14, 1847, Atocha reappeared in Washington, D.C., again bearing confidential dispatches from Santa Anna. By now the United States and Mexico had been at war for seven months and Santa Anna was again president. In this second appearance, Atocha brought several letters written to him by Santa Anna and General Almont. These letters indicated that Santa Anna still desired an honorable peace and that Atocha was "in his confidence." At this time Atocha indicated that the Mexican government would accept the Rio Grande as the boundary, provided that the territory between the Rio Grande and the Nueces remained a no-man's land, a land barrier between the two countries. In addition, he suggested the sale of California. All this would be in exchange for a payment of 15 or 20 million dollars.[6] Atocha made no mention of the sale of the province of New Mexico.

In this January meeting, Atocha succeeded in convincing Polk that he was a genuine agent of Santa Anna. In discussions with Buchanan and the cabinet, the president drafted a letter to the Mexican minister of relations proposing a settlement that ignored the idea of no-man's land, included the purchase of New Mexico, and offered to send commissioners who would have full power to suspend hostilities in the event of an agreement.[7] Polk then dispatched Atocha to Vera Cruz with an offer to open negotiations based on Santa Anna's confidential communications.

By early 1847, President Polk's receptivity to secret and unorthodox peace proposals had been conditioned by the prospect of a long and bloody war. The U.S. Navy was blockading the port of Vera Cruz, and the army had yet to begin its campaign in central Mexico. Congress was increasingly reluctant to vote for war appropriations.[8] Moreover the Atocha affair was concurrent with two other initiatives undertaken by Polk's administration, those of Alexander Mackenzie and Moses Beach.

The Mackenzie mission was a product of Atocha's first conversations with Polk in February 1846. At that time the president had been intrigued by the idea of working through Santa Anna towards a peace settlement, so he dispatched Alexander Slidell Mackenzie (nephew of John Slidell) to Havana to confer with Santa Anna on July 7 and 8, 1846. Mackenzie brought with him the prior understanding that Santa Anna would negotiate a treaty based on the U.S. minimum offer, namely the acquisition of California and New Mexico and the Rio Grande as a boundary.[9] After three hours of conversation, Santa Anna agreed to help bring about this agreement in exchange for American help in his effort to regain presidential power. Again Santa Anna offered his advice to the American army regarding military strategy that would create conditions likely to reinstate him as president. General Taylor, he advised, should move to take Saltillo and San

Luis Potosí in order to put more pressure on the Paredes government. One month after these discussions, Santa Anna boarded a ship bound for Mexico. Mackenzie had arranged for the navy to let the former president pass through the American blockade, and Santa Anna entered Vera Cruz on August 16, 1846. Two weeks later the Paredes government fell, and soon thereafter Santa Anna emerged as president. Later Santa Anna would deny any dealings with the American government in this manner. Nevertheless, although the only remaining evidence is in Mackenzie's notes, the pattern of Santa Anna's behavior in this matter was consistent with his actions during the war. And his masterful manipulation of the American desire for peace and territory worked very much to his own political advantage.[10]

At the same time that Mackenzie was dealing with Santa Anna, Polk was offering to open negotiations with the Paredes government. He made this initiative in response to advise from John Black, the American consul in Mexico City, that such an offer would be well received. By August 30, when the U.S. dispatch arrived in Mexico, the Paredes government had fallen and was replaced by a pro-war faction headed by José Mariano Salas, Valentín Gómez Farías, and Crescencio Rejón. Santa Anna soon replaced that faction. Another secret peace feeler sent out from Washington involved Moses Y. Beach, publisher of the *New York Sun*, who had many highly placed friends in Mexican political circles. On November 21, 1846, because Beach indicated that a treaty might be concluded, President Polk commissioned him as a confidential agent to Mexico. The president instructed him to communicate with high officials in Mexico "only after you have clearly discovered that this may smoothe the way to peace," and cautioned, "Be upon your guard against their wily diplomacy, and take care they shall obtain no advantage over you."[11]

The Beach mission to Mexico was inspired by a bundle of captured dispatches purportedly drawn up by a group of clerics in the Catholic Church in Mexico and by unidentified high officials in the Mexican government. These documents urged an end to the war in order to prevent a monarchist coup. In their letters they proposed three points for a peace settlement: (1) the United States would occupy California above 26 degrees latitude and would protect the Mexican side of the frontier from Indian incursions; (2) the United States would assume all the claims of its citizens against Mexico and pay three million dollars in reparations; and (3) forts and public buildings would be restored and all forced loans renounced.[12] After authenticating these dispatches, Polk sent Beach to Mexico to investigate whether the proposals could be the basis of a peace settlement.

In one of the ironies of history, on April 14, 1847, Polk wrote in his diary his secret hope that Beach would misconstrue his limited instructions and end by making a treaty with Mexico. "Should he do so," the president wrote, "and it [the treaty] is a good one, I will waive his authority to make it, and submit it to the Senate for ratification. It will be a good joke if he will assume the authority and take the whole country by surprise and make a treaty."[13] This is exactly what the president's next peace envoy, Nicholas Trist, achieved nine months later, but the president regarded Trist's initiative as an affront to his authority.

Traveling to Mexico with his daughter to disguise his mission as a business and pleasure trip, Beach met with the pro-clerical factions in Mexico City and discussed peace terms along the lines of the initial proposal, adding that the United States would also act to protect clerical property in Mexico.

As Beach conversed with the pro-clerical groups, General Winfield Scott occupied the strategic port of Vera Cruz. Borrowing a page from Santa Anna, the pro-clerical factions stipulated that a peace treaty would be more compelling if the American army would prepare for a march on Mexico City. Unfortunately for Beach, his peace initiative fell victim to the political fortunes of Mexican party strife. President Gómez Farías, eager to discredit Santa Anna (whose secret envoy, Atocha, was in Mexico City working to present Polk's offer to open negotiations), published Beach's plan and claimed that it was Atocha's, thus making it appear that Santa Anna favored a Mexican Catholic–U.S. government alliance to end the war. A few days later Santa Anna's partisans overthrew Gómez Farías' government, but by then the U.S. peace initiatives had been tainted.

Thus, the two secret U.S. diplomatic initiatives, those of Beach and Atocha, nullified each other. On the other hand, this first stage of diplomacy did facilitate Santa Anna's return to power, and he seemed more disposed to a peace settlement than previous presidents. As Santa Anna resumed the presidency and as General Scott moved to take all of central Mexico, the U.S.–Mexican diplomatic front moved into a new stage.

WAR AND ARMISTICE

The opening sentence in Buchanan's letter to Nicholas Trist, dated April 15, 1847, emphasized that the changed military situation warranted new kinds of diplomacy. "Since the glorious victory at Buena Vista and the Capture of Vera Cruz [sic] and the Castle of San Juan d'ulloa

[sic] by American arms, it is deemed probable that the Mexican Government may be willing to conclude a Treaty of Peace with the United States."[14] After the failure of secret diplomacy, Polk was ready to commit his administration to more formal and open efforts to negotiate an acceptable end to the war.

Polk chose Nicholas P. Trist as commissioner to Mexico and gave him full powers to conclude a treaty. Trist, acting undersecretary of state and chief clerk, came highly recommended by Buchanan. As a southerner imbued with sentiments of Manifest Destiny, Trist seemed a perfect choice. He knew Spanish, was familiar with Latin American culture, and had acquired some diplomatic experience with the American consulate in Cuba during the 1830s. Most important, Trist was a Jacksonian Democrat who promised to be loyal to the president. Polk regarded the issue of loyalty as particularly important, because most U.S. generals fighting the Mexican War were Whigs, enemies of his administration. He needed some means of countering their glories and rising political fortunes. The Trist mission seemed to be perfect for this purpose.[15] Polk's choice of Trist proved to be of the utmost importance, because Trist's unique abilities and idiosyncratic character greatly influenced the final negotiation of the treaty.

In a cabinet meeting of April 13, 1847, Polk and his advisors drew up a draft treaty that Trist was to transmit to the Mexican government as a basis for negotiation. This project treaty along with detailed instructions significantly enlarged John Slidell's earlier demands. In the draft treaty, the United States demanded the cession of Alta and Baja California and New Mexico, the right of transit across the Gulf of Tehuantepec, and the Rio Grande as the southwestern border of Texas. In exchange the United States agreed to pay 15 million dollars and to assume up to 3 million dollars in claims of U.S. citizens against Mexico.[16]

The documents, the draft treaty, and the instructions were important in several respects. A comparison of the final treaty with the original demands reveals how much change there was in the American position during the negotiation. The accompanying instructions gave Trist a great deal of latitude in offering various amounts of money for different areas of territory. Buchanan instructed Trist not to regard Baja California or the rights of transit of the Gulf of Tehuantepec as sine qua non. If a treaty could be signed without these concessions, he should proceed. The absolute minimum, from which there would be no retreat, was the cession of upper California and New Mexico and recognition of the Rio Grande boundary.

Buchanan's instructions made reference to the possibility that the Mexican government might want special protection for its citizens, although "the rights of persons and property of the inhabitants . . . will be amply protected by the Constitution and laws of the U.S." If this was a concern, Trist was instructed to adapt the third article of the Louisiana Purchase treaty, which read: "The inhabitants of the territory over which the jurisdiction of the U.S. had been extended . . . shall be incorporated in the Union of the U.S. and admitted as soon as possible, according to the principles of the Federal Constitution, to the enjoyment of all rights, advantages and immunities of citizens of the United States: and in the meantime, they shall be maintained and protected in the full enjoyment of their liberty, property, and religion which they possess."[17]

Trist was further instructed that if Baja California could not be obtained through diplomacy, the land boundary between the United States and Mexico should be "directly opposite the division line between upper and lower California," which was assumed to be a line north of parallel 32 degrees and south of mission San Miguel (south of Tijuana, Mexico). Buchanan later modified the boundary line so that it would include the mission of San Miguel.[18]

Trist received the project treaty as a guide to negotiations, not as a finished document to be imposed on the defeated Mexicans. From the Mexican point of view, however, the treaty drafted in Washington differed little from the final version negotiated at Guadalupe Hidalgo. Mexico, still threatened by military occupation, was being coerced to cede a large part of its northern territory. It made small difference that the final version of the treaty was not word for word the same as the draft that Polk and Buchanan had dictated to Trist.

One of the reasons for sending Trist rather than Buchanan was that Trist was relatively obscure. His mission would be less conspicuous and have a better chance to achieve its objectives before the political opposition in the United States could sabotage the diplomacy.

The Whig reaction to Trist's mission proved this fear to be well grounded. Trist's mission was not secret for long. A news leak within the White House resulted in the publication of the major points of the draft treaty even before Trist had reached Mexico. The Whigs, opponents of the war and of Polk, engaged in a lengthy analysis of the proposed treaty, especially after learning of the Mexican government's response to it in November 1847. "A forced sale is a robbery," the Whigs wrote. "We are forcing Mexico to a sale of her territory as pleases ourselves." The very terminology of the proposed settlement, they asserted, admitted to the legitimacy of the Mexican claims to the Nueces River boundary, which made a lie of the president's claim that the United States had been invaded by Mexico.[19] In print the Whigs lamented the moral bankruptcy of the American proposals. Not only was it immoral to force a defeated nation to "sell" her territory, but this acquisition would be full of danger for the future. With prophetic and strident tones they forecast dire consequences resulting from acquisition of Mexican territory. "What then follows? An immense national debt—deep taxation—a steady augmentation and extension of the central power—corrupt election—the rapid waste of public funds—neglect of all improvements—moral fanaticism roused and irritated to action—civil war—and that last and greatest of evils, the disunion of the states."[20]

Trist landed in Vera Cruz on May 6, 1847. The secretary of state, Buchanan, had instructed him to give the American commander, General Winfield Scott, a letter from the U.S. government addressed to the Mexican minister of foreign relations. This letter introduced Trist as a special peace commissioner, and also stated that the United States refused to withdraw its troops prior to a negotiated peace.

Along with this official letter, Trist brought with him instructions from the government authorizing him to notify the American commander in Mexico to suspend hostilities should the Mexican government sign a treaty with the U.S.[21] This special power, along with Trist's somewhat conceited attitude regarding his status, rankled Scott, who correctly suspected that the president had sent Trist to undercut his authority. In a short time Scott and Trist were arguing, writing numerous letters to each other and to their respective departments at home. Scott refused to transmit Trist's letter of introduction to the Mexican government, and not until the early part of June did the official document finally arrive in the capital.

Despite ominous signs of impending disaster, the official rhetoric of the Mexican government continued to be bellicose. Secretly, however, various Mexican political factions put out peace feelers to Scott through the British diplomatic mission, while Santa Anna briefly considered resigning his command.[22] A dramatic move on the part of the Americans, which might have had positive results, was not, however, forthcoming from the bickering Scott and Trist.

A secret bribery initiative undertaken by Santa Anna finally drew Scott and Trist together. On June 24, 1847, members of the British diplomatic mission—Edward Thornton, attaché to the legation in Mexico; Mr. Mackintosh, consul in Puebla; and Mr. Turnbull, a local British merchant—visited Scott's headquarters to deliver the Mexican government's reply to Buchanan's message. Santa Anna, now president of Mexico suggested that a peace treaty was possible but only if the American army remained in Puebla. Any military advance on the capital, he said, would destroy the ability of the peace faction to work within the congress for a treaty. In addition, Turnbull confided, Santa Anna would be more able to appoint peace commissioners and sway the Mexican congressmen to endorse a peace settlement if ten thousand dollars were paid to the Mexican government and if an additional secret payment of one million dollars were made upon conclusion of a treaty of peace.[23]

Trist wanted to consider this offer seriously and coordinate it with the movement of the American army, but for several weeks he became too ill to conduct business. Scott, solicitous of Trist's health, now volunteered to share responsibility for negotiating with the Mexicans. When he became privy to diplomatic decisions, he supported the idea of offering the bribe money, even volunteering to help pay it out of his own contingency fund.

Accordingly, Scott, with Trist's agreement, paid Santa Anna's agents ten thousand dollars between July 12 and 14, 1847. A few days later, Scott called a meeting of his officers to seek their support for his actions. General Hitchcock, who was present at that meeting, remembered that "it was represented that Santa Anna was disposed to make a treaty, but could not do it without safety to himself and the presentations of his government without having the means at his disposal to 'satisfy' certain persons of influence who looked for a consideration of sort."[24] Of the five generals meeting with Scott, three voiced opposition to the project on moral grounds, saying that it was "no more than a plan to induce officials of a nation to betray their country through bribery."[25] Within a few days Trist received word through his secret agents that Santa Anna had been unsuccessful in convincing the members of congress to accept peace discussions. Now Santa Anna recommended that the U.S. army advance on Mexico City to pressure the politicians into acceding to peace. Amazingly, Scott decided to follow Santa Anna's advice and ordered the army to march on the capital. Before the march began, another message arrived from the cunning dictator suggesting that the Americans should "attack and capture the outer defenses of the city, halting upon the attainment of this objective to await the arrival of the Mexican commissioners to discuss terms for peace."[26]

Scott obliquely agreed to this arrangement. A few days later, after two decisive battles in which the Americans defeated the Mexican army near Mexico City, Scott ordered a halt to the American advance. Following Santa Anna's script Scott asked for an armistice to discuss peace.

In this most unusual turn of events, the commanding general of the Mexican Army and president of the Mexican Republic gave the American enemy advice on the military strategy to follow during the defeat of his own forces. It appeared that both Santa Anna and Scott so desired peace that they were willing to risk military losses and accusations of treason. Later, most Mexican historians held that Santa Anna was a traitor who orchestrated the final American conquest of Mexico. Americans who have studied this phase of the war concluded that Scott was at best naïve in halting his army's advance on the capital.[27] In any case, with the signing of the armistice agreement, peace negotiations entered a more formal phase. Not since the discussions surrounding the Treaty of Amity and Commerce in 1831 had Mexican and U.S. representatives met to formally discuss boundaries. It took a war and an American invasion to bring the Mexican government to the bargaining table.

CHAPTER 3

Striking the Bargain:
From Armistice to Treaty

It was a painful but not an ignominious agreement. The peace treaties between France and Germany in Frankfort and between Spain and the United States in Paris compel us, by comparison, to be less harsh in our judgment of this unavoidable act of our fathers. They did as much as they could; they accomplished as much as they should have.

JUSTO SIERRA
THE POLITICAL EVOLUTION OF THE MEXICAN PEOPLE

On August 22, 1847, with the U.S. army poised on the outskirts of Mexico City, General Santa Anna and General Scott agreed to an armistice. Representatives of the two countries then entered into a more formal, open stage of negotiation. With a good idea of its opponent's objectives, each side presented its own position at the conference table and engaged in diplomatic trade-offs, the importance of which was magnified by the possibility of a protracted, bloody conflict looming ahead.[1]

Following declaration of the armistice, Santa Anna appointed four men as peace commissioners to meet with Nicholas Trist. Two of them, Bernardo Couto and Miguel Atristain, were lawyers who later participated in the meetings that led to the final draft of the Treaty of Guadalupe Hidalgo. The other two were General Ignacio Mora y Villamil and former President José Joaquín Herrera. Trist met with the Mexican commissioners on August 27 and gave them a copy of the draft treaty. The Mexican commissioners already knew the American terms, however, and in addition they had intercepted notes from Secretary of State Buchanan instructing Trist not to regard Baja California as a sine qua non. As a result, the Mexican diplomats steadfastly refused to agree to its cession. Some historians have blamed Trist for the loss of Baja California in later negotiations, but clearly the fault lay in the failure of American security.[2]

The Mexican foreign minister, José Ramón Pacheco, sent uncompromising instructions to his delegates. They could agree to give up claim to Texas, but only as far as the Nueces River. The Mexican government would not give up California or New Mexico. In addition, the United States would have to pay for settlement of the Texas boundary by releasing the Mexican government from the claims against it by American citizens and by paying an additional amount. When the commissioners first learned of these demands they threatened to resign, arguing that "it is impossible for us to take charge of the negotiations upon said basis and instructions." They correctly felt that if they were to present these terms to Trist, the armistice would come to an end. Rather than have his diplomats resign, Santa Anna modified the instructions, telling the commissioners that they were to use these terms only as a guide.[3]

Some historians have cited the original Mexican position as proof that Santa Anna was not truly interested in peace but was merely using the armistice to buy time to prepare for the defense of the capital. By comparison with diplomatic bargaining conducted under similar conditions elsewhere in the world, the fact that the Mexican demands (like those of the United States) were extreme was to be expected. Because each belligerent expected to have to make concessions, either side would have been foolish to begin with its minimum demand.[4]

Establishing Santa Anna's motives for entering into the armistice is crucial to understanding the diplomatic talks. In a confidential interview with the Spanish minister to Mexico a month before the armistice, Santa Anna reportedly was eager to end the war so as to consolidate his dictatorship. At the same time, he admitted to the Spanish minister that Alta California was expendable because "we cannot populate or defend it," but that Mexico would never agree to the Rio Grande as a boundary. Santa Anna considered a land buffer between the two republics to be absolutely essential. This idea of a buffer zone along the frontier came from the Spanish era, when officials viewed the northern territories as a source of invasion and danger to the more populous central core.[5]

Trist was convinced that Santa Anna genuinely desired peace. After the end of the armistice, Trist wrote of Santa Anna, "I am perfectly convinced that no man was ever more sincere in anything, than he was, in his wish to make peace." Trist maintained that Santa Anna had "allowed himself to be carried along by a flood of circumstance" and that he had been forced into rejecting a peace settlement by the war party, especially by General Tornel and Foreign Minister José Ramón Pacheco.[6]

Santa Anna was indeed in a difficult situation as both General of the Army and President of Mexico. During the armistice he had to prepare for the worst possibilities and maintain the army's morale while conducting peace negotiations, the results of which promised to destroy his political future. The Mexican press frequently asserted that whoever signed a treaty with the Americans would be forever branded a traitor; the Mexican Congress had passed legislation to that effect.

The day before the armistice became official, Santa

Anna explained his dual purpose in entering into the discussions: "to give my troops rest, re-establish morale," and "strengthen the justice of our cause by listening to the propositions of the United States; because, to speak frankly, our obstinancy in refusing . . . placed them in the right in continuing the war."[7]

During the armistice, undisciplined Mexican troops and civilian mobs violated the agreement on a number of occasions. This did little to improve the prospects for peace and gave support to those who doubted the Mexican government's sincerity. The negotiations began in earnest on September 1, 1847, and lasted several days. The results of the wide-ranging discussions were a frank exchange of views and, finally, a tentative agreement. The United States would annex Alta California and New Mexico, and in exchange Mexico would retain the Nueces River as a boundary. The agreement provided that the United States would pay 30 million dollars in exchange for a boundary that would run up the Nueces River to a point north of El Paso del Norte (today Ciudad Juárez), along the southern boundary of New Mexico, down the Gila and Colorado rivers to 33 degrees north latitude, then along this latitude to the Pacific. This boundary enabled Mexico to retain the port of San Diego. By agreeing to the Nueces boundary, however, the United States would tacitly be admitting responsibility for starting the war, because the first battles were south of this river.

The fate of this initial agreement reached by Trist and the Mexican commissioners revealed an essential truth about bilateral diplomacy: that any settlement is really three agreements, "one across the table and one on each side of the table."[8] Even though the negotiators had agreed, they still had to secure the compliance of their respective governments. As it turned out, both Polk and Santa Anna rejected this settlement. Trist agreed to submit the proposal to his government for their approval. The agreement violated the explicit terms of Polk's instructions, that a boundary north of the Rio Grande would be unacceptable. Actually Trist never had a chance to submit the proposal; before he could do so Santa Anna rejected it.

On September 5, the Mexican commissioners returned to the table with their counter offer, which Trist interpreted as a rejection of the basic agreement. Santa Anna's new proposal was for the cession of Alta California north of 37 degrees latitude, giving the United States San Francisco but not Monterey Bay. He refused to consider the annexation of New Mexico, arguing that the Mexican population of that region had expressed no desire to be a part of the United States. Texas would be ceded, but only to the Nueces River. The whole agreement would be guaranteed by Great Britain.[9] Santa Anna argued that because the war had been brought about by the illegal American annexation of Texas, the United States could be given this territory only if Mexico were adequately indemnified and hostilities ended. This counterproposal was essentially what Santa Anna had been forced to modify late in August to keep his commissioners from resigning. With some justification, Trist considered the general's counterproposal evidence of bad faith. Trist's formal reply to the Mexican offer was that Mexico had been the aggressor in the war, that Texas had chosen to join the United States by its own free will, that the role of the United States in the war was one of self-defense, and that as a result, the United States must break off negotiations. The term of the armistice expired, and neither the Mexican nor the American officials asked for a renewal.

The two-week period of peace talks produced a negotiated settlement that was rather easy for the commissioners to conclude. From a political standpoint, however, neither Santa Anna nor Polk could afford to endorse the territorial provisions of the armistice agreement. Polk never received a formal agreement from Trist, but undoubtedly he would have rejected it; in fact, when he learned of his minister's willingness to submit such a proposal, it added to his desire to recall Trist. The armistice negotiations effectively clarified the minimum demands of the United States. When negotiations resumed two months later, neither the rights of transit across Tehuantepec nor the annexation of Baja California were issues for discussion. From Trist's point of view, the armistice talks showed that, given a less intransigent Mexican government, a settlement could easily be reached. All that was lacking was the proper motivation for the Mexican government to cede the territory the United States wanted.

For the Mexican government, the armistice talks afforded an opportunity to present arguments and language that would eventually appear in the final treaty. The discussions resulted in a lengthy published letter presenting the Mexican case for continuing the war.[10] Written by the governor of Jalisco, Mariano Otero, the letter argued against accepting a treaty and proposed that congress pass a law making it illegal for the government to discuss peace proposals that could lead to the alienation of national territory. The arguments developed in this letter later became part of the debate surrounding the ratification of the Treaty of Guadalupe Hidalgo. Ultimately, however, the tone of this "Casa de Alfaro" letter convinced Polk to conclude that Trist's presence was "encouraging the illusive hopes and false impressions of the Mexicans" and that he should be recalled until the Mexican government was more amenable to American demands.[11]

The final stage in the negotiations lasted from the end of the armistice, on September 7, 1847, to February 2, 1848,when the final draft of the Treaty of Guadalupe Hidalgo was signed. The United States applied maximum military pressure to force the Mexican government to reevaluate their position. A day after Scott's formal announcement that the armistice was ended, the American army advanced on Mexico City and fought the bloodiest battle of the war at Molino del Rey. On September 13 they captured Chapultepec Castle and entered the city. Santa Anna fled with his army and resigned the presidency. On September 14 the city surrendered.

At this point the ad interim presidency, as provided in Mexico's 1824 Constitution, devolved upon Manuel de la Peña y Peña, the presiding justice of the Supreme Court. He reestablished the seat of the national government at Querétaro, about one hundred miles north of Mexico City where, for about a month, the new government wrestled with various factions. Within the peace faction, the foreign minister, Luis de la Rosa fought with Luis G. Cuevas. Opposed to them both and in favor of continuing the war were Gómez Farías, leader of the liberal faction known as the Puros, and the more moderate Mariano Otero.

In the meantime Trist sent a note to Peña y Peña offering to reopen negotiations. The Mexican president had difficulty in assembling a congressional quorum but finally the congress assembled to elect a new president, General Pedro María Anaya, who appointed Peña y Peña minister of relations, along with three peace commissioners, Luis G. Cuevas, Bernardo Couto, and Miguel Atristain.[12]

By the time this had been arranged and it appeared that the peace talks were about to begin anew, Trist received a note (on November 16, 1847) from Buchanan instructing him to break off all diplomatic talks and return to Washington. Trist immediately sent word to the Mexican government through the British legation, informing them that he had been recalled and that "if the Mexican government would immediately make some proposition which he could take to Washington . . . he would defer the official announcement of his recall for a few days."[13] Peña y Peña replied that his government bound Trist to his original (October 20, 1847) offer to open negotiations and that a change in his status did not affect the contractual relationship that had been created by a positive Mexican response to this offer. A number of influential people in Mexico attempted to persuade Trist to disregard his recall and stay. Bernardo Couto, one of the Mexican peace commissioners, urged him to persevere, and Scott spoke strongly in favor of Trist's continuing his mission despite his lack of credentials. Nevertheless, on November 24, Trist officially notified the Mexican government of his recall and he continued preparations to leave the capital.

Between November 24 and December 4, Trist changed his mind about obeying his recall order. Later he explained that James L. Freaner, a correspondent for the *New Orleans Delta*, had convinced him to stay on. Freaner had become Trist's valued friend and confidant during the long months of waiting for a renewal of diplomatic discussions. Freaner visited Trist about noon on December 4 and argued that Trist's departure would damage the chances for peace and prolong the war. After a long meeting, the minister announced to the Mexican government his willingness to stay and continue the negotiations.[14] Then, on December 6, he wrote a long, sixty-five-page message to Secretary of State Buchanan explaining his decision. He argued that failure to seize the present opportunity might make it impossible to draft a treaty. The Puro (the pro-war faction) wanted the war to continue in order to use the American occupation to bring about economic and political reforms. A delay in peace would give them a chance to take over the government. In any case, Trist reasoned in his message to Buchanan, the boundaries the Mexicans were prepared to discuss were the minimum they were likely to accept.

Trist's decision not to obey his recall orders, along with the insolent tone of his dispatch (for he assumed that the president did not truly want peace), infuriated Polk and made Trist an outlaw within his administration. In his diary Polk termed Trist's letter "arrogant, imprudent, and very insulting to his government, and even personally offensive to the President." For unknown reasons, however, Polk took no action to terminate Trist's activities for more than a month after learning of his ambassador's insubordination. Polk did not comment publicly on Trist's dealings with the Mexican government. Although officially recalled, Trist continued to send Buchanan dispatches describing the various stages of his diplomacy.[15]

Nicholas Trist's precarious diplomatic status eventually worked to his advantage. He could now more easily and with greater credibility threaten to quit the bargaining table if the Mexican commissioners did not agree to the American terms. From the Mexican point of view, it was easier to explain their negotiations with the Americans by citing Trist's unofficial status.

Before Trist agreed to resume discussions, he asked for and received from the Mexican government assurances that the minimum territorial demands of the United States would be met. This concession was reflected in President Anaya's instructions to his commissioners. Gone were the demands for the Nueces River as a boundary and for the retention of New Mexico and Alta California.[16] The boundary proposed by President Anaya was eventually that adopted by the Treaty of Guadalupe Hidalgo.

One point of contention, however, was the location of the western boundary between the junction of the Gila and Colorado rivers and the Pacific Ocean. The Mexican Commissioners had instructions to work for a boundary that would be two leagues north of the port of San Diego, so that this valuable port would remain part of Mexico. After a delay caused by another change in the Mexican political leadership that brought Peña y Peña to power as president, the final negotiations began on January 2, 1848, and lasted most of the month. With the larger issues of the Rio Grande boundary and the cession of Alta California and New Mexico settled, the discussions first focused on the San Diego issue. Trist had unequivocal instructions from Buchanan: San Diego was to be included in the cession because it was "for every commercial purpose of nearly equal importance to us with that of San Francisco."[17]

The Mexican commissioners, following the instructions of their government, sought to prove that San Diego had always been part of Lower California, citing as evidence a map in Mofras' *Atlas*. Lt. Robert E. Lee, Edward Thornton (the British consul), and General Percifer F. Smith assisted Trist by doing historical research to provide evidence showing that San Diego had always been part of the Alta California and, in fact, had briefly been that province's capital. The Mexican commissioners had to agree with the evidence and settled with Trist that the western terminus of the international boundary would be one marine league south of the southernmost point of the bay of San Diego.[18]

In exchange for the major Mexican concession of the port of San Diego, the Rio Grande boundary, and the acquisition of New Mexico, Trist conceded that the southern boundary of New Mexico would be the Gila River, not the 32d parallel, and that the United States would abandon its demand for the rights of transit across the Isthmus of Tehuantapec. According to Trist's own account of the negotiations, the fate of the inhabitants of the ceded territory "constituted a subject upon which it was all important that the Treaty should be guarded at all points."[19] They spent a good deal of time on various drafts of Articles VIII and IX, which dealt with the property rights of Mexican citizens and American citizenship for the Mexican citizens. The Mexican commissioners succeeded in amplifying the texts of the two articles. They also introduced Article XI, which provided that the United States would be responsible for controlling hostile Indian incursions originating from its side of the border. (This article, which proved to be a source of irritation between the two nations, was negated by the Gadsden Treaty of 1854).

On his own initiative, Trist reduced the amount of the indemnity from 20 to 15 million dollars, judging that this would gain acceptance for the treaty among those who felt that the United States had already paid enough in blood and treasure.

After a full discussion of all these issues, Trist drew up an English-language draft of the treaty. Then Cuevas translated it into Spanish, preserving the idiom and thought rather than the literal meaning.[20]

The Mexican government considered the treaty a last chance to "salvage the nation." A number of antigovernment rebellions had broken out; Justo Sierra's government in Yucatán had proclaimed its independence, and the national government desperately needed funds to pay the army. The British *agiotistas* (money brokers) who had loaned the Mexican government large sums, were pressuring the Mexican officials to terminate the war and begin paying off the country's debts.[21] Barbara Tenenbaum has suggested that the British money interests in Mexico played a key role in pressuring the Mexican government to sign a treaty. The British Minister Percy Doyle asked Trist to stay longer in Mexico while he worked to persuade the Mexican government to sign. Doyle then promised the Mexican government at Querétaro that the U.S. troops would protect them against revolts after the treaty was signed (he had no authority to

Figure 1. La Villa de Guadalupe, 1848. The Treaty of Guadalupe Hidalgo was so named because it was signed in the Villa de Guadalupe. The villa was named for the shrine located there dedicated to the Virgen de Guadalupe, the patron saint of Mexico. This rare 1848 photo of the Villa de Guadalupe shows Colegiata de Guadalupe along with several buildings. The one on the extreme left has above it the partial words "DE PAZ." This was probably the building where the treaty was signed. It is no longer standing. (Photograph Courtesy Museo de la Basilica de Guadalupe)

make this promise). Additionally he reminded them of their financial obligation to foreign countries that would be met if they signed the treaty.[22]

Finally, on February 2, 1848, the Mexican government yielded to financial and political pressures. The commissioners met Trist in the Villa of Guadalupe Hidalgo (see figure 1) across from the shrine of the patron saint of Mexico, the Virgen de Guadalupe. They signed the treaty and then celebrated a mass together at the basilica.

The signing of the treaty was only the beginning of a process. It still had to be ratified by the congresses of both United States and Mexico. No one could foresee how the Polk administration would receive a treaty negotiated by an unofficial agent; nor could they know the twists and turns of the Mexican political scene for the next few months. The Treaty of Guadalupe Hidalgo marked the end of international diplomacy and the beginning of domestic political debate.

CHAPTER 4

Finalizing the Treaty, 1848–1854

*We remain as free, after accepting the treaty, to look to
our own interests and to hold to a purely Mexican policy,
as we were the moment we became independent. The
loss we have sustained in this adjustment of peace was
necessary and inevitable.*

REPORT TO THE SUPREME GOVERNMENT
OF THE COMMISSIONERS WHO SIGNED THE
TREATY OF PEACE WITH THE UNITED STATES,
IN *SIGLO XIX*, JUNE 2, 1848

The final stage in the making of the Treaty of Guadalupe
Hidalgo lasted from the signing of the treaty on February
2, 1848, to the exchange of ratifications on May 30, 1848.
During this period both Mexican and U.S. statesmen de-
liberated over the articles in the treaty. The U.S. Congress made several significant changes that the Mexican
government accepted only after a protocol was drafted. In
its final form the Treaty of Guadalupe Hidalgo was still
an imperfect document. Ambiguities and errors in the
treaty led to boundary disputes, a near renewal of warfare, and the drafting of another treaty, in 1853, that
ceded even more territory to the United States.

U.S. RATIFICATION

An immediate consequence of the signing of the treaty
on February 2, 1848, was to initiate a debate in Washing-

ton, D.C., over the desirability of ratification. President Polk, after a long consultation with his cabinet on Sunday and Monday, February 20 and 21, decided to accept the treaty and to ask Congress to ratify it. This was a decision based primarily on his appraisal of the likelihood of continued congressional support for the war. Polk's view was that Congress would probably reject requests for further war appropriations and that this would lead to an even less favorable treaty.[1] In his message to Congress he recommended not only ratification but also the deletion of Article X, which dealt with land grants (see appendix 1) and a secret article relating to the extension of the period for ratification.

Article X was an explicit statement protecting Mexican land grants, particularly those in Texas. Polk objected to the provision on the grounds that it would revive old land grants and throw into question the grants made by the Texas government since their declaration of independence in 1836. Further, Polk argued, "public lands within the limits of Texas belong to that state, and this government has no power to dispose of them, or to change the conditions of grants already made."[2]

Even with the president's endorsement, when the treaty came before the Senate, it was not assured of passage. Secretary of State Buchanan and Secretary of the Treasury Walker openly opposed it because it would not gain enough territory for the Republic. The opposition party, the Whigs, were against the treaty for the opposite reason: It would annex too much territory, which eventually would increase the slavocracy's power in Congress. Upon a motion by Sam Houston the Senate voted to conduct its deliberations in secret and as a result there are no exact records of the debate.[3]

One roadblock to a speedy passage of the treaty was the possibility that the Senate Foreign Relations Committee, which had to issue its report prior to the debate, might recommend rejection of the document on the basis that Nicholas Trist had been an unauthorized agent. Only Polk's personal intervention with the committee chair, Ambrose H. Sevier, resulted in a noncommittal rather than a negative report.

Finally, on February 28, the Senate met in executive session. For eleven days the various factions traded arguments. The Whigs led by Daniel Webster, who feared a growth of the southern section and slavery, opposed the treaty. Some northern Democrats rejected the treaty because they were morally against the war. Some opposed it because they were political rivals of the president. Others like Sam Houston and Jefferson Davis did not want the treaty because it did not annex more of the Mexican territories; Houston favored retaining the territory as far south as the state of Vera Cruz while Davis wanted to annex most of the northern Mexican states.

The treaty remained largely intact because of each faction's opposition to the proposals of the others. Motions to modify, to either expand or retract, the boundary were defeated. The Senate defeated an attempt to insert the language of the Wilmot Proviso, restricting slavery in the new territories. Article X was stricken as recommended by the President; language in Article IX was changed by substituting language from the Louisiana and Florida treaties; Article XI was changed to allow the United States to sell arms and ammunition to Indians in its territories; and the secret article lengthening the time allowed for ratification was omitted. The Senate made a few other minor changes that did not affect the substance of the treaty. During the debate, President Polk exerted his influence on a number of senators by personal visits and pledges of support. Just before the final vote, a powerful opponent of the treaty, former President John

Quincy Adams, died. This removed a major rallying point for the opposition, and the mourning period that followed delayed the Senate debate long enough for the senators to assess the mood of public opinion, which was strongly in favor of the treaty and an end to the war.

On March 10, 1848, the Senate voted to ratify the modified version by a vote of 38 to 14, four more than the required two-thirds majority. The vote followed sectional rather than party lines, with the majority of northerners opposing.[4]

MEXICAN RATIFICATION

It now remained for Mexico to ratify the treaty. Buchanan attempted to gain Mexican acceptance by writing a letter of explanation to the Mexican minister of foreign relations, Luis de la Rosa. Buchanan argued that changes in Article IX dealing with the rights of citizenship were primarily the result of the Senate's wish not to violate precedents established in treaties negotiated with France and Spain. Article IX in its original form forcefully maintained the civil and property rights of the former Mexican citizens (see appendix 1). The key portion of that article originally read:

> The Mexicans who, in the territories aforesaid, shall not preserve the character of citizens of the Mexican Republic, conformably with what is stipulated in the preceding Article, shall be incorporated into the Union of the United States as soon as possible. . . . In the meantime, they shall be maintained and protected in the enjoyment of their liberty, their property, and the civil rights now vested in them according to the Mexican laws. With respect to political rights, their condition shall be on an equality with that of the inhabitants of the other territories of the United States.[5]

The U.S. Senate struck this language from the treaty and replaced it with a more general and ambiguous statement:

> [Mexicans not choosing to remain citizens of Mexico] shall be incorporated into the Union of the United States and be admitted, at the proper time (to be judged of by the Congress of the United States) to the enjoyment of all the rights of citizens of the United States according to the principles of the Constitution; and in the meantime shall be maintained and protected in the free enjoyment of their liberty and property, and secured in the free exercise of their religion without restriction.[6]

Buchanan maintained that the Senate amendment of the original was justified because in Florida and Louisiana, "no complaint has ever been made by the original or other inhabitants that their civil or religious rights have not been amply protected."[7] In this he chose to ignore the litigious territorial history of Louisiana where there had been numerous public complaints and lawsuits by the native French against the American administration of New Orleans in the early years.[8] Buchanan's overestimation of the benefits of protection afforded ethnic minorities under the Constitution extended to his rationale for the deletion of Article X from the treaty. In its original form, Article X had read:

> All grants of land made by the Mexican government or by the competent authorities, in territories previously appertaining to Mexico . . . shall be respected as valid, to the same extent if said territories had remained within the limits of Mexico. But the grantees of lands in Texas . . . [who] may have been prevented from fulfilling all the conditions of their grants, shall be under the obligation to fulfill the said conditions within the periods limited in the same respec-

tively; such periods to be now counted from the date of the exchange of ratifications.[9]

This article struck to the heart of a question that would be the basis for hundreds of lawsuits and many instances of injustice against the former Mexican land holders. The treaty makers knew well that most of the Mexican citizens occupying land grants in the ceded territories did not have perfect title to their lands and that the majority were in the process of fulfilling the requirements of Mexican law. Frequent changes in political administrations, the notorious slowness of the Mexican bureaucracy, and many individual circumstances had made it difficult for Mexican landholders to obtain clear title in an expedient way. Article X would have allowed them to complete the process under an American administration. The article specifically recognized the unique condition of the Mexican land-grant claimants in Texas, most of whom had been dispossessed of their lands by Anglo Texans following Texas Independence. The article would allow them to resurrect their claims and fulfill the conditions of Mexican law.[10]

In his letter to the Mexican minister, Buchanan said that Article X was so outrageous that if it were a part of the treaty "it would be a mere nullity" and that "the Judges of our courts would be compelled to disregard it." He went on in prolix fashion: "It is to our glory that no human power exists in this country which can deprive the individual of his property without his consent and transfer it to another. If the grantees of lands in Texas, under the Mexican government, possess valid titles, they can maintain their claims before our courts of justice."[11] The language of Article X applied to New Mexico and California as well. For the next five decades the territorial, state, and supreme courts would be occupied with sorting out "perfect" and "imperfect" land grants and dispossessing those who occupied the land in 1848. The absence of specific treaty protections for the holder of unperfected grants threw them on the mercy of the American courts. In 1848 Buchanan had an unbridled optimism about the ability of the judicial system to dispense justice; subsequent decisions, however, created a heritage of ill will between Mexican settlers and Anglo immigrants.

Realizing that these amendments and deletions might prevent the Mexican Congress from ratifying the treaty, President Polk sent with the modified document two commissioners to explain the changes and to accept the Mexican ratification on the spot. Senator Ambrose Sevier, chair of the Senate Foreign Relations Committee, and Nathan Clifford, the attorney general, arrived in Mexico in mid-April, and on May 3, 1848, the Mexican Congress convened to debate the modified version of the treaty.

In the period following the signing of the treaty, a vocal opposition formed. Before the congressional debates, the opponents of the treaty, led by Manuel Crescencio Rejón, published their arguments against ratification and stimulated debate over whether to continue the war. Rejón, a liberal from Yucatán, had helped draft the 1824 constitution and had served as minister of relations under Herrera and Santa Anna. Rejón believed that Mexico could win a protracted guerrilla war. Other liberals such as Melchor Ocampo and Benito Juárez, shared this view and opposed the Treaty of Guadalupe Hidalgo.

Rejón's opposition was published in an 1848 broadside entitled "Observations on the Treaty of Guadalupe Hidalgo."[12] His argument against the treaty was contained in fifteen closely reasoned juridical sections of this treatise. Rejón believed that the treaty would mean the inevitable economic subordination of Mexico by the United

States. He predicted that the new boundary, by bringing American commerce closer to the heartland of Mexico, would lead the Americanization of Mexico. He said, "We will never be able to compete in our own markets with the North American imports. . . . The treaty is our sentence of death."[13] Rejón criticized those who thought that the Mexican citizens in the ceded territories would be protected. He believed that American racism would prevent their being treated justly: "The North Americans hate us, their orators deprecate us even in speeches in which they recognize the justice of our cause, and they consider us unable to form a single nation or society with them." For Rejón the treaty would only delay "the absolute loss of our political existence as a republic."[14]

The juridical arguments Rejón advanced were that the treaty violated Mexican laws because it had been drafted clandestinely without input from Congress or the states. There had been no open discussion of the treaty prior to the debates over ratification. The treaty had not been published, and the signing of the treaty violated the constitution. In a word, Rejón argued that the government had exceeded its authority in agreeing to alienate its national territory. The Mexican government also had violated international law and precedent.[15] Although the government had argued that the territory being ceded was worthless, Rejón placed a high value on the lands, especially California. In his argument he called California "our priceless flower" and "our inestimable jewel."[16] By coincidence gold had been discovered a few weeks before Rejón wrote these words, but neither he nor the rest of the world would learn of it until the midsummer of 1848.[17]

In reponse to Rejón's arguments, Bernardo Couto, one of the original commissioners, published the commissioners arguments in favor of the treaty. The recurring theme in the writings of treaty advocates was that, by ending the war, the treaty had saved Mexico from possible obliteration as a nation. If the war had continued, they argued, all of Mexico probably would have been annexed by the United States. The negotiators wrote: "The treaty not only prevents any increase of our losses by a continuation of the war, but recovers the greater part of that which was subjected to the arms of the conquerors; it may be more properly called a treaty of recovery rather than one of alienation."[18]

Regarding the territory and people being lost, the commissioners adopted a stoic attitude: "It can hardly be said that we lose any power, since that which we cede is almost all uninhabited and uncultivated. . . . We lose in our rich hopes for the future, but if we know how to cultivate and defend the territory that the treaty preserves or has rescued for us, we shall find it sufficient to console us for our past misfortunes."[19]

Couto naïvely argued that the rights of the former Mexican citizens would be protected because, in American law, "every treaty has a superiority and preference under civil legislation." The proponents asserted that the treaty provisions for citizenship and property rights in Articles VIII and IX would be sufficient to protect the former Mexican citizens. They were wrong: American local, state, and national courts later ruled that the provisions of the treaty could be superseded by local laws.[20]

Manuel de la Peña y Peña also published his arguments in favor of the treaty. He emphasized the extraordinary concern he and his fellow commissioners had felt for their abandoned Mexican populations. "If it had been possible," he wrote, "I would have enlarged the territorial cession with the condition of freeing the Mexican population living there." To resume the war, he continued would endanger their safety and condition; terrible sacrifices were necessary to end the war.[21]

On May 7, 1847, the Mexican Congress opened its debates on the treaty. At that time Peña y Peña, another commissioner, was acting president. His support for ratification was important, especially because he addressed freshman deputies and senators whose future political life might depend on their alliance with the president.

In considering the treaty, the Congress heard a report from Minister of War Anaya outlining the military situation. They then listened to a detailed report from Luis de la Rosa, minister of the treasury, outlining financial justifications for a treaty. Finally, the Chamber heard a report from the commissioners explaining the provisions of the treaty.[22]

The military situation was not good. Besides the American occupation, factions opposing the treaty had made sporadic attempts at rebellion against the federal government. In Aguascalientes, General Paredes y Arrillaga pronounced against the government and captured Guanajuato for a few months until the city was recaptured by federal troops.[23] In early May 1848 the governments of Coahuila and Tamaulipas declared that they would not recognize the Treaty of Guadalupe if it were ratified.[24] Benito Juárez, then governor of Oaxaca, formally announced that his state would oppose the treaty and keep fighting.[25] In addition protests against the treaty came from the state governments of Chihuahua, Zacatecas, Jalisco, and Mexico. As if this were not sufficient, several potentially dangerous Indian rebellions called for immediate action; in San Luis Potosí the Xichu Indians razed missions and buildings throughout a hundred-square-mile area.

Opposition to the treaty was strongest in the Chamber

of Deputies. José María Cuevas, brother of the Luis Cuevas who had signed the treaty, spoke eloquently in opposition, moving the delegates to a standing ovation and lengthy demonstration.[26] The published arguments of Senators Mariano Otero and Manuel Crescencio Rejón against the treaty were influential. Oral arguments in favor of ratification came from the minister of foreign relations, Luis de la Rosa, the minister of war, Pedro Anaya; and the president of the Chamber, Francisco Elorriaga.[27] Finally, on May 19, the deputies met and voted 51 to 35 for ratification. Then the Senate took up the debate. There was less intense opposition in this body, the principal leader being Mariano Otero. After three days of discussion, the modified treaty passed by a vote of 33 to 4.[28]

In ratifying the Treaty of Guadalupe Hidalgo, the majority of the Mexican Congress chose the lesser of two evils. Not to ratify the document would have meant continued American military occupation, a prolonged financial disaster for the Mexican government, and the probable loss of additional territory. In accepting the treaty, the politicians admitted that the loss of territory was inevitable and that a treaty would liberate Mexico from foreign domination while preventing further erosion of national territory. Most of the delegates probably accepted Peña y Peña's characterization: It was a treaty of recovery rather than of cession.[29]

PROTOCOL OF QUERÉTARO

Prior to the exchange of ratifications, Luis de la Rosa, the minister of foreign relations, requested a meeting with the American commissioners Clifford and Sevier to draft a protocol that would clearly explain what was intended by the U.S. Senate modification of the original treaty. Also attending the meeting were two former signatories of the treaty, Bernardo Couto and Luis Cuevas. The result of these conversations was the drafting of the Protocol of Querétaro (see appendix 1). This document sought to clarify the intentions of the American government in modifying Article IX and deleting Article X.[30] The first part of the protocol stated that the changes in Article IX (dealing with citizenship rights) "did not intend to diminish in any way what was agreed upon by the aforesaid [original] article."[31] The second part of the protocol affirmed that in deleting Article X (land grants), the U.S. government "did not in any way intend to annul grants of land made by Mexico in the ceded territories."[32]

Later this protocol became a source of political controversy within the United States and cause for further disagreement with Mexico. The protocol was not included with the treaty papers sent to the Congress when the president proclaimed the ratification process complete on July 4, 1848. Six months later, Whig Congressmen embarrassed the administration by raising the issue of the secrecy and meaning of the Protocol of Querétaro. Congress debated it, the Whigs arguing that the protocol language restored guarantees respecting Texas land grants, and the Democrats arguing that the protocol did not enlarge on the meaning of the treaty. The intensity of the debate suggested the importance of the treaty's relationship to incomplete titles in the new territories. Luis de la Rosa, the Mexican envoy to the United States, enlarged the discussion on February 10, 1849, by objecting to Buchanan's assertion that the protocol had "no value" and that the document was merely a record of conversations, having no legal force. Later, the new secretary of state, John Clayton, reaffirmed this view to de la Rosa, saying that the U.S. government "at no time regarded the Protocol as obligatory."[33] In Mexico City, Nathan Clifford met with the minister of foreign relations, José María de Lacunza, and agreed to a three-point interpretation: (1) the protocol was not an addition to the treaty; (2) it did not change any of its provisions; and (3) it was a correct interpretation of the treaty. In a short time the State Department vociferously objected to this last point. The difference of opinion between Mexico City and Washington, D.C., remains to this day.[34]

BOUNDARY DISPUTES

The final ratified version of the Treaty of Guadalupe Hidalgo (see appendix 2) substantially resolved the issue of the status of the Rio Grande as the southern border between Texas and Mexico, but it also created a new boundary dispute in its designation of the southern border between the territory of New Mexico (including Arizona) Sonora and Chihuahua. Article V in the treaty specified that the new dividing line for this region would proceed up the Rio Grande "to the point where it strikes the southern boundary of New Mexico; thence, westward along the whole southern boundary of New Mexico (which runs north of the town called Paso) to its western termination; thence, northward along the western line of New Mexico until it intersects the first branch of the River Gila," and down the Gila to the Colorado.[35] The boundary in California would be a line drawn eastward starting one marine league south of the bay of San Diego.

In July 1849 the commissioners from each country met in San Diego to begin the task of surveying and marking the new international boundary. A year later they finished tracing and marking the line between the two Californias. But when the commissioners met in El Paso in December 1850 to begin surveying the boundary between the New Mexico territory and Chihuahua and Sonora they discovered that there were serious geographical er-

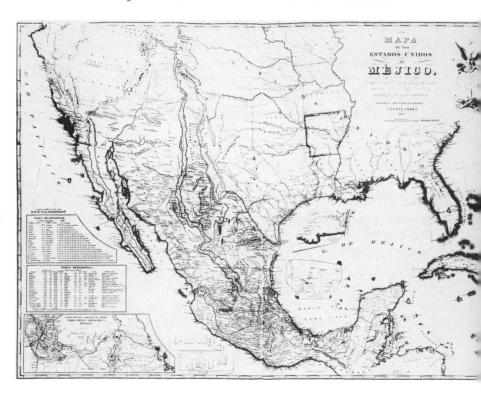

Map 2. Disturnell's *Map of Mexico*, published in 1847. This map was appended to the Treaty of Guadalupe Hidalgo to help identify the boundary. The cartographic errors in this map were the basis for a prolonged dispute that resulted in the Gadsden Treaty in 1853. This map was a reprint of an 1828 plagiarism of an 1826 reproduction of an 1822 publication entitled *Mapa de los Estados Unidos de Méjico*, published by H. S. Tanner, of Philadelphia. Disturnell used modified plates to put out twenty-three editions of this map. The twelfth edition, which contained minor differences from the official seventh version as specified in the Treaty of Guadalupe Hidalgo, was deposited with the treaty in the U.S. National Archives. (Courtesy Bancroft Library, University of California, Berkeley)

rors in Disturnell's 1847 *Map of Mexico* (see map 2), which was cited in the Treaty of Guadalupe Hidalgo. The map placed El Paso half a degree too far north and the Rio Grande two degrees too far east. If the map were followed literally, the rich Mesilla Valley and the Santa Rita de Cobre mines would remain in Mexican territory. Thus, the boundary commissioners charged with surveying the line were confronted with a dilemma: Should they follow the latitudes of the boundary as marked on the map, or should they, using the relationship of the line to the town of El Paso shown on the map, mark the boundary eight miles north of the town? The difference between the two methods for determining the southern line between New Mexico and Chihuahua would mean a loss or gain of about six thousand square miles of territory along with about three thousand persons.

In 1851, when the commissioners met to discuss the problem, the Mexican representative, General García Conde, argued to accept the northern latitude, and the U.S. representative, John R. Bartlett, argued for a more southerly one. After four months of discussion they agreed to a compromise that set the New Mexican–Chihuahua border at 32 degrees, 22 minutes north latitude (see map 3).[36]

Political pressures from American expansionists who wanted a more southerly line for a transcontinental railroad and land access to the Mesilla region's rich mines prevented acceptance of the Bartlett-Conde agreement Southerners anxious to secure the route for their section voted to withhold further money for the survey unless a more southerly line were agreed upon.

In 1852 the situation in the Mesilla Strip became explosive as Mexican repatriates and Anglo-Texan and New Mexican cattle ranchers moved into the area. The governor of Chihuahua claimed jurisdiction and the gover-

The Disturnell Map of 1847 & the Boundary Controversy 1848 - 54

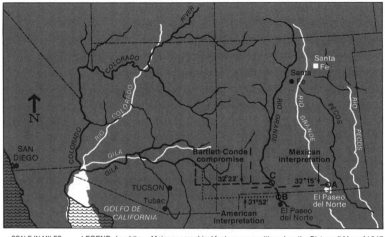

SCALE IN MILES
0   50   100   150

LEGEND: In white— Major geographical features as positioned on the Disturnell Map of 1847
In black— True relationship of geographical features

A— Point of boundary shown on Disturnell Map (Mexican View)
B— Point of boundary if longitude and latitude of Disturnell Map is followed (American view)
C— Compromise position

Source: Henry P. Walker and Don Bufkin, HISTORICAL ATLAS OF ARIZONA, (Norman: University of Oklahoma Press, 1979) opposite plate 19.

Map 3. The Disturnell Map of 1847 and the Boundary Controversy of 1848–1854. (Map by Bardy Anderson and Ann Brook)

nor of New Mexico threatened to occupy the area with force.[37] Further provocation came when American troops occupied the Mexican communities of Isleta, Socorro, and San Elizario claiming that the changes in the Rio Grande's water course now made them part of the United States. These three communities, which included almost six thousand people, had been on the Mexican side of the river in 1848.[38]

The U.S. government's rejection of the Bartlett-Conde agreement was not the only source of conflict between the two countries. Under Article XI of the Treaty of Guadalupe Hidalgo, the United States was bound to prevent

Indian raids into Mexico from the U.S. side of the border. This task turned out to be impossibly expensive. More than 160,000 Indians lived in the border region, and many of them, particularly the Apaches and Comanches, had a long history of raiding pueblos on the Mexican side. In an attempt to comply with its obligations, the United States stationed more than eight thousand troops along the border. The cost of keeping the peace turned out to be more than the cost of the original treaty. Between 1848 and 1853, military expenditures in New Mexico alone rose to 12 million dollars and the raids continued.[39] In 1868 the Mexican government presented claims for damages that amounted to more than 31 million dollars.[40] Needless to say, the U.S. government was anxious to be released from the provisions of Article XI.

THE GADSDEN TREATY

This volatile situation along the border, confusion over the international boundaries, U.S. desire for rights of transit across the Isthmus of Tehuantepec, and a release from the obligations of the Treaty of Guadalupe Hidalgo's Article XI, led to the U.S. dispatch of James Gadsden to Mexico. The Tehuantepec issue had increased in importance since the discovery of gold in California in 1848. Various U.S. investors had been granted concessions to construct a trans-isthmus railroad, but they were not willing to proceed until the United States and Mexico agreed to protect the project. After conversations with President Santa Anna and threats of military force, Mexico signed the Gadsden Treaty, or Tratado de Mesilla. As eventually modified by the American Congress, the United States agreed to pay 10 million dollars and Mexico ceded the territory the Americans wanted for a railroad (see map 4) while allowing the United States to abro-

The Gadsden Purchase, 1853

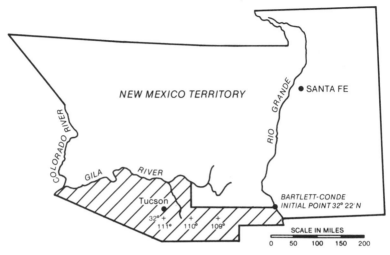

Source: Henry P. Walker and Don Bufkin, HISTORICAL ATLAS OF ARIZONA, (Norman: University of Oklahoma Press, 1979) opposite plate 22.

Map 4. The Gadsden Purchase, 1853. (Map by Bardy Anderson and Ann Brook)

gate Article XI in the Treaty of Guadalupe Hidalgo and granting the rights of transit across the Isthmus of Tehuantepec. The new treaty granted the United States an additional 29,142,000 acres of Mexican territory and released it from the obligation of policing the border Indians.

The Treaty of Guadalupe Hidalgo was imperfect, and it became a source of continuing ill will and misunderstanding on both sides of the border. The Gadsden Purchase did not end the boundary problems. In later years an International Boundary Commisssion would have to deal with unforeseen geographical and political issues. The problem of violence along the border did not disappear. Indian warfare, banditry, smuggling, and filibustering expeditions persisted. The last decades of the nineteenth century witnessed numerous occasions on which American troops pursued outlaw bands of Indians and Mexicans across the border. This chronic condition required additional negotiations between the two countries. In 1910 the Mexican revolution further destabilized conditions along the border.[41]

Thus the Treaty of Guadalupe Hidalgo solved some problems but created others that would become a source of continuing dialogue between the two nations. One of the most pressing issues created by the treaty was dealt with inadequately by both parties: the failure of the U.S. government to provide for the civil and property rights of the Mexican population in the newly annexed territory.

CHAPTER 5

Citizenship and Property Rights: U.S. Interpretations of the Treaty

> We have come here under this treaty; gentlemen sit in
> this convention under this treaty; it is in virtue of this
> treaty alone that we are possessed of this territory.... If
> we violate the stipulations of this treaty, we violate the
> constitution.
>
> MR. HASTINGS
> DEBATES IN THE CONVENTION OF CALIFORNIA

Articles VIII and IX of the Treaty of Guadalupe Hidalgo oset forth the terms by which the former Mexican citizens and their property would be incorporated politically into the United States. These articles in the treaty affected some 100,000 Mexicans in the newly acquired territories, including a large number of Hispanicized as well as nomadic Indians in New Mexico and California.[1] As provided by Article VIII, a person had one year to "elect" his or her preference for Mexican citizenship. If this were not done, it was stipulated that they had elected to become United States citizens and that they would be granted citizenship by Congress at some future time. The two articles also treated the property rights of the conquered people. Absentee Mexican landholders would have their property "inviolably respected," and others would "be maintained and protected in the free enjoyment of their liberty and property" (see appendix 2). In the six decades following the ratification of the treaty, its provisions regarding citizenship and property were complicated by legislative and judicial interpretations. In the end the U.S. application of the treaty to the realities of life in the Southwest violated its spirit.

MEXICAN CITIZENSHIP AND REPATRIATION

A number of persons living in the territories ceded to the United States chose to remain Mexican citizens, either by announcing their intent before judicial officials or by returning to Mexico. No one knows their exact number, but they were probably few in comparison to the total population in the Southwestern states and territories. The Mexican government was anxious to encourage its nationals to return to Mexico in order to populate the sparsely settled northern frontier regions. Since colonial times, Mexican governmental officials had looked toward their far northern frontier with apprehension and had tried to populate it with hardy settlers. The idea of the northern frontier as a buffer zone protecting the more civilized and wealthy settlements to the south emerged time and again in imperial planning. During the negotiation of the Treaty of Guadalupe Hidalgo, General Santa Anna proposed the creation of a buffer zone to separate the two republics. The year 1848 presented the Mexican administration with an opportunity to reorganize frontier defenses. The Mexican government hoped that new colonists migrating from the American Southwest would defend their frontier from Indian attacks as well as from U.S. incursions.

In the governmental decrees of July and of August 1848, Herrera's administration drew up detailed plans to establish eighteen military colonies along the newly

defined U.S.–Mexico border, which were to be popu-
lated with repatriated Mexican citizens.[2] The resettle-
ment zone was to be divided into three sectors of coloni-
zation. Families from New Mexico would have lands
reserved for them in Chihuahua; those from Texas would
settle in Tamaulipas and Nuevo Leon; and those from
California, in Baja California or Sonora. As an incentive,
each settler over the age of fourteen would be given
twenty-five pesos and his children twelve pesos each.
Land, transportation, and initial living expenses were to
be paid from a fund of $200,000, to come from the U.S.
payments provided for under the treaty.[3]

To implement this ambitious plan, beginning in 1849,
the Mexican government sent three commissioners who
would receive, in addition to expense money, a bounty of
one peso for each settler they encouraged to move. In California several repatriation expeditions were organized
but the numbers who actually left were few.[4] The Californios were unwilling to give up their mild climate for
the barren deserts of Baja California or Sonora. Besides,
the gold rush was a powerful reason to remain. The two
commissioners to the more populous province of New
Mexico, Padre Ramón Ortiz and Manuel Armendarias,
met with somewhat more success. After a few months of
activity, between fifteen hundred and two thousand New
Mexicans reportedly left the territory, taking with them
their slaves and property. According to Ortiz's report,
there was a great interest in repatriation; he estimated
that up to eighty thousand might be induced to leave.
Without doubt this number was exaggerated, but it indicated that there was widespread dissatisfaction with the
U.S. administration of the territory. The military governor of New Mexico, fearful that the Mexican commissioners might instigate a rebellion, refused to allow them
to visit other New Mexico counties.[5] Repatriation ef-

forts from New Mexico continued sporadically into the next decade, with the Mexican government making occasional protests regarding the American government's lack of cooperation in the project. Nevertheless a number of frontier towns were founded in Chihuahua by the New Mexicans who returned to Mexico: Guadalupe, La Mesilla, Santo Tomás, and Refugio.[6] In Texas the repatriation program was a qualified success. At least 150 families left that state before the ratification of the treaty, settling on lands set aside by the government. On June 22, 1850, Commissioner Antonio Menchaca brought 618 people and more than 100 families from Nacogdoches to Coahuila and requested 20,602 pesos in expenses. Other groups from Texas moved to establish new border towns or settled in existing ones on the south bank of the Rio Grande. In this way the Mexican border towns of Guerrero, Mier, Camargo, Reynosa, and Matamoros grew in size, and new towns of Nuevo Laredo, Guadalupe, and Ascensión were founded.[7]

Under the provisions of the treaty, the conquered peoples of the new territories could elect to remain Mexican citizens and continue to reside in the U.S. territories. In New Mexico "a large number" chose to appear before the local county official as provided for by the governor to announce their continued Mexican citizenship. This was despite the very short interval allowed for them to declare their intention of remaining Mexican citizens (between April 21, 1849 and May 30, 1849). Their names were published and circulated among the county officials to prevent future voter frauds. There were, however, a number of problems that arose when those who declared their Mexican citizenship changed their mind later on and petitioned to become U.S. citizens without success. Approximately two thousand New Mexicans declared to retain their Mexican citizenship. There is no record that

Mexicans in California or Texas chose to remain Mexican citizens.[8]

UNITED STATES CITIZENSHIP

Article IX provided that those who did not choose to remain Mexican citizens would be considered "to have elected" to become U.S. citizens. As early as 1849 the nature of the citizenship rights of these Mexicans became the subject of controversy. In California the delegates to the state constitutional convention wrestled with the problems of race, rights of citizenship, and the Treaty of Guadalupe Hidalgo. Six of the delegates were native Californios (former Mexican citizens) who were aware that Mexicans who looked like Indians faced the prospect of racial discrimination. Ultimately they argued for the protection of their class even if it meant endorsing the racist views of their Anglo colleagues towards Indians and blacks. Mexico had granted citizenship to "civilized" Indians and to Blacks, and the Treaty of Guadalupe Hidalgo clearly stated that former Mexican citizens would be given the opportunity to become citizens of the United States. Following the biases of their age, the framers of the state constitution sought wording that would exclude Blacks and Indians while including Mexicans. A Mr. Edward Gilbert introduced a proposal that eventually became the first section of the state constitution defining suffrage. It extended the vote to "every white, male citizen of Mexico who shall have elected to become a citizen of the United States." The convention agreed that Indians and Blacks might at some future date be given the franchise but that because voting was not an absolute right of citizenship, they could be excluded. There was some concern over whether in fact the Mexicans remaining were citizens of the United States. Ultimately the delegates agreed that "it would seem that they are not in fact American citizens, but require some further action of Congress to make them citizens of the United States."[9] California's admission as a state presumably would be that conferring act. (Later court cases challenged this assumption.) The ambiguous citizenship of the Californios meant that they could not expect the full protection of the laws during a stressful and violent period in California's history.

The discovery of gold in 1848 created a situation in which thousands of Yankee immigrants were competing with native-born Californio miners in the gold fields. One estimate is that about thirteen hundred native Californios were in the gold regions in 1848 and that probably an equal number returned in 1849.[10] Xenophobia, nativism, residuals of war-time patriotism, and racism resulted in violent confrontations between English-speaking immigrants and other residents. Eventually, most of the latter were driven from the most profitable gold fields. As a consequence of vigilantism and its attendant lynchings, harassment, and abuse of "foreigners," several countries lodged diplomatic protests and financial claims against the U.S. government. The Mexican government was active in lodging formal complaints in Washington, D.C., even though many of them lacked specificity. As late as 1853 the Mexican ambassador to Washington, Larráinzar, protested the treatment of Mexican miners in California, invoking the protections of the Treaty of Guadalupe Hidalgo. The American secretary of state responded that it was not clear that the treaty was being violated since there was a legal distinction between the Mexicans who had migrated to California after 1848 and those who were there before the gold rush.[11] Generally the Mexican government failed to present clear evidence that native Californios were being deprived of their property and civil rights in violation of the treaty. There was evidence to substantiate the charges. In 1849 the military governor of California, General Percifor Smith, responding to nativist fears that foreigners were taking all the gold out of the mining regions, announced his "trespass" orders prohibiting non-citizens from mining gold on public property. He appealed to Americans to help him enforce his policy and under the protection of the military, Anglo-American miners robbed and harassed foreigners. In his reminiscences, Antonio Coronel, a native Californio from Los Angeles, vividly described stabbings, extortions, and lynchings as commonplace American reactions to native Californios, whom they regarded as interlopers. Some Spanish-speaking natives were issued passes, supposed proof of their new status as citizens of the United States, but this had little effect on the hordes of people crowding into the mining district from the eastern United States. Because neither the mass of Americans nor the Mexican government considered the Californios citizens, they were without the juridical protection of either nation.

The violations of their rights under the Treaty of Guadalupe Hidalgo were finally tested in the U.S. courts. In the California Supreme Court case of *People v. Naglee* (1851), the issue was whether or not a newly enacted Foreign Miner's Tax Law violated the U.S. Constitution, the Treaty of Guadalupe Hidalgo, or the California State Constitution.[12] The defense argued, "It does not appear that this act [the Foreign Miner's Tax Law] has ever been enforced against any person entitled to the benefit of this treaty or even against any citizen of Mexico." The Foreign Miner's Tax Law specifically exempted Mexicans who had become U.S. citizens under the treaty. In the

Naglee case the defense did not introduce evidence of the violation of treaty rights.[13] The prosecution, on the other hand, argued that the law should apply to Mexican Americans because they were not yet officially U.S. citizens. This view was rejected by the court but it reemerged twenty years later in the case of *People v. de la Guerra* (1870).

In *People v. de la Guerra,* the status of the former Mexican citizens finally was resolved. Pablo de la Guerra, a venerable Californio landholder who signed the California Constitution, ran for district judge in 1869. His political opponents in that election challenged his right to office based on the argument that he, along with thousands of other Californios, had only elected to become a citizen of the United States under the provisions in the treaty. In fact, none of these people were yet citizens because Congress had not yet formally given them citizenship. The California Supreme Court ruled against this view and in de la Guerra's favor, stating that the admission of California as a state constituted the positive act that confered citizenship on former Mexican nationals.[14]

The fate of the California Indians is further evidence of the violation of the spirit of the treaty. Under the Mexican Constitution of 1824, Indians were considered full Mexican citizens. Upon the transfer of territory to the U.S. government, however, the Indians received neither U.S. citizenship nor the protections of the treaty as specified in Article VIII. The California state constitutional convention recoiled from the idea of granting Indians full citizenship. In violation of the treaty, the California Indian tribes were deprived of the protections specified in the treaty. Consequently they became the victims of murder, slavery, land theft, and starvation. The Indian population within the state declined by more than 100,000 in two decades. Whites overran tribal lands and people were exterminated. Genocide is not too strong a word to use in describing what happened to the California Indians during that period.[15]

In New Mexico, where the largest Hispanicized Indian population lived, there was little debate about the citizenship rights of these people. In the territorial framework the franchise was limited to whites only. On September 24, 1849, a convention met to draw up an organic act to govern the territory during its wait for statehood. A majority of the delegates were from old line Hispano families. They declared that the rights of citizenship would be restricted to "free white male inhabitants residing within the limits of the United States, but who [were residents] on the 2nd day of February, 1848."[16] They specified that former Mexican citizens would have to take an oath of affirmation before a territorial or federal court renouncing allegiance to the Mexican Republic before they would be considered citizens of the territory. This stipulation was approved with no debate and approved by the U.S. Congress the next year.[17]

Because New Mexico became a territory rather than a state, the civil rights of its inhabitants were less than those in California. Following the pattern established under the Northwest Ordinances of 1787 and the Wisconsin Organic Act of 1836, the people resident in the territories were conceived of as a dependent people who were not entitled to full participation in the national body politic. The laws and administration of the territory were subject to controls of Congress. The citizens of the New Mexico Territory (which, until 1863, included Arizona) did not have full civil rights: they were not allowed to vote for their governor or for the president of the United States; the decisions of their elected representatives were subject to federal approval; and they did not have an independent judiciary. It was not until the period from 1901 to

1922, when the Supreme Court heard the Insular Cases, that the rights of the residents in the territories of the United States were articulated. The high court determined that the Constitution did not necessarily apply with full force to the residents in the U.S. territories. As Secretary of War Elihu Root put it, "The Constitution follows the flag—but doesn't quite catch up with it."[18]

The Hispanos of New Mexico did not obtain all the rights of U.S. citizens under the terms of the Treaty of Guadalupe Hidalgo until statehood in 1912. For them the key phrase in the treaty was contained in Article IX: "and in the meantime [they shall] be maintained and protected in the free enjoyment of their liberty and property, and secured in the free exercise of their religion." Essentially these "citizens-in-waiting" had their rights guaranteed by the treaty until they gained full citizenship status.

As in California, the most obvious victims of the transfer of sovereignty in New Mexico were the Indians. Approximately eight thousand Pueblo Indians who had been Mexican citizens in 1848 were disenfranchized. In 1849 several pueblo villagers had participated in local elections under the assumption that they were citizens. U.S. officials believed, however, that the Indian vote was too easily manipulated by various factions and moved to convince the residents of the nineteen Pueblo villages that it would be in their interest to reject full citizenship and accept a ward status under the 1834 Indian Intercourse Act. Accordingly, in 1849 the presidentially appointed Indian Agent at Santa Fe, James S. Calhoun, traveled to visit all the Pueblos to convince them to accept federal protection under the Intercourse Act. In 1851, as a result of Calhoun's labors, representatives of several tribes met and voted not to participate in New Mexican politics, apparently rejecting their rights under the Treaty of Guadalupe Hidalgo. In 1854 the legislature passed a law prohibiting the Pueblo tribes from voting except in the election of local water officials.

Despite this early history of disenfranchisement, some of it voluntary on the part of the Indians, the New Mexico Territorial Courts later decided cases that confirmed the citizenship of the Pueblo Indians. The *Lucero* case in 1869, the *Santistevan* case in 1874, the *Joseph* case in 1876, the *Delinquent Taxpayers* case in 1904, and the *Mares* case in 1907 were all decisions of the Territorial Supreme Court that confirmed the citizenship rights of the Pueblos. This judicial tradition, however, had little effect on the ward-like status of the Pueblos. A U.S. Supreme Court decision in 1913, *United States v. Sandoval* 231 U.S. 28 (1913), found that the Pueblos were entitled to federal protection and that their citizenship status was not clear. When New Mexico was admitted as a state in 1912, its constitution contained a provision denying voting rights to "Indians not taxed," which included the Pueblo tribes. It was not until 1948 that this provision was declared unconstitutional and not until 1953 that the New Mexican Constitution was changed to allow Pueblo Indians the vote.[19]

There was little argument about the citizenship status of the other Indian groups in New Mexico. The Apaches and Navajos, who had fought so long to escape Hispanicization, remained the traditional enemies of the whites well into the 1870s and 1880s. They were eventually defeated in battle, placed on reservations, and treated as conquered nations with separate peace treaties. They were given citizenship at the same time as the Pueblo tribes.[20]

LAND

Admittedly the rights and benefits of U.S. citizenship were somewhat abstract blessings for Mexican Americans, considering that for a long time the Anglo Americans treated them all as foreigners. A more tangible promise offered by the treaty, included in Articles VIII and IX and the Protocol of Querétaro, was the promise of protection for private property. It was in the realm of property rights that the greatest controversies erupted. In California thousands of gold-rush migrants encroached on the Californio land grants and demanded that something be done to "liberate" the land. The result was the passage in Congress of the Land Act of 1851. This law set up a Board of Land Commissioners whose job would be to adjudicate the validity of Mexican land grants in California. Every grantee was required to present evidence supporting title within two years, or their property would pass into the public domain. The land commissioners were instructed by law to govern their decisions according to the Treaty of Guadalupe Hidalgo, the law of nations, Spanish and Mexican laws, and previous decisions of the U.S. Supreme Court.

A basic principle underlying the establishment of the Land Commission and the land-confirmation processes in New Mexico and Texas was that the vast majority of Mexican land grants in the ceded territory were "imperfect," meaning that the claimants had not fulfilled Mexican regulations for legal land ownership. In years subsequent to the treaty, American courts ruled that the U.S. government had inherited the Mexican government's sovereignty and thereby the right to complete the processes of land confirmation.[21]

Under this assumption the Land Commission in California examined 813 claims and eventually confirmed 604 of them involving approximately nine million acres. This, however, did not mean that the majority of Mexican landholders were ulitmately protected by the courts. On the contrary, most Californio landholders lost their lands because of the tremendous expense of litigation and legal fees. To pay for the legal defense of their lands, the Californios were forced to mortgage their ranchos. Falling cattle prices and usurous rates of interest conspired to wipe them out as a landholding class. Pablo de la Guerra summarized the dilemma for the California legislature: "Sir, if he gained his suit—if his title was confirmed, the expenses of the suit would confiscate his property, and millions have already been spent in carrying up cases that have been confirmed by the (Land Commission), and land owners in California have been obligated to dispose of their property at half its value, in order to pay for the expenses of the suit."[22]

Even if some landholders were able to fulfill the terms of the 1851 land law, they soon encountered tremendous pressure from Anglo-American squatters to vacate their rights. Perhaps one of the most celebrated and controversial cases was that of Joseph Yves Limantour. Limantour was a Frenchman whose son later became a famous secretary of treasury under President Porfirio Díaz. In 1843 the governor of California, Manuel Micheltorrena, gave Limantour a grant of four square leagues comprising about half of the unpopulated area known as Yerba Buena, land that later became part of the city of San Francisco. When gold was discovered in northern California in 1848, thousands of immigrants flooded San Francisco, settling on lots carved from Limantour's grant. To protect his rights Limantour presented his case before the Land Commission, and in 1856 that body confirmed his title. Limantour was an absentee landholder whose rights were ostensibly protected under Article VIII of the treaty, as well as under Mexican law. Because he did not intend to reside in California, Limantour offered to sell his land rights to settlers at 10 percent of their true market value. A number of squatters settled along these lines but a majority formed an Anti-Limantour party to challenge his ownership. The political pressure of the squatters, many of them wealthy and influential San Franciscans, resulted in accusations of fraud. Following an indictment by a grand jury, Limantour was jailed on charges of fraud and perjury in 1857. Released on bond after a few months, he returned to Mexico to gather evidence to substantiate his case. He returned in 1858 for the trial with new documents and witnesses. Nevertheless the court decided against him, and he lost his land.[23]

Other individuals who held perfect titles to their land under the Mexican government and who were able to survive economically lost their holdings because they had not fulfilled the terms of the 1851 land law. A number of court cases in this regard involving Mexican and Spanish grants emerged, but the most famous one pertaining to the Treaty of Guadalupe Hidalgo was *Botiller et al. v. Dominguez* (1883).

In 1848, Dominga Dominguez, owner of Rancho Los Virgenes, just east of Mission San Fernando in California, had a perfect title to her land, a grant from the government of Mexico dated August 28, 1835. Her ancestors had taken all the steps required to legalize this claim. For some reason she and her relatives neglected to bring their papers before the Land Commission within the specified time provided for in the 1851 law. For the next thirty years a number of Mexican-American and European immigrant families settled on the rancho assuming that the land was part of the public domain and that it had been opened for homesteading. Finally, in 1883, Brigido Botiller, a French-born Mexican citizen headed a group of squatters to oust Dominguez from her land, claiming that by the 1851 law she had no legal title to it.[24] Dominga then sued Botiller and the other squatters for reclamation of her land and back rents. In the 1880s both the district court and the California State Supreme Court ruled in her favor. Both courts were convinced that her title was legitimate because the provisions in the Treaty of Guadalupe Hidalgo meant that the Dominguez family was "not compelled to submit the same for confirmation . . . nor did the grantee Nemecio Dominguez forfeit the land described."[25]

Botiller and the squatters appealed their case to the U.S. Supreme Court, where, in a decision issued on April 1, 1889, the Court reversed the California Supreme Court decision ruling that, despite the Treaty of Guadalupe Hidalgo guarantees, Dominguez did not have legal title. The Court reasoned that by admitting the legality of this title under this treaty, the government would open the floodgates to others who had perfect titles but had not presented them to the Land Commission. The result would be to wreak havoc on California land ownership. Further, the justices argued that the Supreme Court had no power to enforce the Treaty of Guadaulpe Hidalgo and that matters of treaty violation were subject to international negotiation and more treaties. Specifically, they stated, "This court has no power to set itself up as the intrumentality for enforcing provisions of a treaty with a foreign nation." They held that the Land Law of 1851 did not violate the due process provision of the Constitution because property holders were "at all times liable to be called into a court of justice to contest [their] title to it." Congress, the court ruled, had the power to require landholders to verify their claims and to fix penalties for failing to follow the law.[26]

In *Botiller et al. v. Dominguez* the Supreme Court held that the sovereign laws of the United States took precedence over international treaties. This appeared to contradict the Constitution, which (in Article VI, Section 2, and Article III, Section 2, Clause 1) gave treaties the same status as the Constitution. The ruling thus sparked learned debate. John Currey, a San Francisco attorney, published a booklet challenging the court's logic.[27] The Supreme Court's decision, he argued, sanctioned the confiscation of property and violated the due process provision of the Constitution: "The fact of the existence of a title in fee simple to land cannot be destroyed by a sweep of the pen, nor by the *obiter dictum* of a learned judge."[28] *Botiller et al. v. Dominguez* was an important precedent, guiding the court in its future interpretation of conflicts between treaty obligations and domestic laws. In this case the protection of private property ostensibly guaranteed by the Treaty of Guadalupe Hidalgo was essentially invalidated.

The Compromise of 1850 made New Mexico a territory while California entered the Union as a state. This difference in political status produced different resolutions of land-tenure problems. In California a state judiciary functioned to render relatively swift interpretations of the Treaty of Guadalupe Hidago; in New Mexico federally appointed officials had to have their decisions approved by Congress, a lengthy and often politicized process. Ironically, New Mexico's more direct link to the national government meant that the property-rights guarantees under the Treaty of Guadalupe Hidalgo would be even less important than in California.

In 1848 private and communal land grants in New Mexico covered about 15 million square miles. To determine the federal domain, Congress established the Office of Surveyor General, who was given broad powers to "issue notices, summon witnesses, administer oaths, etc.," and to report to the secretary of the interior and, ultimately, to Congress regarding the status of New Mexico land grants. Until Congress acted to confirm the findings of the surveyor general, all lands were to be withheld from sale.[29]

In August 1854, Congress appointed William Pelham to the office of surveyor general. Once in New Mexico, Pelham had considerable trouble getting the Hispano land-grant owners to file their claims with his office; as a result, by 1863, only twenty-five town and private claims and seventeen Pueblo Indian grants had been confirmed by Congress. By 1880, 1,000 claims had been filed by the surveyor general but only 150 had been acted upon by the federal government. As the number of unconfirmed grants in litigation before the surveyor general and the Congress lengthened, so too did the legal expenses incurred by the Hispano pueblos and ranchers. Such lawyers and politicians as Stephen Benson Elkins and Thomas Benton Catron formed the nucleus of the Santa Fe Ring, a confederation of opportunists who used the long legal battles over land grants to acquire empires extending over millions of acres. The most famous example of the land-grabbing activities of the ring was the creation of the Maxwell Land Grant, a Spanish claim of 97,000 acres that became inflated through the actions of the ring to a final patent of 1,714,074 acres.[30]

In addition to losing their lands to rapacious lawyers and politicians, the Hispanos suffered the changing whims of national politics. In 1885 the newly elected Democratic president, Grover Cleveland, removed the Republican surveyor general of New Mexico and replaced him with his own man, William Andrew Sparks, an individual described by historian Ralph Emerson Twitchell as "steeped in prejudice against New Mexico, its people and their property rights."[31] The new surveyor general decided that his predecessor had been corrupt and had given away far too much federal land and that his decisions and those of the Congress regarding land should be reviewed. In the name of reform, the new surveyor general revoked the approval of twenty-three grants. The process of reviewing the New Mexico claims gave no assurance that the Treaty of Guadalupe Hidalgo, or indeed the rule of law, outweighed the political influence of those behind the scenes.

When Benjamin Harrison became president in 1889, the federal land policies in New Mexico changed again. Under pressure from developers and New Mexico Hispanos, Congress in 1890 began to consider legislation that would settle the outstanding land claims. Railroad interests wanted to have the public domain established, so that they could get federal grants. Hispano landholders in New Mexico sought to speed up the land-confirmation process or to reverse previously adverse rulings. Writing to Matias Romero, the Mexican minister plenipotentiary to the United States in 1890, the predominantly Hispano Commercial Club of Las Vegas, New Mexico, laid out their complaints. They urged Minister Romero to use his influence to secure passage of a new land law.

> The American government has thus far, though over 40 years have elapsed, neglected to provide a competent court to pass on the validity of the claims of those who were once Mexican citizens. . . . We, with great respect petition you to champion the cause of our people and again represent to the State Department at Washington evil inflicted on us by the failure of the U.S. government to fulfill in this respect its obligations incurred by the Treaty of Guadalupe Hidalgo.[32]

For its part, the Mexican government followed the proposed legislation with interest but was unable, for diplomatic reasons, to advocate the Hispanos' cause in Congress. The Mexican government did instruct Romero to react to court cases when it appeared that there was prejudice against former Mexican citizens in the application of the law once it passed Congress. Romero, for his part, suggested that his government publicize its concern for its former citizens so that they would be better able to oppose unjust actions taken against them in violation of the Treaty of Guadalupe Hidalgo.[33]

On March 3, 1891, the president signed into law a bill to establish a Court of Private Land Claims. The Treaty of Guadalupe Hidalgo was specifically invoked as a guiding document for this court, although wording in the act provided that it would apply only to "persons who became citizens by reason of the Treaty of Guadalupe Hidalgo and who have been in the actual adverse possession of tracts not to exceed 160 acres."[34] The court was made up of five judges plus an attorney representing the interests of the U.S. government. Unlike the California Land Commission, the New Mexico Court of Private Land Claims did not require those holding perfect titles to apply to the court for confirmation—only those who had not fulfilled all the regulations of the Spanish and Mexican laws. Those not presenting their claims within two years would be considered to have abandoned their grant. The law also restricted to eleven square leagues (about thirty-six square miles) the amount of land that would be allowed for a communal or town grant and stipulated that errors in previous decisions by Congress would be indemnified at not more than $1.25 per acre.

Meeting in Denver, Colorado and in Santa Fe, New Mexico, between 1891 and 1904, the New Mexico Court operated by the strict rule that confirmation of a land grant required proof that the Spanish or Mexican granting official had legal authority. There had been a good deal of confusion in Mexico's political history; therefore, many

New Mexican grants were held not to be legitimate because of the "illegitimacy" of the Mexican governing bodies.[35] The court was also very strict regarding what it considered a proper survey, documentation, and full compliance with every Mexican law regarding land tenure. As a result of this less-than-liberal interpretation of Spanish and Mexican laws, the New Mexico court rejected two-thirds of the claims presented before it. Ultimately only eighty-two grants received congressional confirmation. This represented only 6 percent of the total area sought by land claimants. Thus, using the Court of Private Land Claims, the U.S. government enlarged the national domain at the expense of hundreds of Hispano villages, leaving a bitter legacy that continued to fester.[36]

In 1856 the U.S. Supreme Court ruled that the Treaty of Guadalupe Hidalgo did not apply to Texas. In *McKinney v. Saviego* the justices ruled that Articles VIII and IX of the treaty referring to property rights and citizenship, "did not refer to any portion of the acknowledged limits of Texas. The territories alluded to (in Articles VIII and IX of the treaty) are those which previous to the treaty had belonged to Mexico. . . . The Republic of Texas had been many years before acknowledged by the United States as existing separately and independently of Mexico."[37]

This decision seemed to invalidate the meaning of the Protocol of Querétaro, which specifically identified Texas land grants as being protected. Under this agreement (see appendix 1) grants made before March 2, 1836—the date of Texas' self-proclaimed independence from Mexico—would remain as legal land grants.[38] Thus, according to the Supreme Court, Texas was not to be considered part of the Mexican Cession. Congress had admitted Texas into the Union in 1845, and that state's constitution ran counter to the Treaty of Guadalupe Hidalgo (Article VIII) in forbidding aliens from holding property. (The Texas government had already declared as aliens those Tejanos who had left the Republic during the Texas Rebellion.) The Mexican government took exception to this interpretation. In 1895, R. S. Sanchez, a legal consultant to the Secretaría de Relaciones Exteriores published his views, arguing that U.S. courts were in violation of the Treaty of Guadalupe Hidalgo because Mexico had never recognized the independence of Texas and the treaty specifically and formally recognized Texas as part of the United States by the delineation of the boundary (in Article IV).[39] The issue of Texas and the treaty remained a point of contention well into the twentieth century. U.S. courts discounted arguments that cited the treaty when arguing for Texas land claims. In 1911, in *State v. Gallardo et al.*, a Texas Civil Appeals Court reaffirmed the Supreme Court view that "the validity of the title under consideration should be determined without reference to any provision of the treaty," but, at the same time, recognized that prior decisions of the local courts in Texas had upheld grants of land based, in part, on interpretations of the Treaty of Guadalupe Hidalgo and the Protocol.[40]

During the Bucareli Conferences held in 1923 between the United States and Mexico, the issue of the status of the Texas land grants and the applicability of the Treaty of Guadalupe Hidalgo resurfaced. This conference was convened to settle the outstanding claims of both countries and to pave the way for U.S. diplomatic recognition of Mexico's revolutionary government. To counter U.S. claims for damages suffered by Americans during the revolution of 1910, the Mexican government decided to present the claims of its former citizens in the Southwest. Initially they presented 836 claims amounting to 245 million dollars. Almost 193 million of this amount was for Texas land claims invalidated in violation of the Treaty of Guadalupe Hidalgo.[41] The Mexican government, through its consulate in Texas, actively solicited land claims from heirs of the original land-grant owners who had been dispossessed of their lands after 1848. Increased Anglo-American migration into South Texas after 1848 was the origin of a large number of these claims. This was the area of Texas in which the first battles of the Mexican War had occurred and over which there had been much diplomatic disagreement prior to the signing of the Treaty of Guadalupe Hidalgo. Many Tejano grants in this region were perfected Spanish claims that had been recognized by the Mexican government.[42]

Unlike New Mexico or California, Texas had been admitted to the Union with full control over its public lands. Instead of federal laws guiding the settlement of land disputes, state laws and courts played a dominant role. It is difficult to generalize about the Texas claims because of the decades of litigation surrounding them. Two Texas historians, Arnoldo De Leon and Kenneth Stewart, concluded that most Tejanos lost portions of their patrimony or all of it through "a combination of methods including, litigation, chicanery, robbery, fraud, and threat."[43] As early as 1847 the citizens of Laredo, Texas, fearing how they would fare under the Texas administration, requested assurances from the state government that their property rights would be protected. Receiving no reply, they petitioned to be allowed to remain part of Mexico.[44] Many violent episodes marked the struggle between Tejanos and Anglo-Texans for control of the land. The Cortina Rebellion, in the Brownsville-Matamoros area in the 1850s and 1860s and the El Paso Salt War in the 1870s pitted entire communities against the Texas rangers in a struggle for the land. Hundreds of lesser struggles that resulted in lynchings, beatings, and riots also had their origin in conflicts over the land.[45] Tejanos had good reason to distrust the Texas government in its implementation of laws.

Tejano families found their lands in jeopardy because they had been forced to flee Texas during the Mexican war. The Las Mestenas grant near Reynosa is one example. The original heirs vacated their lands between 1846 and 1848. Their decision to reoccupy the grant in 1848 was an expensive one, for it meant selling their lands to pay back taxes and paying the expense of rounding up stolen or stray cattle. The large families and the Hispanic tradition of equal inheritance worked against continuing land ownership. There were numerous heirs, some of whom had never seen the grant. American speculators bought up interests from these absentee owners, made high-interest loans, assumed mortgages on portions of the ranch, and purchased sections at tax sales. Tejano sued Tejano and Anglo-Texan sued Tejano over conflicting claims until 1915, when a million-dollar lawsuit finally cleared title with few of the original claimants retaining an interest.[46]

Other Tejano grantees lost their lands because they had left Texas during the Texas rebellion in 1836. The Republic declared their lands vacant and issued certificates of land ownership to individuals who had fought in the Texan army. Litigation between these certificate holders and recipients of older Mexican and Spanish grants resulted in further violations of the Treaty of Guadalupe Hidalgo. Andrew A. Tijerina, who studied the process up to 1850, concluded, "Across the state, Tejano emigres lost their lands to 'fictitious law suits,' sheriff's auctions, and dubious transfer of titles."[47]

David Montejano, who has also studied the loss of Tejano lands, concluded that the process was a complex one involving fraud, confiscation, and the operation of the mechanisms of market competition. In the late nineteenth century the Tejanos did not have access to capital to develop their lands so that they could remain solvent during the changes in the ranching industry. They also inherited the traditional noncapitalist view of the use of their lands. The death of a patriarch often meant the dismemberment of the ranch as it was sold for back taxes and old debts. A large portion of the famous King ranch in south Texas was pieced together during the forced sale of Tejano ranches during unfavorable market conditions in the period 1886–1889.[48]

The conflicts between Spanish and Mexican claims and those granted by the Republic and State of Texas resulted in various legislative attempts to clear titles. In 1850, Governor P. H. Bell appointed a commission to investigate land claims arising from the Treaty of Guadalupe Hidalgo in South Texas.[49] The Bourland-Miller Commission, created by the legislature, gathered abstracts of titles and made recommendations to the Texas legislature. More than 135 claims were reviewed and presented to the legislature for confirmation. In 1854, 1861, 1866, 1870, 1881, and 1901, the Texas legislature passed laws providing mechanisms for the examination and confirmation of Spanish and Mexican grants. A number of claims rejected by the Texas legislature became issues for further litigation.

In the nineteenth century, Texas courts regularly considered the Treaty of Guadalupe Hidalgo as it applied to Spanish and Mexican grants made before March 2, 1836. In *Texas v Gallardo et al.* (1911), the Texas Supreme Court ruled that the validation acts passed in earlier decades should not apply to titles that were valid under the Treaty of Guadalupe Hidalgo—meaning those that were legitimate prior to March 2, 1836. The court ruled that "a title to lands within the original Mexican states of Tamaulipas and the present boundaries of Texas . . . is within the protection of the Treaty and entitled to recognition in the Supreme Courts." Subsequent court decisions affirmed the point of view that the treaty took precedence over state legislation, but many Tejanos became landless because they could not afford lengthy legal appeals.[50]

Whether by laws, force, foreclosure, or litigation, many Tejanos lost title to their ancestral lands in the period from 1848 to 1923. Many had their cases presented on their behalf by the Mexican government during the Bucareli negotiations. On September 8, 1923, the United States and Mexico agreed to establish a commission to review the Texas land grants. Eventually 433 cases, valued at 121 million dollars, were presented on behalf of the heirs. In 1941, after much delay, the Texas land claims were settled on the international level with the Mexican government assuming the obligation of compensating the Texas heirs. The issue was not resolved, however, for although both the United States and Mexico recognized the legitimacy of the Texas claims under the Treaty of Guadalupe Hidalgo, the Mexican government refused to carry out its financial obligations—this despite constant pressure from the Tejano land-grant heirs.[51]

In the first half century after ratification of the Treaty of Guadalupe Hidalgo, hundreds of state, territorial, and federal legal bodies produced a complex tapestry of conflicting opinions and decisions. The citizenship rights seemingly guaranteed in Articles VIII and IX were not all they seemed. The property rights for former Mexican citizens in California, New Mexico, and Texas proved to be fragile. Within a generation the Mexican Americans who had been under the ostensible protection of the treaty became a disenfranchised, poverty-stricken minority.

CHAPTER 6

The U.S. Courts and the Treaty

If the treaty was violated by this general statute enacted for the purpose of ascertaining the validity of claims derived from the Mexican government, it was a matter of international concern, which the two states must determine by treaty or by other such means.

BARKER V. HARVEY (1901)

Conquest gives a title which the courts of the conqueror cannot deny, whatever the private or speculative opinion of individuals may be.

CHIEF JUSTICE MARSHALL
UNITED STATES V. ALCEA BAND OF TILLAMOKS (1946)

When it was promulgated by President James K. Polk on July 4, 1848, the Treaty of Guadalupe Hidalgo achieved the status of a law of the United States. Since its ratification more than two hundred federal, state, and district court decisions have interpreted the treaty, expanding and changing the meaning of the original treaty.

A review of selected U.S. court cases shows that Anglo-American land corporations and the state and federal governments were the primary beneficiaries of the legal system's interpretation of the Treaty of Guadalupe Hidalgo.[1] Although some Indians and Hispanics lodged lawsuits citing the treaty guarantees, the vast majority of them were unsuccessful in their efforts.

The U.S. courts' interpretation of the treaty roughly

paralleled the political history of the United States. The Civil War and Reconstruction period was one of great expansion in civil and political rights in American jurisprudence with the ratification of the 13th, 14th, and 15th amendments, abolishing slavery, defining citizenship, and expanding the electoral franchise. The period after Reconstruction until the early 1930s was largely one of conservative politics, with the exception of a progressive reform movement in the first two decades of the twentieth century. Juridical settlements mirrored a society caught up in a struggle for wealth and preoccupied with the supremacy of the white race. Examples of this conservative trend include *Plessy v. Ferguson*, which affirmed segregation in public facilities; *In re Debs*, which undercut labor unions; and *United States v. E. C. Knight Co.*, which vitiated anti-trust legislation. Since 1930, there has been periodic resurgence and decline of liberal and conservative political philosophies. During this period the U.S. Supreme Court lost its liberal majority and became more balanced politically, and neither political party has enjoyed a monopoly of both the legislature and the presidency.

The U.S. Supreme Court decided almost half the major cases interpreting the Treaty of Guadalupe Hidalgo. The political evolution of the Court influenced how the justices regarded the treaty. Prior to the Civil War, the Supreme Court had been concerned primarily with the nation-state relationship and the preservation of the union. During the tenure of Chief Justice Taney, the Court sought ways to avoid a civil war over the issue of slavery and sectionalism. The sanctity of property was foremost in their reasoning. For example, when they rendered their famous *Dred Scott* opinion in 1857, they stated that Congress had no power to exclude slaves as property from the territories.

After the Civil War the Court turned to the relationship between government and private business and tended to favor the latter. Many Supreme Court decisions opposed the government's attempts to regulate or restrain the excesses of capitalism. Not surprisingly, in the decades following Reconstruction, the Court opposed interpretations of the Treaty of Guadalupe Hidalgo that might hinder the growth of the American economy in the Southwest.

The Supreme Court changed its views in 1937 when it abandoned its opposition to government programs that challenged private business. Increasingly thereafter the Court adopted a more balanced opinion of the role of government in the economy.[2] After World War II the Court was more inclined to concentrate on the relationship of the individual to the government, and specifically on civil rights.

The court cases decided by district, territorial, and state supreme courts usually reflected the pressures of regional interests and local concerns. Most cases came from courts in California and dealt with the issue of property rights, a concern emerging out of that state's growing population pressures on natural resources. Court cases coming from Arizona and New Mexico focused on Indian- and tribal-rights questions as well as challenges to Hispano community grants. Cases decided in Texas reflected a recognition of the Mexican common-law traditions in that state but only those that did not conflict with Anglo-American rule.

1848–1889

In the first period of juridical interpretation, federal and state courts issued judgments that tended to interpret the treaty liberally. Generally the courts bolstered the status of the treaty as a document confirming and protecting rights. On the subject of property rights, the courts sought to clarify the meaning of the language in Article VIII and the Protocol of Querétaro. In 1850 the California Supreme Court ruled that an inchoate title (i.e., not clearly a legal Mexican title) was protected by the treaty and that its legitimacy could be affected or questioned only by the federal government. This construction went far beyond the implied guarantees in the stricken Article X and the Protocol of Querétaro. Even landholders lacking clear titles would be protected until the grants could be examined by the U.S. courts.³ Sixteen years later, in *Mintern v. Bower et al.*, the California court further expanded this concept to include perfected land grants. In that case the court decided "that perfect titles to lands which existed at the date of the treaty of Guadalupe Hidalgo in Mexicans then established in California, were guaranteed and secured to such persons not only by the law of nations, but also by the stipulations of that treaty."⁴ This meant that those individuals who held perfect titles need not submit them before the Board of Land Commissioners established in 1851 to validate titles. This position, which recognized the primacy of federal treaty obligation over congressional legislation, guided California until it was overturned in the federal case of *Botiller v. Dominguez* in 1889.

Other court findings also interpreted the Treaty of Guadalupe Hidalgo liberally. In *United States v. Reading* (1855) the Supreme Court ruled that the treaty protected the property rights of a Mexican citizen who had fought in the U.S. Army against Mexico at the very time his land grant was pending certification by the Mexican government. Because of the treaty's protection, the Court ruled that his military action did not result in a forfeit of land rights. In *Palmer v. United States* (1857), the Court argued that the dates given in the Protocol of Querétaro were not limiting and that in New Mexico and California legitimate titles might have been made by Mexican officials after May 13, 1846. In *Townsend et al. v. Greeley* (1866) the Court held that town or community grants as well as private ones were protected by the treaty.[5]

In other rulings the Court interpreted the treaty to legitimize the transfer of Mexican law to the conquered Southwest. In *United States v. Moreno* (1863), the Supreme Court affirmed that the treaty protected land grants that were legitimate under Mexican law; in 1884 the Court ruled that treaty stipulations did not invalidate the powers of local officials, acting under Mexican law, to make legitimate land grants prior to the implementation of American laws; and in *Philips v. Mound City* the Court advanced the position that the treaty also protected partitions and divisions of land made under Mexican law prior to July 4, 1848.[6]

In this period the implications of the treaty for the civil rights of former Mexican citizens were also a concern of the courts. In the 1870 *De la Guerra* case, the California court interpreted the treaty as confirming U.S. citizenship for Mexicans. In New Mexico the presence of a large group of Hispanicized Pueblo Indians complicated the issue of citizenship. The territorial government in New Mexico did not give Indians citizenship, but in 1869 the New Mexico Supreme Court ruled that by virtue of the treaty, the Pueblo Indians were citizens of the territory and of the United States. In *United States v. Lucero* the justices analyzed the treaty extensively to support this view. After reviewing Article 9, Justice Watts, writing for the court, stated: "This court, under this section of the treaty of Guadalupe Hidalgo, does not consider it proper to assent to the withdrawal of eight thousand citizens of New Mexico from the operation of the law, made to secure and maintain them in their liberty and property, and consign their liberty and property to a system of laws and trade made for wandering savages."[7] The justices thus proposed that the Pueblo Indians were not tribal Indians subject to laws administered by the Department of Indian Affairs. This interpretation regarding the treaty status of the Pueblo Indians was reaffirmed by the New Mexico Supreme Court in 1874 but reversed in 1940.[8]

A narrower view of the meaning of the treaty in this period was largely limited to the question of the application of the treaty to Texas. In 1856 the Supreme Court heard a case involving a land-grant claim in Texas that sought remedy under the treaty. In *McKinney v. Saviego* the Court decided that that the treaty did not apply to Texas lands. Justice Campbell, writing for the Court, summarized Article VIII in the treaty and asked: "To what territories did the high contracting parties refer to in this article? We think it clear that they did not refer to any portion of the acknowledged limits of Texas." The Court argued that Texas had been recognized by the U.S. government as an independent country and had been annexed as a state prior to the Mexican War. Therefore, the Treaty of Guadalupe applied only to those territories annexed by the United States in 1848. This interpretation was sustained by several subsequent decisions, and it stands as law today.[9]

1889–1930

A liberal view of the meaning of the Treaty of Guadalupe Hidalgo prevailed in the period prior to the landmark judgment of *Botiller v. Dominguez* in 1889. This case inaugurated a decidedly conservative attitude regarding the extent to which the treaty was important in protecting the property of the former Mexican citizens. The most far-reaching impact of the *Botiller* case was summarized in the statement written by Justice Miller for the Court.

> If the treaty was violated by this general statute [the Land Law of 1851], enacted for the purpose of ascertaining the validity of claims derived from the Mexican government, it was a matter of international concern, which the two states must determine by treaty or by such other means as enables one state to enforce upon another the obligations of a treaty. This court, in cases like the present, has no power to set itself up as the instrumentality for enforcing the provisions of a treaty with a foreign nation which the government of the United States, as a sovereign power, chooses to disregard.[10]

In *Botiller v. Dominguez* the Supreme Court held that the sovereign laws of the United States took precedence over international treaties. This appeared to be in direct contradiction of the Constitution, which (in Article VI, Section 2 and Article III, Section 2, Clause 1) gave treaties the same status as the Constitution. The Supreme Court's decision, some argued, sanctioned the confiscation of property and violated the due process provision of the Constitution. Nevertheless the case became an important precedent guiding the Court in its future interpretation of conflicts between treaty obligations and domestic laws.[11] The judgment in *Botiller* declared that the American courts had no responsibility to hear cases involving violations of the Treaty of Guadalupe Hidalgo. To resolve conflicts arising over the treaty there was no recourse but to international diplomatic negotiation.

Eventually the *Botiller* case was cited as a basis for denying lands to the California Mission Indians, who had legal title to their ancestral lands under Mexican law but had not filed their title before the Land Commission as stipulated in the 1851 law. For the Court the right of the government to provide "reasonable means for determining the validity of all titles within the ceded territory" superseded the inhabitant's treaty rights.[12] Just as the *Botiller* decree became a rule of law in subsequent years, the courts continually reconfirmed the right of Congress and the courts to implement the treaty through laws "to ascertain the legitimacy of title." If these implementing laws ran counter to the protections of the treaty, the congressional laws would take precedence. This principle was affirmed in *California Powderworks v. Davis* (1894), in *United States v. Sandoval et al.* (1897), and in *Arisa v. New Mexico and Arizona Railroad* (1899).[13]

The courts also interpreted the treaty so that it would be more restrictive as to the land rights claimed by former Mexican citizens and those who had acquired their lands. The Supreme Court determined that the treaty "did not increase rights" and that "no duty rests on this government to recognize the validity of a grant to any area of greater extent than was recognized by the government of Mexico."[14] This in itself might have been a reasonable assertion but it hinged on the government's view of the scope of legitimate Mexican laws, and increasingly the courts took a narrow view. One question that arose was whether Mexican landholders would be protected from squatters and speculators during the time it took for the U.S. courts to determine the validity of their Mexican titles. In 1901, in *Lockhart v. Johnson*, the Supreme Court ruled that neither Articles VIII or IX gave such protection. In this case a portion of the Cañada de Cochiti land-grant in New Mexico had been purchased from the U.S. government by a mining company while the grant was pending action by the Surveyor General's Office. An American who had purchased the original grant argued that the mining company's occupancy had violated the

Treaty of Guadalupe Hidalgo. Justice Peckham stated for the Supreme Court: "[T]here are no words in the treaty with Mexico expressly withdrawing from sale all lands within claimed limits of a Mexican grant, and we do not think there is any language in the treaty which implies a reservation of any kind."[15]

This 1901 doctrine, that the treaty did not protect land claims from public sale, differed from the long-standing policy of the General Land Office, which had interpreted the treaty to mean that "all lands embraced within the Mexican and Spanish grants were placed in a state of reservation for the ascertainment of rights claimed under said grant."[16] In California the courts also ruled that the treaty would not provide special protection for Mexicans who owned property. In 1913 the California State Supreme Court argued that "the treaty of Guadalupe Hidalgo requires only that the rights of Mexican grantees in their property shall be equal to that of citizens of the United States." And in 1930 it ruled that the treaty did not bind the government to follow the Spanish or Mexican statute of limitations with regard to land or water rights.[17]

Article X in the original treaty, which was stricken out by the U.S. Senate, was not part of the official document proclaimed as law in 1848. Among other things Article X had specified that "all grants of land made by the Mexican government . . . shall be respected as valid, to the same extent that the same grants would be valid, if the said territories had remained within the limits of Mexico" (see appendix 1). The striking of this article emerged as a point of law for the courts and became a basis for rejecting land claims.

In *Interstate Land Co. v. Maxwell Land Co.* (1891) the U.S. Supreme Court rejected the assertion that a grant was invalid because it had been declared so by a Mexican law prior to 1848. After analyzing the circumstances surrounding the removal of Article X by the Senate, including President Polk's message to Congress, the Court stated that "this claim was one of the class which was expressly refused to be recognized by the treaty" (more accurately by the absence of Article X).[18] In another case, *Cessna v. United States et al.* in 1898, the Supreme Court interpreted the absence of Article X to rule against a New Mexican land claimant whose grant had been rejected by the Court of Private Land Claims. Accordingly, "when the U.S. received this territory under the Treaty of Guadalupe Hidalgo, they refused to recognize as still valid and enforceable all grants which had been assumed to be made prior thereto by the Mexican authorities. Article X, as proposed by the commissioners, was rejected by this government."[19]

Thus the absence of Article X, with its specific guarantees of due process after 1848 under Mexican law provided a basis for the courts to restrict further the meaning of the treaty. The Protocol of Querétaro, which had been drafted to assure the Mexican government that the spirit of Article X would be retained, was not a matter for future juridical consideration.

The final area of conservative interpretation of the treaty in the period 1889–1930 was in Indian affairs. Three cases illustrate the trend. In 1897 the Supreme Court construed the treaty so as to benefit the government and undercut historic understandings between Mexican and Indian communities in New Mexico. The pueblo of Zia claimed proprietory and grazing rights in northern New Mexico by virtue of their use of land with the agreement of the Mexican settlers. The Court, however, ruled that, by ceding Mexican lands to the public domain the treaty provided the basis for revoking these prior concessions as well as for denying any claims of land ownership on the part of the Indians.

The Court also moved to question any extension of citizenship rights to Indians. In an 1869 judgment the New Mexican territorial court ruled that the treaty conferred U.S. citizenship on Pueblo Indians. In a 1913 case the Supreme Court stated that "it remains an open question whether they have become citizens of the U.S." Also, "we need not determine it now, because citizenship is not in itself an obstacle to the exercise by Congress of its power to enact laws for the benefit and protection of tribal Indians as dependent peoples."[20] The next year the Court ruled that the California Indians had not been given citizenship by the Treaty of Guadalupe Hidalgo. Chief Justice White attacked the argument that the California Indians were entitled to citizenship by virtue of the treaty as "so devoid of merit as not in any real sense to involve the construction of the treaty." A later court arrived at similar conclusions regarding the status of the Pueblo Indians in New Mexico.[21]

Although the bulk of court constructions of the treaty from 1880 to 1930 were based on a conservative reading of the document, there were a few cases in which the courts expanded its meaning. Despite earlier indications by the U.S. Supreme Court, in *McKinney v. Saviego*, that the treaty would not apply to Texas, the Texas Supreme Court made a series of rulings that validated the treaty as applying to certain regions of the state. In *Texas Mexican Rail Road v. Locke*, the Texas Supreme Court ruled that Mexicans holding valid titles on March 2, 1836, and continuing to hold them until July 4, 1848, "were protected in them by Article 8 of the Treaty of Guadalupe Hidalgo." In a 1914 verdict the same court ruled that the treaty had the "force of law in Texas," and this same principle was affirmed by at least two other Texas rulings.[22] In these decisions the Texas Supreme Court asserted the right of the state to incorporate the treaty into its local laws even though the U.S. Supreme Court refused to do so with respect to the national law. One basis for this difference of interpretation was that in Texas the treaty was being invoked to preserve the rights of property owners who had purchased the lands of former Mexican title holders.

In a similar vein the treaty became a weapon in a struggle between the state and the federal government over the use of the Rio Grande. In 1897 commercial interests in New Mexico sought to construct a dam near Las Cruces to divert water for irrigation projects. The federal government sued the private company, charging that, among other things, the dam would violate Article VII of the Treaty of Guadalupe Hidalgo, which had stated that "the navigation of the Gila and of the Bravo [Rio Grande] . . . shall be free and common to the vessels and citizens of both countries; and neither shall, without the consent of the other, construct any work that may impede or interrupt, in whole or in part, the exercise of this right." Although it did not address the international question directly, the Supreme Court did find that "if the proposed dam and appropriation of the waters of the Rio Grande constitute a breach of treaty obligations or of international duty to Mexico, they also constitute an equal injury and wrong to the people of the United States."[23] The U.S. government was concerned for the rights of the people of the El Paso region to the water and was using the treaty to buttress their position. The result was that the Supreme Court found in favor of the U.S. government and the project was halted. A subsequent lawsuit, in 1902, reconfirmed this opinion. Finally, in 1914, after securing an agreement with Mexico through an international treaty, the federal government undertook the project, constructing the Elephant Butte Dam.[24]

1930 TO THE PRESENT

The Great Depression, which began in 1929, marked the beginning of a liberal political response that lasted well into the 1960s. Conservative reaction to the social and economic policies of the Democrats occurred during the 1950s, 1970s, and 1980s. Thus the political environment surrounding the juridical interpretation of the treaty became more polarized. Neither strict nor liberal interpretations predominated. Increasingly the treaty became a tool for advancing the interests of various interest groups. Various governmental agencies used the treaty with mixed success to enlarge their powers. Corporate interests sought to interpret the treaty to bolster their positions. Native Americans, mobilized by the New Deal and Vietnam War eras, sought redress for past injustices. Mexican Americans began to use the treaty as a weapon to reclaim lands and rights.

The treaty became part of the struggle between the federal government and the western states. As early as 1922 the states of the Colorado River basin had agreed to a division of the waters of that great river system, and in the early 1930s the federal government neared completion of the Hoover Dam project. In 1931 the federal government successfully asserted its control of the nonnavigable sections of the Colorado River in *United States v. Utah*, citing the Treaty of Guadalupe Hidalgo as a basis for its claim against the rights of the states. The treaty provided the legal basis for federal control of dam projects on the river. Similarly, in this same period, the federal government used the treaty to justify its rights to the California tidelands.[25] In the 1960s the federal government sued the gulf states of Louisiana, Alabama, Florida, and Texas in an attempt to control oil-rich lands beyond the three-mile limit. The states of Texas and Florida cited the treaties that had settled their international boundaries to successfully retain control of lands beyond three miles off shore. The state of Texas cited Article V of the treaty, which stipulated that the Texas–Mexico boundary would begin "three leagues from land opposite the mouth of the Rio Grande." The Florida treaty with Spain contained similar language. Since a league was approximately two miles, both states could claim a six-mile limit. Using this same wording in the treaty, the Mexican government had, since 1936, asserted a three-league offshore limit on its gulf coast. Consequently the Supreme Court found in favor of Texas and Florida but against the other states citing the Treaty of Guadalupe Hidalgo as a major basis for its decision.[26]

Corporate interests have also had some success in using the treaty to their benefit. In 1940 in *Chadwick et al. v. Campbell* the Circuit Court of Appeals for New Mexico gave a lengthy interpretation of the treaty in deciding a corporate struggle over land containing valuable oil and gas leases. Campbell, representing one group of investors, successfully sued Chadwick and the trustees of the Sevilleta de la Joya grant, who controlled 215,000 acres in Socorro County. The trustees had lost title to the lands following nonpayment of taxes. Chadwick argued that the treaty guaranteed protection of Mexican land grants. The court ruled that the treaty did not exempt Mexican landholders from taxes but that "under the Treaty of Guadalupe Hidalgo, private rights of property within the ceded territory were unaffected by the change in sovereignty"[27] In *Summa Corporation v. California* (1984) an investment corporation successfully challenged an attempt by the State of California to declare their lands part of the public domain. The corporation persuaded the court that the treaty had been legitimately implemented in the actions of the California Land Commission. The court ruled that the corporation's land rights derived from Congress's interpretation of the treaty in law.[28] This was the same argument employed by the federal government in earlier periods to justify its appropriation of the public domain.

During this period (1930 to the present), Native Americans seeking redress for the loss of their tribal lands and liberties used the treaty as one of many treaties that courts might consider. On the whole their efforts were frustrated. Most judicial decisions were against the Indians' rights and in favor of a limited interpretation of the treaty.

In *Tenorio v. Tenorio* (1940) the New Mexico Supreme Court echoed an earlier suggestion of the federal court that the Treaty of Guadalupe Hidalgo did not embrace Pueblo Indians. This judgment reversed an earlier territorial court position in the *Lucero* case, which had applied the treaty to the Pueblo peoples. In 1945 the Supreme Court also ruled that the treaty could not be used to give support to the land claims of the Shoshonean Indians, many of whom had lived within the Mexican Cession in Utah, Nevada, and California. The courts also rejected California Indian claims, refusing to agree that the treaty was a substantive basis for a fiduciary duty towards these people. In *Pitt River Tribe et al. v. United States* (1973) two members of this California tribe sued the government to recover the true value of lands that had been settled in a financial agreement in 1964. The court rejected their appeal, which had been based largely on the treaty.[29]

Two of the most significant interpretations of the Treaty of Guadalupe Hidalgo as it affected American Indians were made in April and May of 1986. They represented both a victory and a defeat for Indian rights.

On January 4, 1985, an officer of the Department of the Interior charged José Abeyta, an Isleta Pueblo Indian, with violating the Bald Eagle Protection Act because he had killed one of these birds to use its feathers in religious ceremonies. Abeyta defended himself before the U.S. District Court in New Mexico, asserting that Indians were protected in the exercise of their religion by Article IX of the Treaty of Guadalupe Hidalgo, which had promised that all Mexican nationals would be "secured in the free exercise of their religion without restriction." The District Court again overruled the 1945 *Tenorio* ruling that the Pueblo Indians were not protected by the Treaty of Guadalupe Hidalgo. Judge Burciaga ruled for the court: "Because the Treaty of Guadalupe Hidalgo afforded protections to the Pueblos, however, it is in this dimension more than a settlement between two hostile nations: it is a living Indian treaty."[30] The court then moved to dismiss the charges against Abeyta based entirely upon the protections of religious liberty contained in the 1st Amendment and the Treaty of Guadalupe Hidalgo. This was a significant finding in that, for the first time, the language of the treaty itself was the primary basis for a legal decision.

One month later, on May 5, 1986, the U.S. Court of Appeals in California decided another case involving Indian rights, specifically the claim of the members of the Chumash tribe to the Santa Barbara, Santa Cruz, and Santa Rosa islands. The Chumash peoples claimed that they had occupied the islands since "time immemorial" and that the Treaty of Guadalupe Hidalgo, by failing to mention the islands as part of the ceded territories, left the tribe in legal possession. The court, in a footnote, issued its opinion of this argument: "While the court generally must assume the factual allegations to be true, it need not assume the truth of the legal conclusions cast in the form of factual allegations."[31] The Indians further argued that if the treaty did apply to them, then "the aboriginal title of the Chumash Indians to the islands came to be recognized by Article VIII and IX of the 1848 Treaty of Guadalupe Hidalgo." The court responded that this argument was "novel and creative but does not appear to have any merit." In rejecting the tribal claims, Judge Fletcher maintained (1) that Indian title to land "derives from their presence on land before the arrival of white settlers" and (2) that the treaty did not convert Indians' claims into recognized titles, because only the Land Commission could do this, and the Chumash had failed to present their claim within the stipulated time limits.

Since the 1930s the treaty has been an instrument most widely used by plaintiffs of non-Mexican origin seeking a variety of remedies. Only a few court cases have been initiated by those whom the treaty was intended to protect. In this period, six court cases citing the treaty directly impinged on the fate of the Mexican-American population. In the 1940s the state of Texas and the Balli family engaged in a series of legal battles over ownership of Padre Island. Alberto Balli had inherited what he thought was a legal Mexican land grant from his family. In 1943 the state of Texas sued the Balli family to recover the land grant, arguing that it had not fulfilled the technical requirements of Mexican statutes. The District Court in Texas found that the Balli family had met most of the requirements of the law and that their rights were protected under the Treaty of Guadalupe Hidalgo. In a series of rulings, the court resoundingly supported Balli against the state. The Texas Supreme Court later affirmed this verdict on appeal. This was a major land-grant victory for Tejanos, and it was based squarely on an interpretation of the treaty. It also was an indication that, notwithstanding previous court decisions exempting Texas from application of the treaty, it was still possible to interpret the document as applying to land-grant cases in that state.[32]

A few years later the courts faced this issue again but ruled in the opposite direction, to divest a Mexican family of its land. In 1946 Amos Amaya and his family, all citizens of Mexico, sued the Texas-based Stanolind Oil and Gas Company to recover lands allegedly taken illegally under the Treaty of Guadalupe Hidalgo. Circuit Court Judge Waller, in his ruling, cited Article VIII of the treaty, specifically that portion requiring the title of Mexican citizens to be inviolably respected: "We regard the phrase as a covenant on the part of the United States to respect from thenceforth any title that Mexicans had, or might thereafter acquire, to property with the region, but not that it would guarantee that those Mexicans would never lose title to persons by foreclosure, sales under execution, trespass, adverse possession, and other non-government acts."[33] Because the Amaya family failed to follow the timetable for land recovery under Texas statutes, the judge sustained the lower court's ruling against recovery of their lands. As he put it, "The provisions of the treaty do not save the Appellants from the fatal effect of the passage of time under the statutes of limitations in the State of Texas."[34]

The issue of the property rights of Mexican citizens reemerged in 1954 during the height of a nationwide campaign to deport or repatriate Mexican immigrants. Robert Galván, a legal Mexican immigrant accused of being a communist, was brought for deportation hearings before the U.S. District Court in Southern California. He in turn filed for a writ of habeas corpus, arguing that his deportation would violate the Treaty of Guadalupe Hidalgo provision protecting the property of Mexican citizens. The court responded that although the treaty was entitled to "juridical obeisance," it did not specify that Mexicans were entitled to remain in the United States to manage their property.[35]

Another Mexican-American land-rights issue came before the court in a series of cases launched by Reies Tijerina and the Alianza Federal de Mercedes Libres in New Mexico. In the 1960s a group of Hispano land-grant claimants led by the charismatic Reies López Tijerina sought to regain their lost community grants. Concurrent with their court battles, the organization sponsored a series of meetings and rallies that eventually erupted in violent confrontations, a take-over of Tierra Amarilla courthouse, shootings, and a statewide manhunt for the leaders of the Alianza. In 1969, with the land-grant struggle still fresh, Tijerina launched another campaign to change the public-school system in New Mexico by forcing reapportionment on local school boards of education and by requiring the teaching of all subjects in both Spanish and English. As in the land-grant wars, Tijerina relied heavily on the legal and moral force of the Treaty of Guadalupe Hidalgo. In a class-action lawsuit on behalf of the "Indio-Hispano" poor people of New Mexico, Tijerina sued the State Board of Education. On December 4, 1969, the District Court dismissed the suit for a variety of causes, including the court opinion that Tijerina had misinterpreted the scope of the treaty. Tijerina had based his suit for bilingual education on Articles VIII and IX of the treaty, but the court found that the treaty "does not contemplate in any way the administration of public schools. In addition we are not of the opinion that the treaty confers any proprietary right to have the Spanish language and culture preserved and continued in the public schools at public expense."[36] Addressing Tijerina's contention that the rights of poor people were being violated, the court ruled, "This is an unsound position as that treaty has nothing to do with any rights that 'poor' people may have."

Tijerina appealed the District Court ruling to the Supreme Court, and on May 25, 1970, that court also dismissed the appeal. Justice Douglas wrote a dissenting opinion, arguing that although the treaty was not a sound basis for the case, it could be argued on civil rights under the 14th and 15th amendments.[37]

Another land-rights case occured in 1984, when the Texas Mexican property holders who were members of the Asociación de Reclamantes brought a case before the federal courts. They sought reimbursement for lands taken from them in violation of the treaty. As a result of counterbalancing international claims, the Mexican government had become liable to compensate the heirs of Tejano landholders for their losses. In the 1984 case the Asociación members outlined the damages they sought from the Mexican government. The U.S. Court of Appeals, however, declined to hear the case on the basis that the violation had not occurred within the United States. Of significance, however, was the statement of the judge recognizing that the Tejano landholders had rights that "were explicitly protected by the Treaty of Guadalupe Hidalgo." This suggested a reversal of the *McKinney v. Saviego* (1856) opinion in which the treaty was interpreted as not being applicable to Texas. U.S. acceptance that the 1941 treaty with Mexico settled the outstanding claims against Mexico appeared to be an admission of the validity of the Tejano land claims under the treaty.[38] This point has not, however, been explicitly tested in the courts.

CONCLUSION

It is difficult to characterize in a few words the direction the American courts have taken in interpreting the Treaty of Guadalupe Hidalgo. The courts have changed their opinions several times on a number of issues, most notably regarding the applicability of the treaty to Texas and the Pueblo Indians. About half of the cases entailing a major interpretation of the treaty have involved Mexican American or Indian litigants. In these cases, defeats outnumbered victories by about two to one. The treaty has been more important in legitimizing the status quo, particularly in justifying federal, state, and corporate ownership of former Spanish and Mexican land grants. About three-fourths of the cases decided since 1848 have been about land-ownership rights, and only a small percentage have been about civil rights under the treaty.[39]

The Treaty of Guadalupe Hidalgo has remained a viable part of the U.S. system of laws, having been interpreted again and again by the federal and state courts. Unfortunately, the treaty has not effectively protected and enlarged the civil and property rights of Mexican Americans. This apparently unfulfilled promise of the treaty fueled a Mexican-American political movement in the 1960s and 1970s that sought to achieve a justice denied them by the American courts.

CHAPTER 7

Historical Interpretations of 1848

Of all conquerors we were perhaps the most excusable, the most reasonable, the most beneficent. The Mexicans had come far short of their duty to the world. Being what they were, they had forfeited a large share of their national rights.

JUSTIN H. SMITH
THE WAR WITH MEXICO

Peace, on the other hand, gave us an occasion to take advantage of acquired experience . . . waking from the dream of illusions, putting aside our war expenses, balancing our treasury with war indemnities, reestablishing public credit, and creating a spirit of union and concord.

JOSE MARÍA ROA BÁRCENA
RECUERDOS DE LA INVASIÓN NORTEAMERICANA
(1846–1848)

The Mexican War was a pivotal event in the relationship between the United States and Mexico, creating new boundaries and problems as well as setting in motion forces that influenced the histories of both countries. As a result of this conflict the United States acquired the valuable lands and natural resources that accelerated its industrial growth in the twentieth century. Disputes over the territory acquired also affected a larger conflict—the U.S. Civil War—which dramatically changed American politics.

In Mexico, the disastrous military defeat in 1848 forced a reevaluation of the national leadership, which led to a reform movement headed by Benito Juárez. This also generated a civil war in Mexico, which began in 1857, an invasion by the French in 1862, and ultimately the restructuring of the Mexican state under a dictatorship that lasted until the Mexican Revolution in 1910. Historians in both countries have interpreted the importance of the Mexican War and especially the Treaty of Guadalupe Hidalgo. The interpretations on both sides of the Rio Grande have changed over time, according to the climate of the political culture.

U.S. VIEWS

U.S. historians have largely been concerned with studying how the Treaty of Guadalupe Hidalgo came to be drafted. As a result, the historiography in the United States regarding the impacts of the treaty is not very substantial. If American historians have not been much concerned with the long-term legal and historical significance of this document, it is probably because the historical presence of Mexican Americans within the United States is of relatively recent interest.[1]

Historical views of the Treaty of Guadalupe Hidalgo from north of the Rio Grande are largely included in military and diplomatic histories of the Mexican War. Here the historiography is better developed. Hundreds of books and articles have appeared since 1848 on the subject of the Mexican War and these have been annotated by Norman Tutorow in his encyclopedic reference book, *The Mexican-American War: An Annotated Bibliography*.[2] Nevertheless, in comparison with other eras in U.S. history, the Mexican War has been neglected, overshadowed in importance by the Civil War.

As might be expected most of the early studies of the Mexican War saw the treaty as an entirely justified end to a conflict that the Mexican government had provoked. Perhaps the most ambitious of these early accounts was Roswell Sabine Ripley's two-volume history *The War With Mexico*, which was written by a participant who had been involved in the political intrigues against General Scott.[3] Written in 1849, book had much to say about the political and military maneuvers of the American army and little of consequence to offer in the way of evaluating the significance of the treaty. Along with most of his contemporaries, Ripley interpreted the war and its conclusion in terms of Manifest Destiny. He thought that the war had benefited Mexico since it reduced the disruptive political influence of the army and introduced American commerce and culture.[4] Overall the treaty was seen as an entirely just and fair settlement to a patriotic war.

A more critical perspective on the war and the treaty was offered in 1849 by William Jay in his widely read book *A Review of the Causes and Consequences of the Mexican War*.[5] This book and several others like it were the result of a competition sponsored by the American Peace Society, and it reflected an anti-war, abolitionist perspective, critical of American policy towards Mexico and the conduct of the war. Jay advanced a conspiracy theory of history involving president Polk's "war mongering" on behalf of slave owners. He did not directly analyze the treaty, but devoted a chapter to the acquisition of new territory where he pointedly observed that thirteen large slave states could be carved from the Mexican lands acquired by the treaty. He did not think this territory worth the loss of human life and increased corruption of the nation's morals. Even the gold rush, he felt, could not justify the debasement of character that would inevitably result. The new territory, he asserted, was not worth 15 million dollars since "not only Texas but all New Mexico, will for a long period be doomed to the ignorance, degradation and misery which are inseparable from human bondage."[6]

Perhaps the most thoroughly researched book dealing with the Mexican War was Justin Smith's two volume work *The War With Mexico*, which was published in 1919.[7] This study, based on many sources that have since disappeared, continued Ripley's pro-Manifest Destiny interpretation of the war and treaty. It was the first book in English to give a detailed discussion and interpretation of the negotiation and ratification of the treaty but the account was marred with florid prejudices. Trist was a man of "goodwill, self-sacrifice and courage" while the Mexican negotiators were factious, inefficient, and punctilious. For Smith "our real title was conquest" and the treaty merely was "an acknowledgement of our title." And in return "we gave her not only peace, which meant vastly more to Mexico than to us, but the extensive lands, the renunciation of all American claims antedating the treaty, and fifteen million dollars in money—a wealth of gold that her treasury had never seen before." The conclusion Smith reached was that the war was entirely justified given Mexico's lack of civilization—"Being what they were, they had forfeited a large share of their national rights"—and the American conduct of the war and imposition of a peace was "the most excusable, the most reasonable, the most beneficent."[8]

The very impressive, if sometimes questionable, scholarship that went into the book made *The Mexican War* a benchmark. But the most important studies in English dealing with the Treaty of Guadalupe Hidaglo were yet to be written. The most thorough histories of the treaty's origins appeared in David Hunter Miller's *Treaties and Other International Acts of the United States*, published in 1937, and David M. Pletcher's *The Diplomacy of Annexation: Texas, Oregon and the Mexican War*, which appeared in 1973.[9] Both of these works were much more detailed than any previous scholarship dealing with the negotiation process. Both tended to view the treaty as an antiquarian artifact of the conflict, however, not as a document that had continuing importance after 1848. Miller's discussion, written as part of a Department of State treaty series, was exhaustive in its description of the legal and diplomatic details that went into the actual drafting process. Scrupulously objective, his main purpose was to describe and chronicle the twists and turns of diplomatic exchanges without evaluating their long range importance. This approach tended to slight a larger historical interpretation of the military and political events surrounding the war. David Pletcher's book remedied this problem admirably as he interpreted rather than described the documents relating to the story of the Mexican annexation.

For Pletcher the real significance of this period could be told in terms of the failures and successes of diplomacy. Most causes of the war had been due to breakdown in diplomacy; President Polk's major weakness was his inability to be patient and rely on his diplomats; the crises engendered by war for both the United States and Mexico were finally resolved by the civilian diplomats. The treaty, he thought, was "a blend of compromise, persuasion, and coercion . . . in most respects a credit to all concerned." Pletcher did not question the morality of the war and annexation as had Ripley and his successors, nor did he run up the flag as blatantly as had Smith. Pletcher's view was that annexation might have been accomplished more humanely and at less cost through conventional diplomacy rather than through war.[10]

Recent scholarship surrounding the war and treaty, as

limited as it has been, is partially incorporated into the textbooks used by American high school and college students. With few exceptions they have continued to neglect the consequences the war and the treaty had for Mexican Americans, although they recognize American responsibility for the war. One recent text alluded to the aggressive American diplomatic and military maneuvers just prior to the war in 1846 and quoted Ulysses S. Grant as saying, "We were sent to provoke a fight, but it was essential that Mexico should commence it." After a brief narrative about the course of the war, the text cursorily mentioned the treaty of Guadalupe Hidalgo without any reference to the key articles dealing with the transfer of people. The authors gave the war and treaty minor treatment; basically this era was seen as a prelude to the Civil War.[11] This emphasis, with some variation, has continued in more advanced texts.

The influential college reader *The Jacksonian Era 1828–1848*, by Glyndon G. Van Deusen, was published in 1963 and presented a detailed account of the political and military maneuvers surrounding the negotiation of the treaty. The emphasis was on the events in Washington, D.C., and conflicts between northern Whigs and Southern Democrats that led to the Civil War. No mention was made of the 100,000 Mexican citizens annexed in the bargain and there was no discussion of how the treaty promised to protect their land and liberties. Mexican Americans remained invisible in this national history.[12]

Some U.S. history texts published in the 1980s have incorporated Mexican Americans into the national history. The college level text by Gary B. Nash and Julie Roy Jeffrey, *The American People: Creating a Nation and a Society*, gives a more balanced interpretation of the war and treaty, setting these events within the context of the westward expansion of the Anglo Americans and their encounter with other civilizations. The cause of the Mexican war was Manifest Destiny and American expansionism; the Treaty of Guadalupe Hidalgo (treated under its own sub heading) "guaranteed the civil and political rights of former Mexican citizens and their rights to land." Subsequent discussion of how this promise was a hollow one makes this textbook one of the most complete discussion of the war and the peace published thus far.[13]

MEXICAN VIEWS

Mexican interpretations of the events of 1848 can be divided arbitrarily into two categories: 1) the historical writings of the late nineteenth century, including those made by the participants; and 2) the interpretations of Mexican historians writing after World War II. There is a gap in the Mexican historiography of the Mexican War period. The generation of historians that came to maturity during the period of the Mexican Revolution (1910–1940) wrote few works focusing on this period.

In general, Mexican historiography regarding the war and treaty has been influenced by the development of history as a profession and by the rise of Mexican nationalism. Along with many other Latin American historians, Mexican writers in the nineteenth century were self-educated, multifaceted people who worked in many professions—as journalists, educators, administrators, clerics, politicians, and lawyers. All wrote history as an avocation. They were intensely political, and both liberal and conservative points of view can be found in their interpretations of the past. Many writers of Mexican history in the nineteenth century developed a research interest in the Spanish colonial era and independence movements. Conservative writers naturally sided with the centralist, monarchist, and anti-liberal factions while the liberals criticized the Spanish colonial administration and defied revolutionary leaders.[14]

Soon after the war, fifteen Mexican journalists, politicians, military officers, and businessmen headed by Ramón Alcaraz formed a historical association in order to write an unbiased collective account of the conflict.[15] The group pooled their archives and reminscences and divided the labors of writing a survey history of the war. They made every attempt to remain factual and nonpartisan. They reviewed and criticized each other's work, and they omitted accounts about which there was significant disagreement. The result, modestly entitled *Apuntes para la historia de la guerra entre Mexico y los Estados Unidos*, was published on August 11, 1848, soon after the Mexican Congress had approved the treaty.[16]

Alcaraz and the other authors wrote a prosaic and detailed history, but they clearly indicted the Americans as aggressors, identifying American expansionism as a cause: "They desired from the beginning to extend their dominion in such a manner as to become the absolute owners of all this continent." The drift toward war with Mexico they characterized as a "conscious plan," not a series of accidents or misunderstandings. The Americans' "spirit of aggrandizement" propelled them to invade Mexico (the territory between the Rio Grande and the Nucces River). The bulk of the *Notas* came from accounts written by participants in the original battles and official government documents of that time that have since been lost or destroyed. In evaluating the treaty the authors succinctly described the arguments advanced by Peña y Peña and Réjon respectively, but they refrained both from commenting on the treaty itself and from revealing their own position in the debate. They explained: "Being sadly affected by an event that has reduced us to the most frightful debasement of misfortune and discredit, we feel incapable of expressing ourselves with the impartiality that ought to characterize the historian."[17] Two other contemporary interpretations of the war were those of José Fernando Ramírez and Carlos María de Bustamante. Ramírez wrote a series of lengthy letters and notes about the political and military events in Mexico City during the war. His notes, *Mexico durante su guerra con los Estados Unidos*, were published posthumously in 1905 in a larger volume edited by Genaro García entitled *Documentos ineditos o muy raros para la historia de México*. Ramírez's account ends on September 30, 1847, and so therefore does not include an interpretation of the Treaty of Guadalupe Hidalgo. In his account, Ramírez expresses disgust with the factional politics that plagued Mexico and that made a peace treaty impossible. Clearly he favored an end to the war, but he heaped blame for the conflict on "the corrupt governments of the past."[18]

Carlos María de Bustamante's contemporary account also ended in 1847. He wrote a two-volume, detailed history of the origin and progress of the war based on documents of the period. Even though Bustamante was writing before a formal end to hostilities, he blamed General Santa Anna for his treachery and ineptness in losing the war. There is no analysis of treaty negotiations.[19]

Criticism of Mexico's disordered political factions and a lack of criticism of the United States characterized the historical view of 1848 put forth during the era of Porfirio Díaz. During the Porfirato, conservative Mexican historians began to view 1848 as the well-deserved end to ineffectual liberal government. One such conservative writer was the Priest Francisco de Paula Arrangoiz (1812–1899). Born in Jalapa, Veracruz, of a middle-class family, he had a career as a politician in various administrations and became a fervent supporter of General Santa Anna. In 1848 he served as minister of hacienda under Peña y Peña. After the war, Arrangoiz served as consul general to the United States, where he was in charge of distributing and investing the money paid Mexico by the United States for the Gadsden Purchase (1854). After Santa Anna's final fall from power, Arrangoiz went to Europe, where he embraced monarchism. When the puppet Emperor Maximilian came to Mexico in the 1860s, Arrangoiz served as his minister to England and Belgium. In 1872 he wrote his history of Mexico.[20]

His interpretation of the events of 1848 was that the real traitors to Mexico were the republicans who had opened the City of Mexico to the conquerors, specifically the members of the municipal assembly (ayuntamiento). These politicians, Arrangoiz believed, were working for the "prosperity of the United States and the Annexation of Mexico to it."[21] According to this view, the liberals were the natural allies of the Americans because they shared the same anticlerical, democratic ideals. The conservatives were the only true enemies of the Americans because they were monarchists. Reflecting his career as a pro-French diplomat, Arrangoiz praised the French for their opposition to the American invasion and their criticism of the Treaty of Guadalupe.

For Arrangoiz the Mexican government had no choice but to sign the treaty, not only because its armies were totally defeated and there was a lack of popular support for continuing the war but also, and perhaps primarily, because the Americans were actively involved in fomenting Indian uprisings—a "guerra de las castas." The specter of an Indian rebellion haunted Arrangoiz. He cited several such uprisings—in Guanajuato, San Luis Potosí, and Querétaro—that occurred in 1848 and were allegedly inspired by the Americans. Arrangoiz's view of 1848, then, was that the nation had been defeated from within, primarily by the treasonous liberals, and that the dangers of a race war made a humiliating peace treaty a necessity.[22] One of the most important historians to write about the Mexican War and treaty negotiations was José María Roa Bárcena (1827–1908). Born in Jalapa, Veracruz, tropical home of so many other conservatives in the nineteenth century, Roa Bárcena established himself early as a businessman and part-time journalist. He supported conservative causes, Santa Anna's presidency among them. In 1853 he moved to Mexico City, where he devoted most of his energies to collaborative publication in a variety of journals and newspapers. In the 1860s he supported the monarchy of Maximilian, for which he later spent several years in prison. In his declining years he survived by managing a wealthy widow's estate, writing poetry and essays, and putting the finishing touches on his magnum opus, a three-volume study, entitled *Recuerdos de la invasión Norte Americana (1846–1848)*, which appeared in 1887.[23] This multivolume work stands alone today as the definitive Mexican history of the war with the United States and the treaty negotiations. Based mostly on primary sources and notes gathered by the author during the war it contains many quotations and little-known facts from rare and now-destroyed or missing archival documents. What was remarkable about the book, in addition to its originality and detail, was its relatively dispassionate interpretation of events. His work was more than just a compendium of facts. Some of his interpretations remain penetrating and astute to this day.

Roa Bárcena's account of the treaty negotiations is a case in point. In discussing the flow of events during the last two months of the talks between Nicholas Trist and the Mexican government, Roa Bárcena saw that the continuation of the war pressured Mexican politicians in a very direct way to sign the treaty. The lack of a treaty meant that elections and congressional sessions could not be conducted. This in turn affected the future careers of all politicians then in power. Most important, to pay its army the Mexican government desperately needed the money promised by the treaty and by the resumption of revenue collection. Quoting officials in de la Rosa's government, Roa Bárcena directly traced the end of the war to economic pressures on the government.

Roa Bárcena also emphasized that a considerable body of Mexican politicians did not favor the treaty. His own state, Veracruz, along with San Luis Potosí, Zacatecas, Chihuahua, and Jalisco opposed the treaty. Roa Bárcena outlined their arguments along with those of advocates of the treaty.

In his evaluation of the war and the treaty, he viewed the United States as the aggressor, consciously planning to take over Mexican territories. The Americans saw the northern frontier of Mexico as "indispensible to the security and well being of the United States." Once at war, Mexico was bound to lose because of the weakened condition of the social, political, and economic systems of the country. Roa Bárcena's view of 1848 was that the treaty was an honorable document that prevented Mexico from being dismembered entirely. The end of the war served, he thought, to awaken the Mexican people to new realities and to establish a "new spirit of union."[24]

A contemporary of Roa Bárcena, Justo Sierra (1848–1912), was perhaps the most influential man of letters during the age of Porfirio Díaz. Sierra was prolific. His works included volumes of poetry, literature, essays, plays, and historical writings. In his widely read book *Evolución política del pueblo Mexicano* he presented an urbane analysis of Mexico's history that is now consid-

ered a classic work, less for its original scholarship than
for its literary brilliance.[25]

To understand Sierra's perspective on the Mexican War
and the treaty, it helps to know that during the war his
father led the Yucatán faction that sought alliances with
the United States and European powers to help end a
caste war. The family supported official neutrality in the
war. In his book, Sierra presented the Mexican War as
an avoidable tragedy brought on by Mexican weakness
and ignorance. The issue of Texas, he argued forcefully,
should have been settled by negotiation in 1836. Instead,
led by General Santa Anna, who "personified all the
Mexican defects of character," the nation insisted on retaining what it had never controlled. Texas had "an in-
controvertible right to separate from Mexico." Sierra felt
that the peace settlement was a "sad but not ignominious
agreement" and that the negotiators "did as much as they
could and as much as they should have." By comparison
with other treaties of conquest (the Franco-Prussian War
and the Spanish-American War) the treaty was "more
just." A kind of divine retribution visited the Americans
to punish them for invading Mexico, because the Mexican War led directly to the U. S. Civil War. "Mexico," he
concluded, "has always had a malignant influence on its
invaders."[26]

Sierra's vision of 1848 reflected the Positivist contempt
for weakness and disorder. The treaty was an attempt to
restore some sanity to the nation and as such was a positive influence. The conservative periods in Mexico's history seem to have spawned the best historical writing
about the Mexican War and the treaty. During the period
of violent revolution following the overthrow of Díaz
in 1910 up through the era of Lázaro Cárdenas in the
late 1930s, few significant studies appeared. During the
1920s historical writings were strongly influenced by re-

ligious issues generated by the Cristero rebellion. These included anticlerical polemics by Lazaro Gutierrez de Lara and the proclerical defense by Mariano Cuevas. These authors focused mostly on the role of the Catholic Church during the war. The major historical work of this period, that of Alberto María Carreno, tended to be traditionalist in its interpretation of the causes of the war but gave scant attention to the treaty.[27]

During the 1930s a surge of nationalism, accompanied by antimilitarism inspired by the presidency of Lazaro Cardenas produced histories by José Vasconcelos and the Marxist Rafael Ramos Pedrueza.[28] Both authors discussed the war in general and gave only passing attention to the significance of the treaty. Beginning in the 1940s and coinciding with a conservative resurgence in Mexico, historians turned again to interpreting the meaning of 1848.

In 1940, Jesuit Priest Padre Mariano Cuevas published his *Historia de la nación Mexicana*.[29] Based largely on the writings of Roa Bárcena and Arrangoiz, this was one of the first major national histories to be published since the Porfirato. Cuevas devoted four chapters to the Mexican War and the Treaty of Guadalaupe Hidalgo. As might be expected, his interpretation of the war period reflected the clerical position. For Cuevas the liberals were responsible for both the military and the diplomatic defeats. They controlled the government of the Mexico City *ayuntamiento* and were, according to Cuevas, manipulated by Valentín Gómez Farías. These liberals, Cuevas argued, acted as a fifth column and eventually sold the country to the Americans. The Treaty of Guadalupe Hidalgo was important not primarily because of the vast expanse of land given to the Americans—land that Cuevas characterized as worthless, arid, and indefensible. Rather, its main significance was that it revealed the many corruptions of the liberals. Cuevas argued that Mexico had no alternative but to ratify the treaty, especially because the American government was encouraging revolutionary activity within Mexico. The treaty was the only way to prevent the total disintegration of the social order.[30] In 1947 two significant works appeared commemorating the centennial of the Mexican War, a book by Vicente Fuentes Díaz and a monograph by Francisco Castillo Nájera. Fuentes Díaz, a school teacher who had been active in the politics of his home state of Guerrero, was a member of the Socialist Party. By 1947 he had become a functionary of the newly formed Partido Revolucionario Institucional. His book-length study of the Mexican War and the treaty, based on well-known secondary works, was an analysis of various issues that had influenced Mexico's fate during and after the war: political factionalism, economic problems, the position of the Catholic Church, and the activities of the Mexican fifth column. In discussing issues of American expansionism and aggression against Mexico, Fuentes Díaz reminded the readers that the war had been opposed by such North American leaders as Abraham Lincoln, Ulysses Grant, Henry Clay, and Daniel Webster. He believed that the true work of any historian should be to "promote good relations between the two countries," not to reopen old grievances. He provided a fairly clear exposition of the nature of American expansionism, and his analysis was not overly emotional.

Fuentes Díaz assumed a basic knowledge of events on the part of the reader. There is no attempt to narrate the story of the Mexican War and there is no study of the Treaty of Guadalupe Hidalgo. His book is strongest in its evaluation of the consequences of the treaty. He emphasized that, by giving the United States land and natural resources, the treaty enabled that country to become a world power. The humiliation of Mexico in 1848 helped shape the character of the United States in that henceforth the nation would be more aggressive in its colonial expansion. Fuentes Díaz went so far as to suggest that the war poisoned United States–Mexico relations in subsequent years.[31] In his concluding chapter he quotes extensively from Rejon's analysis of the war and the treaty.

In 1947 the first twentieth-century study of the Treaty of Guadalupe based on archival material also appeared: Francisco Castillo Nájera's "El Tratado de Guadalupe."[32] Using archival sources located in Washington, D.C., Castillo Nájera attached to his modest study Spanish translations of several key documents generated by the negotiations. The first Mexican historian to offer an interpretation of these American sources, Nájera devoted most of his manuscript to tracing the evidence of Santa Anna's treasonous activities and to an exposition of the debate in the Mexican Senate over the ratification of the treaty. His view of 1848 is limited to comments on Mexican rather than American motives and actions.

Nájera's research paved the way for one of the first modern Mexican studies of the Mexican War and the treaty, that of José Bravo Ugarte in "La Guerra a Mexico de Estados Unidos 1846–1848."[33] This author relied heavily on Mexican and U.S. sources, especially on Roa Bárcena and Justin Smith. He told the story of the war and the treaty, narrating the twists and turns of diplomacy without much commentary or interpretation. As a result, it gives the impression that Mexico's loss was part of an inexorable flow of events. The question of blame and war guilt does not surface prominently. Bravo Ugarte's sole critical comment on 1848 was in a final paragraph in his essay: "The United States was formed as a Continental Republic so that its disproportionate power in the hemisphere made impossible juridical equality with the American nations."[34] Bravo Ugarte did call the Mexican War unjust, but he did not suggest any blame.

A major example of this nonideological history written in the 1950s was Carlos Bosch García's survey history of Mexico-United States relations during the period 1819–1848.[35] The concept that seemed to guide Bosch Garcia's work was the importance of momentum in history. Individuals were relatively unimportant in changing centuries of historical tradition. Bosch García saw the Mexican War and the treaty as ending a chapter in a struggle for primacy in Latin America, a struggle that the United States and Mexico had inherited from their colonial forebears. Following a national interest that was a product of history, each country came into conflict over territory. The year 1848 marked both the end of this struggle and the triumph of the United States. According to this thesis, Manifest Destiny was a legitimate expression of national self-interest, as was the policy of the Mexican government to populate its northern provinces.

Bosch García's account is balanced. He became somewhat nationalistic in characterizing the Mexican War as one of American invasion and aggression, but his main theme was the emergence of the United States as a dominant power in response to the impetus of history. His discussion of historical sources is an excellent bibliographic introduction to the subject. In it he identifies American as well as the Mexican biases in interpreting the period. Bosch García judged Hubert Howe Bancroft the best of all historians of the war and the treaty.

The tones of consensus, impartiality, and objectivity during the 1950s could be found in Mexican textbooks used in secondary and university history classes. Two examples are the survey texts by Carlos Pereyra and José C. Válades. Válades's *Breve historia de la guerra con los Es-*

tados Unidos was straightforward, with no mention of the Treaty of Guadalupe Hidalgo. He termed Santa Anna "intelligent and subtle" and judged him undeserving of the charge of treason. Válades saw the United States as caught up in a war of aggression, but this did not have any particular implications for the future; "Mexico," he wrote, "knows how to forgive."[36] Pereyra's text, also a strictly factual narrative, passes over the issue of war guilt and Santa Anna's controversial actions during the conflict. Like Válades and other historians of the 1950s Pereyra offered no critical evaluation of events or sources. This approach to Mexican-U.S. relations, the war, and the treaty, paralleled a period of relative harmony and cooperation between the two nations evident in the presidencies of Miguel Alemán and Adolfo Ruíz Cortines. The mood changed during the turbulent 1960s and 1970s, when radical revolutions in Latin America and other Third World countries—Cuba and Vietnam in particular—created a different environment. In this later period, Mexican historians openly criticized U. S. aggression in Latin America. The anti-war movement, civil-rights protests, and the Chicano movement in the United States made some Mexican historians more aware of the importance of violations of rights guaranteed in the treaty. Reies Tijerina's Alianza movement to regain lands lost by Hispano pueblos in violation of the treaty in New Mexico had an impact on the Mexican intelligentsia. Tijerina traveled and published in Mexico, awakening a sense of outrage among Mexico's elite writers.

One example of a historian influenced by these years was Agustín Cue Cánovas whose strident book *Los estados unidos y el México olvidado* was published in 1970.[37] The importance of 1848 for Cue Cánovas was that it marked the emergence of American imperialism. Cue Cánovas was the first Mexican historian since 1848 to criticize the U.S. government for its violations of the Treaty of Guadalupe Hidalgo. In particular he questioned the morality of the decision by the American Senate to reject Article X of the treaty, which would have protected the validity of Mexican land grants "to the same extent that the same grants would be valid if the said territories had remained within the limits of Mexico." As a result of Senate suppression of Article X, Cue Cánovas argued, thousands of Mexican-American property holders lost their land because ambiguities in the balance of the treaty left the door open for legislative action and court rulings that required Mexican property holders to submit their claims to American courts for validation. Frequently this was a long and expensive process and it usually ended in sale of the land to pay court costs. Article X would have allowed Mexican property holders to fulfill the terms of their grants under Mexican law. The omission of this article "removed the opportunity for Mexican land holders to comply with regulations which they had been prevented from doing as a result of the war." From Cue Cánovas's perspective, 1848 had meaning because it created a group of second-class citizens within the United States. He wrote, "The North American government and the citizens of that country are obligated to respect the rights of Mexicans and their descendants who have remained in the lost territories."[38]

Cue Cánovas also evaluated the American violations of Article VIII and Article IX of the treaty, the articles that deal with property rights for Mexican citizens and the process of gaining U.S. citizenship. Unlike previous historians, Cue Cánovas attempted to translate the meaning of 1848 for the present generation by linking the American violation of the treaty with the larger theme of American imperialism.

Another historian with a radical interpretation of 1848 was Gastón García Cantú who wrote *Las invasiones norteamericanas en México*.[39] In his work he lists and analyzes 285 U.S. interventions and acts of aggression against Mexico during the period 1800–1918. In discussing the period of the Mexican War and the treaty, he quotes extensively from primary documents to make the point that the Mexican government had a deep concern for Mexican citizens remaining in the United States. In García Cantú's words, the diplomats at that time were "very clearly aware that the destiny of thousands of Mexicans in the United States would be that of slavery, discrimination, and contempt" but were powerless to prevent this from happening especially if the Americans ignored their own laws.[40] The violation of the treaty was to be expected. It was only one among hundreds of immoral actions in the expansion of the United States at the expense of Mexico.

Not all historians of this period were radically inclined. In the late 1970s a major work was Luis Zorrilla's two-volume *Historia de las relaciones entre México y los Estados Unidos de America 1800–1958*.[41] Zorrilla's view of 1848 was that of a diplomatic historian interested in chronicling rather than interpreting the political process. His detailed account of the negotiation of the Treaty of Guadalupe Hidalgo, pointing our flaws and errors on both sides, paralleled the writings of Roa Bárcena in the nineteenth century. An evaluation of the treaty and the war appears briefly, buried in hundreds of paragraphs of dense historical narrative. The treaty, Zorrilla thought, was "one of the harshest ones in modern history, with the exception of those of the Second World War, owing to the enormous extent of the territory taken from Mexico."[42] Zorrilla's diplomatic history views 1848 as a particularly troubled year, but not a determining event, in relations between the two countries. Real politique, not abstract morality is what governs relations between nations. In recent years more optimistic views of 1848 have been put forth. César Sepúlveda's interpretive history of the United States– Mexico border is such a work.[43] Sepúlveda, a legal scholar, has worked closely with the Mexican diplomatic corps and with the Instituto de Matías Romero. From his point of view the Mexican negotiators of 1848 were remarkably successful in gaining concessions despite their extremely disadvantageous position. In the face of overwhelming American military power, they managed to keep Baja California and the mouth of the Colorado River and to prevent the annexation of large parts of northern Mexico. The year 1848 represented a confirmation of what had already taken place in fact: the American occupation of Mexico's northern provinces. In his words: "The Rio Grande boundary line had been already conceded since 1836. The inhabitants of California and New Mexico had been practically separated from Mexico and had accepted the North American domination from the start of hostilities."[44] Sepúlveda went so far as to describe the Treaty of Guadalupe Hidalgo as a victory for Mexico. In it, Mexico did not grant the right of transit across the Isthmus of Tehuantapec, American claims against Mexico were cancelled, and the Mexican government gained a large indemnity—this in exchange for territory that the Mexican government had never really controlled. The importance of the treaty was that it served as a fresh start for relations between the United States and Mexico because it settled outstanding border disputes. Thus it became "the foundation on which Mexican and North American relations were based for many decades."[45]

This same optimistic assessment could be found in college-level textbook discussions of the treaty. The *Historia general de México* (1976) devoted several paragraphs to the treaty and characterized it as a partial success in that the negotiators prevented the annexation of Sonora, Chihuahua, and Baja California. Beyond that, the tragedy of 1848 served to awaken in Mexicans a sense of reality and to stimulate a greater national consciousness.[46]

Scholarly writing about the Treaty of Guadalupe Hidalgo has not exerted much influence on the writers of history textbooks that are used by millions of children in the Mexican school system. The majority of texts lack much information at all about the war and the treaty. Those few that do treat this crucial period in the nation's history have mostly unbalanced and personalistic interpretations.

One Mexican history text, published by the Secretaría de Educación Pública in 1970, totally ignores both the war and the treaty, instead devoting many pages to a discussion of "the crucial period, 1821–1867," in which Santa Anna is the chief actor.[47] Another textbook, this one a world history survey published in 1977, devoted fifty pages to a discussion of the war and treaty. The authors called the Treaty of Guadalupe Hidalgo "one of the most delicate and transcendent events in the history of our country." Their analysis of the war and loss laid all blame on Santa Anna, whom they termed a "super coward" and a monstrous *vende patria* (sell out).[48] Much of the discussion of the war and treaty negotiations is a marshaling of evidence to prove Santa Anna's treachery. Entirely absent was a discussion of the U.S. role in causing the conflict and in forcing the treaty.

This survey and critique of Mexican historians and their interpretations of the meaning of the year 1848 can be concluded with a few observations about the function of history in national consciousness. Some of the most bitter critics of Mexican political history have been Mexican historians, whether it was Manuel Crescencio Réjon arguing against Peña y Peña or a world history textbook blaming the entire war on the evil machinations of General Santa Anna. One theme that runs through Mexican literature on the war and the treaty is self-criticism. In part, this criticism is due to the tremendous political strife that has accompanied Mexico's slow emergence as a nation. The Mexican War and the Treaty of Guadalupe Hidalgo provided a rich source of historical ammunition with which to fight political battles after 1848.

The dominant Mexican historiography of 1848 is that of the conservatives, Arrangoiz, Roa Bárcena, Bosch García, Zorrilla. With the notable exception of Justo Sierra, these historians have tended to emphasize the sequence and detail of events more than the interpretation of facts. Conservative history in Mexico has tended to be Positivist in philosophical orientation—letting the facts speak for themselves to illustrate the "natural laws" of political development.[49] Criticism of American aggression has been a rather late development, coinciding with an increased national independence vis à vis U.S. foreign policy.

The year 1848 was important in Mexican history. As a result of the war, Mexican nationalism began to find form, largely through the inspired leadership of Benito Juárez, and the dominance of the army, the church, and the *hacendados* began to be questioned. As Mexico changes economically and politically, new interpretations of the meaning of 1848 certainly will arise.

CHAPTER 8

The Chicano Movement and the Treaty

The Treaty of Guadalupe Hidalgo is the most important document concerning Mexican Americans that exists. From it stem specific guarantees affecting our civil rights, language, culture, and religion.

ARMANDO RENDÓN
CHICANO MANIFESTO

During the 1960s and 1970s a new generation of Mexican Americans sought to redefine their position within the United States using, in part, the Treaty of Guadalupe Hidalgo. They called themselves Chicanos, a term previously used as a derogatory reference to working-class Mexican immigrants. Sparked by a growing civil rights and anti-war movement, Chicano political militants sought to focus world attention on the failed promises of the Treaty of Guadalupe Hidalgo. Beginning with an agrarian revolutionary movement in New Mexico and a farm workers' strike in California, the newly born Chicano movement resurrected the treaty as a primary document in the struggle for social justice. This generation of Mexican Americans learned of the legal basis for reclaiming their lost lands. The political aims of the Chicano movement, to gain representation and recognition, generated a more critical interpretation of the meaning of the Mexican War and the treaty. A lasting legacy of Chicano awareness in the 1960s and 1970s was a consciousness of their history dating from 1848 and the Treaty of Guadalupe Hidalgo.

THE ALIANZA MOVEMENT AND NEW MEXICAN LANDS

One of the first activists to provoke a reassessment of the treaty was Reies Lopez Tijerina. Originally a fundamentalist preacher from Texas, Tijerina became part of the struggle of the Hispanos of New Mexico to regain the community land grants that had been taken from them after 1848 in violation of the treaty. Representing New Mexican land claimants, Tijerina traveled to Mexico City in 1959 and again in 1964 to present memorials to the Mexican authorities, including the president of Mexico. Thousands of Hispanos whose families had lost their lands in violation of the terms of the treaty signed the petitions. Tijerina and the delegation asked the government of Mexico to demand that the United States fulfill the terms of the treaty. On both occasions the Mexican government listened respectfully but did nothing.[1]

During the early 1960s Tijerina traveled throughout New Mexico, organizing La Alianza Federal de Mercedes Libres. The purpose of the organization was "to organize and acquaint the heirs of all Spanish land-grants covered by the Guadalupe Hidalgo Treaty" with their rights.[2] This organization became the catalyst for a number of militant actions by the Hispano villagers: the occupation of Kit Carson National Forest (see figure 2), the proclamation of the Republic of San Joaquín de Chama, the courthouse raid and shootout at Tierra Amarilla, a massive military manhunt for Tijerina and his followers, and

Figure 2. Alianza Member Guarding Treaty Lands. Baltazar Martinez was photographed in 1968, near Canjilon, New Mexico. A member of Reies Tijerina's Alianza Federal de Mercedes Libre, he and others stood guard during the occupation of lands that the group believed had been stolen in violation of the Treaty of Guadalupe Hidalgo. (Photograph Courtesy Victor Nabokov, Special Collections Department, General Library, University of New Mexico, Albuquerque)

lengthy legal battles. Lost in the sensational publicity surrounding Tijerina and the Alianza during the late 1960s was the fact that Alianza leaders justified their movement on the basis of historical and legal interpretations both of the constitutions of New Mexico and the United States and of the Treaty of Guadalupe Hidalgo. Much like the American Indian Movement of the same period, the Alianza claimed that legitimate treaty rights had been violated and demanded compensation. Tijerina's analysis of the land-grant question appeared in a booklet that the Alianza published and distributed throughout the Southwest.[3] Tijerina based his arguments for the reclamation of lost Hispano lands on two documents, the *Recopilación de leyes de las Indias*, which had been the legal framework for the Spanish land grants prior to the nineteenth century, and the Treaty of Guadalupe Hidalgo. He contended that the United States had violated Articles VIII and IX of the treaty, which had guaranteed property and citizenship rights to Mexicans. Ultimately, Tijerina's claims were presented before the U.S. Supreme Court as a class action lawsuit in 1969. Denied a hearing two times in 1970, the case finally received a favorable recommendation, but it was not presented, probably because Tijerina lacked sufficient funding to pursue the issue.[4]

One of the little-known episodes in the Alianza's history was Tijerina's effort to forge an alliance with Mexican popular and governmental organizations.

Early in January 1964 Tijerina and his wife, Rosita, went to Mexico City to meet with Mexican officials. On January 9th he met with a labor leader, Lic. Javier Rojo Gómez, who was the secretary general of the Confederación Nacional Campesina. Tijerina reported that he felt encouraged and that the interview was a great success. On January 14th he met with a secretary who worked with the Relaciones Exteriores (foreign relations) where he left a memorandum for president Adolfo Lopez Mateos. On January 29 he sent a telegram to Lic. Donato Miranda Fonseca, secretary to the president in the National Palace, asking for a meeting, and on February 4 he met with the secretary. Tijerina had a lengthy meeting where he explained the various violations and aggressions suffered by Mexicans in the United States since the Treaty of Guadalupe Hidalgo.

Back in New Mexico, Tijerina set to work to organize a caravan to Mexico City. While doing this he began a letter-writing campaign to remind both the U.S. and Mexican governments of their obligations under the treaty.

In July, Tijerina again went to Mexico with his wife. In Chihuahua he attended a student meeting to promote the upcoming caravan. While he was speaking he was arrested by the Mexican Judicial Police. He was released from jail after a number of strategic phone calls were placed to Mexico City and Washington, D.C. He continued his journey to Mexico City undaunted, making a map for the later caravan. In Mexico City he sent a letter to Luis Echeverría, the secretary of Gobernación, along with memoranda to the president, Adolfo López Mateos, informing them of the caravan's purpose. He received a "positive impression" that the caravan would be permitted to travel to Mexico. He visited the offices of all the political parties in Mexico City, the left as well as the right, explaining his position on the treaty and "pueblo olvidado": "We, the Mexicans in the United States, only want that all Mexico, in the name of the Treaty of Guadalupe, would receive us so that the United States would know of the dear brotherhood between the Mexicans of the South and of those north of the Rio Grande."[5] Tijerina's speeches were reported in the Mexican media and he even appeared before the national syndicate of publishers in Mexico City (Sindicato Nacional de Redactores de la Prensa), where he talked about the upcoming caravan.

Tijerina held a meeting of interested Mexican officials to discuss the caravan, emphasizing that the purpose was to seek Mexican support for Chicanos and their struggles in New Mexico. Mexican federal agents also attended. The next day Tijerina was detained by the police and questioned about his activities. Finally they decided to deport him with the threat that if he returned he would be put in prison for ten years. They took him to the airport and saw him off on the plane. Tijerina was convinced that he had been set up by the U.S. government. Back in New Mexico, with a heavy heart, Tijerina called off the caravan. Tijerina's activities in attempting to gain the support of the Mexican people for the plight of the Hispano villagers had threatened the Mexican government. It was possible that the U.S. government had influenced the deportation but ultimately the Mexican government was responsible. This episode put an end to the Alianza's dream of having the Mexican government act as an advocate within the United Nations.[6]

A few years later the legal and moral issues raised by Tijerina's Alianza movement influenced domestic politics. Senator Joseph Montoya of New Mexico introduced a bill in the U.S. Senate to create a Special Commission on Guadalupe Hidalgo Land Rights. Simultaneously Representative Manuel Lujan (New Mexico) introduced a similar bill in the House. Montoya proposed that the federal government establish a temporary commission that would review violations of property rights guaranteed in the treaty and make recommendations to Congress and the president regarding restitution. One of the first tasks of the commission would be to "make a comprehensive study of the provisions of the Treaty of Guadalupe Hidalgo" to determine violations of the treaty. Senator Montoya, by no means a political ally of Reies Tijerina, adopted what seemed to be a radical plan of questioning established land tenures in his home state. He justified his measure as a means of rectifying past injustices: "If certain lands have been wrongfully taken from people, we must make amends."[7] Montoya's bill reflected the degree to which the long and bitter history of land-grant conflict in New Mexico had emerged as an issue for federal concern. Senator Montoya's bill died in the Insular

and Interior Affairs Committee, as did a similar bill introduced the same year by Congressman Augustus Hawkins
of California.

Hawkins proposed that Congress establish a Community Land Grant Act targeted specifically at the villages
of New Mexico. Like Montoya, he envisioned the establishment of a commission that would hear petitions from
members of villages whose community land grants had
been lost through corruption or deceit. The commission
was to have the power to "reconstitute the community
land-grant" under the Laws of the Indies where it was
consistent with the Constitution or state laws. Additionally the Hawkins Bill provided for 10 million dollars to
finance the operations of the commission.

Unfortunately there are no records of the debate surrounding either Montoya's or Hawkin's bill in these committees. That these measures were defeated is not too
surprising, because any federal investigation into land
tenure in New Mexico would be bound to unsettle powerful commercial and speculative interests. Nevertheless
congressional interest in investigating the violations of
the treaty's provisions continued. Throughout the 1970s
at least three bills were introduced. In 1977 Representative Henry B. Gonzalez (Texas) introduced a resolution to
create a special congressional committee "to investigate
the legal, political, and diplomatic status of lands which
were subject to grants from the King of Spain and the
Government of Mexico prior to the acquisition of the
American Southwest as a result of the Treaty of Guadalupe Hidalgo." In 1979, Representative Ronald V. Del-
lums (California) introduced a similar proposal, but a
House committee rejected it. Finally, in 1979, as a result
of lobbying by Reies Tijerina, the New Mexico legislature instructed its representatives to introduce legisla-

tion to establish a board of review to investigate the theft of communal lands in northern New Mexico.[8] This move, like others before it, was killed by conservative interests in Congress. The motivation for the continued legislative attempts to rectify the land-grant situation in New Mexico came primarily from increased public awareness and pressure originating from a revitalized Alianza movement. Again, the public records are silent on the debates surrounding these measures, because each was squashed without a lengthy hearing.

THE URBAN CHICANO MOVEMENT

Knowledge of the treaty and its violations was widespread among New Mexicans. Collectively they had been fighting for a return of their pueblo lands for more than a century. On the other hand millions of urban Chicanos— sons and daughters of Mexican immigrants who had entered the United States after 1910—had yet to be educated about the treaty. In the 1960s and 1970s this process took place in informal meetings, discussions, and rallies.

In the spring of 1968, urban and rural Mexican-American leaders found a common ground for dialog. Rudolfo "Corky" Gonzales, leader and organizer of the Denver Crusade for Justice, joined forces with Reies Tijerina to participate in the Poor People's March on Washington, D.C. Together with other urban leaders they issued a joint statement, entitled *We Demand*, listing the needs of Mexican Americans throughout the nation. These included bilingual education, adequate housing, job development, more sensitive law enforcement, economic opportunities, and agricultural reforms. The demand for agricultural reforms, inspired by Tijerina's struggle in

New Mexico, called not only for a return of lands stolen from the pueblos in violation of the treaty, but also for "compensation for taxes, legal costs, etc., which pueblo heirs spent trying to save their land."[9]

The Treaty of Guadalupe Hidalgo and its implications became a topic of discussion at the first Annual Youth Conference in Denver, Colorado, which was organized by Gonzales in 1969. Knowledge of treaty violations became a driving force behind the final statement of the conference in "El Plan Espiritual de Aztlan," a document of Chicano solidarity and a declaration of independence. During the 1970s, surveys and critiques of the treaty, and especially of Articles VIII and IX, began to appear in anthologies and books being published to satisfy the demand for more printed materials dealing with Chicanos. One of the most popular of these was Armando Rendon's *Chicano Manifesto*. In the section of the book dealing with the treaty, Rendon summarized his view of the importance of the treaty: "The Treaty of Guadalupe Hidalgo is the most important document concerning Mexican Americans that exists."[10] The terms and spirit of the treaty, he said, had been systematically violated by the U.S. government. Rendon called for Chicanos to become aware of the "exact processes by which the Treaty of Guadalupe Hidalgo was made meaningless over the past century and a half." He had in mind a detailed documentary case that could be made against the federal government so that some kind of compensation could be exacted. He hinted that Chicanos could seek, as the American Indian tribes had, monetary settlements or even a return of territory to Mexico.[11] The probability that the latter would occur was nil, but the prospect of a monetary settlement did not seem wholly impossible, given the political atmosphere of the time. For many militants of the 1970s the treaty legitimized their demands for social and economic justice and provided a cause for radical action.

THE BROWN BERETS' OCCUPATION OF CATALINA ISLAND

The same year that Rendon's *Chicano Manifesto* appeared, the most dramatic attempt to publicize the importance of the treaty took place. In September 1972 the Brown Berets in California began a twenty-four-day occupation of Santa Catalina Island, claiming that it had never been included in the original treaty and thus was still part of Mexico. The Brown Berets were founded in 1967 by David Sanchez, a former chairman of the Los Angeles Mayor's Youth Council. Eventually the Berets claimed five thousand members nationwide. The goal of the Berets was to fulfill the ideals articulated in "El Plan Espiritual de Aztlan," that is to control or at least have a voice in the policies of major institutions in the barrio that affected Chicanos: the schools, police, welfare offices, and the immigration service. As an action-oriented militant organization, the Berets participated in and helped organize most of the major landmarks of the Chicano movement: high-school "blowouts" (walkouts) and moratorium marches in East Los Angeles, La Marcha and Caravana de la Reconquista, as well as other local actions in southern California designed to raise public awareness of oppression and racism.[12]

A particular interpretation of the meaning of the Treaty of Guadalupe Hidalgo influenced the Brown Beret's decision to stage a symbolic occupation of Santa Catalina Island. None of the nine channel islands off the coast of southern California had been mentioned in the treaty as part of the territory ceded to the United States in 1848.

According to popular beliefs in Mexico and in many U.S. barrios, the islands remained part of Mexico until the 1870s, when Benito Juárez, then president of Mexico, leased Catalina Island to Americans. William Wrigley, Jr., of the chewing-gum empire, eventually acquired the ninety-nine-year lease on the property, which expired in 1970. The true history of Catalina Island's title contradicted this folk history. On July 4, 1846, Pio Pico, the last Mexican governor of California granted the island of Catalina to Tomás Robbins. Robbins sold the island to José María Covarrubias of Santa Barbara in 1850, and Covarrubias sold it to Albert Roshard of San Francisco in 1853. Thereafter the title to the island is traceable up to Mr. Wrigley's purchase in 1919.[13]

Although the claim that Catalina had been leased from Mexico had no historical basis, the story reflected a need to keep alive the issue of the illegal seizure of community lands. The legend also reflected a real ambiguity in the treaty regarding the status of the offshore islands. This vagueness had been a source of sporadic public discussion in the 1950s and 1960s.[14]

Some legal experts in Mexico were prepared to argue that the island could be reclaimed by Mexico. A partial basis for argument was that Governor Pico's grant of the island was made after the declaration of war and hence was considered invalid by both the U.S. and the Mexican governments.[15] Late in the nineteenth century the Mexican government had considered making the ownership of the islands an international issue. In 1894 the United States asserted control over Clipperton Island in the Pacific Ocean (called Medanos or La Pasión by Mexico), a small island some thousand miles off the coast of southern Mexico. Mexican newspapers claimed that this island was rightfully Mexico's and that the Catalina Islands should be reclaimed by the Mexican government in retaliation. The issue became an item for official private correspondence but soon died for lack of presidential support.[16] The Brown Berets did not seriously believe that they could regain Catalina for Mexico. The real purpose of the occupation was to provide a forum for discussion of the problems confronting Mexican Americans arising from their colonized status.

After several weeeks of planning at a base near Lancaster, California, the offensive against the island, code named Tecolote, was ready. A primary concern was secrecy. From previous scouting expeditions the Berets knew that there was a Mexican barrio of about four hundred persons on the island. The leaders flew to Catalina and the rest of the contingent took the boat and acted as tourists. On August 30th the Berets assembled twenty-five men and one woman at the Waikiki Motel on Catalina. From there, they rented a jeep, and drove to the top of the hill above the town of Avalon Harbor. At nine o'clock the next morning the citizens of the small town awoke to see a huge Mexican flag flying from the hilltop. Campo Tecolote had been established.[17] The Beret contingent carried no arms but stood in formation, dressed in military fashion (see figure 3). At first some residents, recalling folktales about the controversial title to the islands thought they had been invaded by the Mexican army.[18]

The mayor of Avalon, Raymond Rydell, a former vice-chancellor of the California State College system, had dealt with student militants during the 1960s. He encouraged the sheriff's department to use a low-key approach to the Beret encampment and to leave them alone as long as they caused no trouble. The vice-president of the Santa Catalina Island Company was a Mexican American named Renton. He too advised the sheriffs to

Figure 3. Brown Berets Occupying Avalon Harbor, Catalina Island. David Sanchez, the organizer of the occupation, is in the foreground. (Photograph Courtesy La Causa Publications)

leave the Berets alone; and to show his good will he sent the Beret contingent cold drinks and box lunches. David Sanchez, the Beret leader, issued a press release, which read in part: "As gentlemen who may try to understand other gentlemen, how about a peaceful resolution? . . . We have begun an occupation plan, which is by means of peaceful occupation only. By this plan, we wish to bring you the true plight of the Chicano, and the problems of the people of Mexican descent living in the United States."[19]

The occupation lasted twenty-four days. During that time the Brown Beret camp became something of a tourist attraction. The small Mexican-American population of the island helped provide food and drink for the Chicano demonstrators. Local restauranteur Mike Budd gave them a free meal at his restaurant. As the occupation stretched into weeks, the Berets had a chance to talk to some of the island's Chicano residents. Their message was that the United States was illegally occupying not just Catalina but all of the American Southwest. Mexican Americans were a colonized people, they said, victims of an unjust war of aggression. The occupation of Catalina ended peacefully on September 23, when the city council decided to enforce a local camping ordinance and threatened jail unless the Berets abandoned their campground. The Berets left, vowing to return to occupy other islands at some future date and to engage in more legal research. As it turned out, however, the Catalina occupation was the last organized action of the Brown Berets. A few weeks later their leader, David Sanchez, citing the pervasive presence of police informants within the organization, announced that the Brown Berets had been disbanded.[20]

The Treaty of Guadalupe Hidalgo provided a basis for legitimizing the occupation of Catalina Island, both for the presentation of grievances and the dramatization of *la causa*. In comparison to the Alianza's occupation of Kit Carson National Forest and the shootout at Tierra Amarilla, Catalina Island was a relatively minor incident. Nevertheless, the Santa Catalina occupation demonstrated the degree to which some were willing to take militant action based on the historical violations of the Treaty of Guadalupe Hidalgo.

INTERPRETATION BY CHICANO INTELLIGENCIA

American Indians and Mexican Americans are the only segments of U.S. society that have kept alive the issues raised by the Treaty of Guadalupe Hidalgo. Because of the popular movements of the 1960s and 1970s as well as the institutionalization of Chicano Studies classes in major universities, larger numbers of Mexican Americans have been introduced to the treaty and its significance. More often than not, however, this familiarity did not go beyond a belief that the treaty guaranteed certain rights for Mexican Americans and that these rights had been violated. Only a few scholars writing about Chicano history have attempted to go beyond this generalized view of the implications of the treaty. Perhaps the most detailed, scholarly, and realistic appraisal of the meaning of the treaty for human rights appeared in 1978 as a doctoral dissertation by Fernando Chacon Gómez. Before Gómez, no one had analyzed how the treaty influenced subsequent court cases involving Mexican Americans. This work was a conscious blending of scholarly training and Chicano activism.

Gómez's main argument was that despite decades of "invisibility" and general neglect, the Treaty of Guadalupe Hidalgo had real legal implications for the present. He wanted to explore the legal history of the treaty after 1848 to determine "to what extent it could be used to compel enforcement of contemporary civil rights." He analyzed the cultural and historical background of the legal battles waged in the nineteenth and early twentieth centuries to secure property and civil rights for former Mexican citizens. On a case-by-case basis he pointed to the ethnocentric and racist basis of the arguments and decisions. Manifest Destiny, he concluded, had found its way into the courtroom. This was especially true in New Mexico where, because of the judge's ignorance of local tradition, "the century-old concept of flexibility of the common law may indeed have been 'bastardized.' " Elsewhere in the United States, judges relied on local precedent in making decisions. Not so in New Mexico. Thus, although the treaty was a "rights conferring document," in the courts it remained a dead letter. Chacon Gómez concluded that the most viable avenues for redress were largely in the international arena because the Supreme Court had consistently ruled against interpretations of the treaty that would protect Mexican-American rights. A legal attack on the injustices and inequalities confronted by people of Mexican origin, he thought, could best be pursued in such international forums as the United Nations and the World Court.[21] This approach is currently being followed by a handful of activists.

INTERNATIONALIZATION OF THE TREATY

Since World War II the plight of the Mexican Americans within the United States as been presented before various international forums, primarily agencies of the United Nations concerned with human rights. The Treaty of Guadalupe Hidalgo has figured prominently in these formal presentations; indeed the treaty has provided the legal rationale for discussing Mexican American rights within international bodies.

The earliest attempt to use an international forum to redress wrongs vis à vis Mexican Americans was by the American Committee for the Protection of the Foreign Born in 1959. The committee was a leftist organization that split from the American Civil Liberties Union in 1942. Carey McWilliams, a progressive newspaper reporter, editor, author, and activist was one of its first directors during the 1940s. In the 1950s the committee fell onto the U.S. attorney general's list of subversive, communist infiltrated organizations, and committee members were questioned by the House Un-American Activities Committee in the early 1960s. In 1959 the American Committee for Protection of the Foreign Born submitted a petition to the United Nations entitled "Our Badge of Infamy: A Petition to the United Nations on the Treatment of Mexican Immigrants."[22] The petition was signed by more than sixty individuals, most of them Anglo-American professionals. They charged that the United States had violated provisions of the Universal Declaration of Human Rights, specifically Articles II, III, IV, VII, IX, XV, XXII, and XXV. In their opening statement they stated that U.S. government committees and agencies had investigated the plight of the Mexican immigrant in the United States but no change had come about. "We feel that the United Nations should consider this problem only because repeated attempts over the years by agencies of the United States government and public and private organizations have failed to overcome the serious deprivation of the human rights of the Mexican immigrants living in the United States."[23]

The petition was not limited to defending Mexican immigrants; it also dealt with the violations of the Treaty of Guadalupe Hidalgo affecting the native-born Mexican Americans. "While rights to property, especially land, were safeguarded by the provisions of the Treaty of Guadalupe Hidalgo, in practice Mexicans and Mexican Americans were cheated of most of their properties in a short while."[24] The main orientation of the petition was to present concrete evidence, in the form of historical examples, of how the human rights of Mexicans in the United States had been violated. Instances of mistreatment and murder of bracero workers were documented to show violations of Article III of the U.N. declaration guaranteeing freedoms regardless of race. Cases of wage discrimination were related to violation of Article IV, which forbade slavery and involuntary servitude. The operations of the Immigration and Naturalization Service during Operation Wetback (a repatriation program of

1954) were presented as violations of Article IX, which provided for equal protection under the law. The significance of the committee's petition was that it was the first attempt to go beyond the domestic system to seek redress under international law. It was over twenty years before another organization attempted to internationalize the issues raised by the treaty.

During the 1980s various Native American groups discovered the Treaty of Guadalupe Hidalgo and began to forge alliances with Mexican American organizations and individuals. In July 1980, at the Sixth Annual Conference of the International Indian Treaty Council (IITC) meeting at Fort Belnap, Montana, a resolution was introduced by native delegates to support the Treaty of Guadalupe Hidalgo and Mexican-American rights to self-determination.[25] The International Indian Treaty Council was a San Francisco–based organization dedicated to working for the rights of native peoples throughout the Western Hemisphere. Since 1977 it had been recognized by the United Nations as a Non-Government Organization (N.G.O) and had traveled numerous times to Geneva to present petitions and interventions on behalf of Indian people. In 1981 the IITC introduced the Treaty of Guadalupe Hidalgo as one of the North American treaties that affected Indian peoples before the International Conference of Non-Government Organizations concerning Indigenous Populations and Land. Several U.S. Indian tribes considered the treaty an important part of their claims for redress. The Hopi people, for example, presented a statement at a 1981 Geneva Conference where they cited Article IX and XI of the treaty to support their opposition to the relocation of the Navajo (Dineh) and Hopi elders from their ancestral lands near Big Mountain, Arizona.[26]

According to Hopi prophecy, "most important information" bearing on the fate of their nation would be found at the bottom of a "high stack of papers." The elders reported that they had found this "important information"—Disturnell's 1847 map, which had been appended to the Treaty of Guadalupe Hidalgo. That map contained a notation, "Los Moquis [Hopis] has conservado su independencia desde el año 1680." The meaning of this notation on the treaty map was clear: the Hopis had not been considered subjugated by the Spanish; they were independent and sovereign. In the words of the elders, "From that time forward, the power of the Hopi and our right to sovereign independence should never have been questioned."[27] The 1981 Hopi statement as delivered to the United Nations went on to assert that their rights as Mexican citizens under Article VIII of the treaty had been violated by the U.S. courts and that their religious rights under Article IX had not been protected.

Other Indians also considered the Treaty of Guadalupe Hidalgo as bearing on their claims for compensation. The Tohono O'odham, or Papago, for example, have interpreted the treaty as bearing on their desire to reclaim lands.

The IITC continued to be active in bringing the Treaty of Guadalupe Hidalgo before international bodies. In June 1982 the position of the Chicano Caucus regarding the treaty at the IITC annual conference was presented before the General Assembly, and in September of that year Chicanos presented their case before the First American Indian International Tribunal held at D-Q University near Sacramento, California. In 1984, the IITC representatives presented the Chicano and Indian positions on the treaty before the 40th session of the U.N. Commission on Human Rights meeting in Geneva, Switzerland, and in 1985 the Treaty Council presented a document outlining the Chicano situation before a U.N. Working Group on Indigenous Populations at Geneva. Working with the IITC during these years was a small group of Chicano and Mexican-American activists who saw a community of interest. For years the Chicano movement leaders had attempted to educate Mexican Americans regarding their indigenous roots. Almost every barrio had its contingent of nativists who strongly identified with and attempted to preserve Mexican and Southwestern Indian traditions through song, dance, paintings, and rituals. For them the spiritual lessons of the Indian peoples were all important. One statement of this position during these years was an anonymous pamphlet entitled "Aztlan vs. the United States." It argued that Chicanos in the United States were Indians by blood as well as heritage; they had suffered the same second class treatment as Indians. Aztlan, the Aztec name for their homeland, was a spiritual and biological nation that included Indians as well as Chicanos. "This is the nation of RAZA INDIGENA, and the INDIAN NATIONS, or in other words nosotros los indios de Aztaln."[28]

In the 1980s Chicano intellectuals also began to conceptualize the Treaty of Guadalupe Hidalgo in terms of its potential for mobilizing the declining activism of *el movimiento*. Armando Rendon, the noted author of *Chicano Manifesto*, wrote an essay in 1982 arguing that "the Treaty of Guadalupe Hidalgo is in fact an international human rights document, extending guarantees through the decades which have not been asserted on an international level."[29] He recommended that Chicanos seek redress in forums such as the International American Commission on Human Rights and the Inter-American Court of Human Rights. Rendon argued that the development of human rights law since the 1960s had made the treaty a viable tool for seeking justice.

Rendon's perspective found elaboration and development in the writings of Roberto Barragan, a young undergraduate at Princeton who consulted with Rendon in writing his senior thesis in the Politics Department.[30] In a lengthy, 200-page thesis Barragan argued that in light of the pronouncements of various international bodies, the treaty conferred on Chicanos particular international human rights. "Rights guaranteed by the Constitution as regards Chicanos are no longer solely of domestic character. As they are additionally protected by the Treaty, they are now of international character. As such they are under the jurisdiction of various Inter American forums."[31] Barragan's view was that the effort to protect the human rights of Mexican Americans under the treaty should be part of a three-pronged project aimed toward self-determination. The organized effort to internationalize the treaty would be known as the Treaty of Guadalupe Hidalgo Project that would integrate the various Chicano communities into an organization that would use international forums to support Chicano self determination. Among his many proposals was one that this organization could request that member states of the Organization of American States ask for an advisory opinion on the Treaty of Guadalupe Hidalgo and the status of the land grants. He also opined that the language of Article IX (relating to citizenship) could be construed to apply to Mexican immigrants in the Southwest. Barragan's thesis found a small audience because it was not published but only circulated among interested parties. It did, however, become part of the archive of contemporary thought about the international aspects of the treaty.

Recent events have shown a maturation of Indian-

Chicano efforts to internationalize the issues raised by the treaty. In 1986 the IITC hosted the first National Encuentro on the Treaty of Guadalupe Hidalgo at Flagstaff, Arizona. During the three day meeting, which was attended by over 100 representatives of Indian tribes and Chicano organizations, commitments emerged that led to subsequent planning meetings the next year in Denver, Colorado, and Jemez Springs, New Mexico. The Flagstaff Encuentro also resulted in a commitment to send a delegation of Chicano observers with the IITC delegates to the Geneva U.N. Commission on Human Rights meeting in early 1987.

This was a major step in introducing a small group of Mexican Americans to international politics. For the first time a delegation of Chicano delegates spoke before a U.N. body about the Treaty of Guadalupe and contemporary problems confronting Chicanos. The IITC allowed a Chicano delegate to present an intervention before the commission. It read in part:

> That same Treaty of Guadalupe Hidalgo, in which Mexico tried to guarantee human rights to indigenous people, is continually being violated by injustices toward the Chicano indigenous people by the United States. These people have suffered since the military conquest of their indigenous land of AZTLAN. The treaty right to maintain their language and culture have been denied to Chicanos: their human rights and dignity have been subverted through racism, intended to undermine the cultural ethnicity of indigenous people.[32]

The Chicano delegates presenting formal documents also held press conferences with representatives of the media of Mexico, Brazil, Argentina, and various European nations, where they presented Chicano perspectives on the treaty and issues affecting Mexican Americans. At Geneva, the representatives learned about diplomatic protocol and lobbying to expand their views regarding the role of Mexican Americans within the world community.[33]

The first national attempt to form an organization that would regularize Chicano participation within international forums took place in Santa Cruz, California, on October 10–12, 1987. This meeting brought together international lawyers with Chicano community activists and tribal representatives. The treaty became a point of organizing a larger number of people than had previously participated. Commissions on land grants, international law, and cultural violations were established. As a result of this endeavor further Encuentros were planned to solidify the directions that were established.

The Treaty of Guadalupe Hidalgo became a focal point for claims of social and economic justice during the activist 1960s and 1970s through militant action, popular books, and scholarly studies. An important legacy of the Chicano movement is its fostering of a particular historical awareness: the Southwest is really "occupied Mexico," and Mexican Americans and Indians are a "colonized people" whose rights have been violated despite the guarantees of the treaty. In the 1980s, attempts to use the Treaty of Guadalupe Hidalgo to reach international audiences has increased, primarily through the organizing energies of the International Indian Treaty Council. The result has been that the Chicano movement has gained new international dimensions.

CHAPTER 9

The Treaty and International Relations

[The] Treaty of Guadalupe Hidalgo, in which Mexico tried to guarantee human rights to indigenous people, is continually being violated by injustices toward the Chicano indigeneous people by the United States.

AGENDA ITEM 12, "A QUESTION OF THE VIOLATION OF
HUMAN RIGHTS AND FUNDAMENTAL FREEDOMS"
COMMISSION ON HUMAN RIGHTS, UNITED NATIONS

Since 1848 the United States and Mexico have entered into more than one hundred treaties, conventions, and international agreements regulating many aspects of their relationship.[1] The Treaty of Guadalupe Hidalgo is the oldest international agreement still in force between the two nations. Those portions of the original treaty still binding on their relations today are included in Articles VIII and IX (land and citizenship provisions), Article XVI (the right to fortify ports), and Article XXI (renouncing war as a means of settling future disputes and providing for arbitration of these conflicts) (see appendix 2). Within the context of the range of issues covered by the history of international agreements, the Treaty of Guadalupe Hidalgo is not necessarily the most important treaty between the two nations. Certainly the problems of narcotics control, trade and economic cooperation, telecommunication, and immigration are areas of mutual concern that are not directly related to the Treaty of Guadalupe Hidalgo but are of the most pressing concern and diplomatic activity between the two countries today. Nevertheless the 1848 treaty, by virtue of its scope, has influenced subsequent international agreements over boundaries, territorial waters, and economic claims of citizens affected by the international boundary. Beyond these areas the Treaty of Guadalupe Hidalgo can be interpreted as a platform upon which the superstructure of U.S.-Mexican international accord has been built.

A number of treaty provisions that influenced the international relations of the two countries have been discussed in earlier chapters. Through Article XI of the treaty the United States assumed responsibility for control of Indian raids originating on its national soil. This led to a series of financial claims, which were eventually abrogated by the Gadsden Treaty in 1853. In 1923, at the so-called Bucareli Conferences, the Mexican government presented the claims of the Tejano landholders (the Asociación de Reclamantes) who had suffered violations of their land rights under the Treaty of Guadalupe Hidalgo. Finally, the efforts of Chicanos and Indians to bring the importance of the treaty to international forums for discussion has been chronicled.

The focus of this discussion is on four major areas of conflict that were profoundly influenced by the treaty: the Pious Fund, el Chamizal, territorial waters, and international arbitration.

THE PIOUS FUND

In 1848 the Treaty of Guadalupe Hidalgo divided more than geopolitical territory; it also severed religious jurisdictions, which created a long and complicated dispute over church funds. In the nineteenth and twentieth centuries the American Catholic Church sued the Mexican government for recovery of the interest on the Pious Fund, an ancient trust fund that was established in colonial times to finance missionary activity in the two Californias.

The Pious Fund was started in 1697 by the Jesuit Order, which solicited donations in real estate and other gifts that were in turn invested in income-producing properties around Mexico City. In 1767, fearing their growing independence and power, the Spanish King expelled the Jesuit Order from the New World. Subsequently the fund was split between the Dominican Order in Baja California and the Franciscans in Alta California. When Mexico gained its independence from Spain in 1821, the Pious Fund passed to the Mexican government, which in 1836 allowed the monies to be controlled by the Dioceses of California. In 1842, under General and President Santa Anna, the trust was confiscated, but at the time the Mexican government recognized an obligation to pay an annuity of 6 percent of the fund to the Catholic Church in California.[2]

When the United States acquired Alta California in 1848, the American Catholic Church took over the administration of the former mission properties. In the 1870s, under Joseph Sadoc Alemany, the newly appointed Bishop of Monterey, California, the Catholic Church retained a lawyer, John Thomas Doyle, to begin efforts to claim Alta California's portion of the Pious Fund. In 1870, Doyle filed a one-page brief against the Mexican government, asking for payment of the accrued annuity since 1848. Doyle presented the claim before the Mixed Claims Commission that had been established to settle outstanding financial claims between the two countries.

On November 11, 1875, the umpire for the commission, Sir Edward Thornton, awarded the Bishop of Monterey $904,070 in back interest.[3] The Mexican government under Porfirio Díaz did not contest the award and dutifully paid the obligation off in thirteen installments, making the final payment in 1890.

The Pious Fund controversy did not end there. Soon after the award, Doyle advanced the argument that the Mexican government had a continual and perpetual obligation to pay the 6 percent interest each year subsequent to the award. He began a series of complicated legal maneuvers that eventually led the U.S. government, acting on behalf of the Catholic Church in California, to convince the Mexican government to submit the question before the newly established Permanent Court of Arbitration under the Hague Convention of 1889. The Pious Fund case was one of the first to be heard by this new international court. The lawyers representing the Mexican government at The Hague argued that the Pious Fund suit should be dismissed because it was not presented as a claim in 1848 when the Treaty of Guadalupe Hidalgo (Article XIV) settled all financial claims arising prior to February 2, 1848. The U.S. representatives argued that the claim was not based on illegal acts on the part of the Mexican government prior to 1848, but on the nonpayment of interest since 1875. The Treaty of Guadalupe Hidalgo figured prominently in the legal arguments on both sides.[4]

The Hague Tribunal rendered its judgment on October 12, 1902, deciding that "the government of the Republic of the United Mexican States shall pay to the Government of the United States of America on February 2, 1903 and on each following year on the same date of February 2, perpetually, the annuity of $43,050.99 Mexican, in money having legal currency in Mexico."[5] (February 2 was the date of the signing of the Treaty of Guadalupe Hidalgo.) The Mexican government paid this award annually until 1914 when payments stopped due to the diplomatic crises engendered by the Mexican Revolution. No further payment was made to the Pious Fund account until 1967 when, by mutual agreement, Mexico extinguished its "perpetual obligation" by making a final payment of US $719,546 as a "full and final settlement of all claims."[6] Thus the Pious Fund controversy passed into history but left a residue of bad feelings between the two powers. The litigious approach of the California Catholic hierarchy, working through the U.S. government, continues to be interpreted by Mexican historians as a modernized version of Manifest Destiny. The Pious Fund controversy also illustrated the attitude of the Mexican government toward international arbitration: the Mexican government took the decisions of the international tribunals and arbitration commissions as serious obligations and worked to abide by these decisions even when they were against Mexico. The same respect for arbitration was not evident on the part of the United States in the case of the Chamizal conflict.

EL CHAMIZAL

Article IV of the Treaty of Guadalupe Hidalgo was written to define the geographic boundaries between the United States and Mexico. As already noted, the land boundary between El Paso and San Diego became a source of controversy after the ratification of the treaty, which led to the negotiation of the Gadsden Treaty. The eastern portion of the boundary described by the Treaty of Guadalupe Hidalgo, the Rio Grande, also became a source of conflict between the two countries, largely because of periodic changes in the river's course through flooding and accretion.

The most significant conflict arising from the 1848 treaty boundary involved an area of land known as el Chamizal, a 600-acre tract that eventually became part of downtown El Paso, Texas. El Chamizal, so named for the kind of bush that grew there, was located south of the Rio Grande in 1848, but because of flooding and changes in the river's course (see map 5), the tract was located north of the river by 1910. After the riverbed changed, the city of El Paso, the state of Texas, and the U.S. government exercised political jurisdiction over this section of land, but they were consistently challenged by the Mexican government.

The Chamizal controversy became the impetus for the establishment of a convention of November 12, 1884, to establish rules to govern the political status of *banco* lands, those territories that were transferred from one side of the river to the other through changes in the river channel. Five years after the convention was established the countries set up a joint International Boundary Commission with representatives from Mexico and the United States who would have the responsibility of settling of further disputes involving river and land boundaries. After detailed engineering studies the joint commission recommended transfers of *banco* lands to Mexico or the United States.

On November 14, 1895, the Mexican government sought to test the Mexican-American agreements flowing from the Treaty of Guadalupe Hidalgo by submitting a tract of land within the Chamizal zone for adjudication by the International Boundary Commission.[7] The Commission heard arguments from both sides but was unable to reach agreement. In 1911, the case was finally submit-

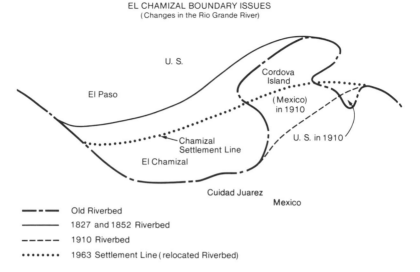

EL CHAMIZAL BOUNDARY ISSUES
(Changes in the Rio Grande River)

U. S.

El Paso

Cordova
Island

(Mexico)
in 1910

Chamizal
Settlement Line

El Chamizal

U. S. in 1910

Cuidad Juarez

Mexico

— ·— Old Riverbed

——— 1827 and 1852 Riverbed

– – – – – 1910 Riverbed

• • • • • • • 1963 Settlement Line (relocated Riverbed)

Map 5. El Chamizal Boundary Issues (Changes in the Rio Grande Channel). (Map by Bardy Anderson and Ann Brook)

ted to an Arbitration Tribunal (a specially enlarged session of the International Boundary Commission) with the prior understanding that both countries would abide by the decision. A major argument for the Mexican case involved reference to the original Treaty of Guadalupe Hidalgo boundary line, which stipulated that the United States was acquiring lands north of the Rio Grande. The tribunal's decision was to divide the tract, giving a portion to Mexico and leaving the rest with the United States. The tribunal's decision leaned heavily on the language and intent of the original Treaty of Guadalupe Hidalgo.[8] The U.S. government refused to accept the results of this arbitration decision, arguing that the river's changed course was not caused by slow accretion as had been maintained by the Mexican government, but had been due to violent flooding. (Under the 1884 convention regulating *banco* lands, both countries agreed that violent changes in the riverbed would not be considered legitimate changes in the boundary). The U.S. negotiator, Anson Mills, held that the arbitration decision was so vague and indeterminate that it was impossible to execute.[9]

For the next fifty years the dispute nagged the relations between the two countries with various proposals being advanced and rejected. The unstable political climate in Mexico during the revolution and the U.S. delay in diplomatic recognition made an early settlement impossible. One effect of this controversy was to create uncertainty about land titles in the Chamizal zone. As a result, the area degenerated into a slum.[10] Finally, in 1963, President John F. Kennedy responded to suggestions from the Mexican government that the issue be laid to rest. As a result, a settlement was reached along the lines of the 1911 arbitration award (see map 5 and figure 4).[11] Under the terms of the settlement, Mexico gained 437 acres of land while the Cordova Island tract was evenly divided between the two countries. Both countries agreed to share the cost of relocating the river by building a concrete channel. The citizenship of the persons living in the zone being transferred would not be affected.

In Mexico there was a tremendous emotional reaction to the Chamizal issue. For the first time since 1848, Mexico was reclaiming part of its national domain from the United States. President Adolfo López Mateos and President Lyndon B. Johnson met in El Paso, and both spoke of how this act signified a new era in U.S.-Mexican cooperation and brotherhood. The ceremonies of transfer were carried live on Mexican television to more than 75 million people, and September 24 was declared Cha-

Figure 4. El Chamizal. An aerial photograph of the relocation project undertaken by the International Boundary and Water Commission under the terms of the 1963 Chamizal settlement. The photo shows the location of the new river channel in 1969 and the old river channel that formed the international boundary before the relocation. (Photograph Courtesy International Boundary and Water Commission, El Paso, Texas)

mizal Day in both Juárez and El Paso. Candlelight parades were held, *corridos* composed, and a massive fiesta celebrated.[12]

For the Mexican press the Chamizal resolution had a rich meaning: it was symbolic of the persistent efforts of Mexico to rectify past injustices, of the emerging international strength of Mexico, of the triumph of rule of law and peaceful negotiation, of the political strength of the ruling party (PRI), and a vindication of an independent

Mexican foreign policy. In a lengthy editorial, Leopoldo Zea, a leading Latin American philosopher, interpreted the end of the Chamizal conflict as a triumph of Mexican dignity over force of arms: "It was not the result of a Machiavellian net but more the clear and natural expression of an old Mexican tradition. And the result was that this pride, far from hurting the country, strengthened and helped it, within the same terrain of prideful dignity, it was possible to grant concessions where politics and power would have failed."[13]

TERRITORIAL WATERS

Mexican diplomatic victories over "the colossus of the north" have been rare in the relations between the two countries. Negotiations involving the international boundary have more often resulted in lengthy complex exchanges and compromises. An example of this has been the issue of international territorial waters. Due to the political conflicts over international rights for oil exploration and fishing grounds, the extent of the offshore territorial seas of Mexico had important economic implications. For many years the Mexican government cited the Treaty of Guadalupe Hidalgo as the authority for claiming a nine-mile territorial sea. Article V in the 1848 treaty stated that "the boundary line between the two Republics shall commence in the Gulf of Mexico, three leagues from land, opposite the mouth of the Rio Grande." A league is approximately three miles. The specific language on this point in the Treaty of Guadalupe Hidalgo was inserted by Trist, borrowed from an 1836 Texas Boundary Act dated December 19, 1836, where the offshore territorial waters were claimed to run "three leagues from land, to the mouth of the Rio Grande." Ironically a Mexican counterproposal to the original treaty language had omitted this proposed three-league stipulaton.[14]

In 1960 a Texas lawsuit, *U.S v. Louisiana et al.* 363 U.S. 1 (1960), cited the Treaty of Guadalupe Hidalgo as an authority for that state's claim to offshore oil lands. The Mexican government followed this case very carefully, because its outcome would either assist or damage Mexico's claim to expand its territory for offshore fishing and oil exploration. In 1961 Alfonso García Robles chaired the Mexican delegation to the Second United Nations Conference on the Law of the Seas and presented an extensive argument in favor of Mexico's claim to a territorial sea larger than the conventional three-mile limit, extensively citing and interpreting the Treaty of Guadalupe Hidalgo.[15] He presented historical evidence to show that in diplomatic dispatches the U.S. government considered the three-league provision valid. On April 30, 1848, the British government sent a note to the United States protesting the language of Article V of the treaty since it violated their understanding of U.S. territorial waters (one league, or three miles). Secretary of State Buchanan wrote back that "the stipulation in the treaty can only affect the rights of Mexico and the United States" and that "the government of the United States never intended by this stipulation to question the rights of Great Britain or any other power may possess under the laws of nations." Thus in 1848 the U.S. government recognized that its maritime boundary with Mexico was three leagues but that this provision was not binding on third parties.[16] In the Gadsden Treaty of 1863 this same three-league or nine-nautical-mile limit was reconfirmed. In a congressional act in 1935, Mexico fixed nine nautical miles as the breadth of its offshore waters. The U.S. government did not accept Mexico's proposed limit.

The U.S. side of the argument was presented by Arthur

H. Dean, president of the American Society of International Law. In the 1961 Law of the Seas Conference, he argued that the much cited case of *U.S. v. Louisiana et al.* applied only to relations between Texas and the U.S. government, not to foreign countries. The Supreme Court, he argued, refused to consider any issue of territorial seas in its review of the 1848 treaty as it applied to this domestic case. Moreover the Treaty of Guadalupe Hidalgo was silent regarding a territorial sea boundary on the Pacific Ocean and this seemed to substantiate the view that the negotiators were not primarily interested in this issue as they delineated the international boundary.[17]

On December 26, 1969, after years of discussion between the United States and Mexico over the meaning of Article V with respect to territorial waters, both countries finally agreed to a twelve-mile limit. This ultimate resolution relied to some degree on the historical interpretation of existing international treaties, especially the Treaty of Guadalupe Hidalgo. The agreement was given detail in a formal treaty signed in Mexico City on November 23, 1970, and ratified in 1971 by the United States. This 1971 comprehensive treaty also resolved long-standing problems arising from the Colorado River and Rio Grande boundaries.[18] By this new treaty, Article V of the Treaty of Guadalupe Hidalgo was formally terminated along with Article I of the Gadsden Treaty. In its place they included a new provision for a twelve-mile offshore limit and a Pacific territorial sea boundary.

INTERNATIONAL ARBITRATION

It was the Treaty of Guadalupe Hidalgo that introduced for the first time the idea of permanent arbitration of disputes in American diplomacy. Article XXI of the treaty read,

If unhappily any disagreement should hereafter arise between the Governments of the two Republics, whether with respect to the interpretation of any stipulation in this treaty, or with respect to any other particular concerning the political or commercial relations of the two nations, the said Governments, in the name of those nations, do promise to each other that they will endeavor, in the most sincere and earnest manner, to settle the differences so arising, and to preserve the state of peace and friendship in which the two countries are not placing themselves, using for this end, mutual representations and pacific negotiations. And if, by these means, they should not be enabled to come to an agreement, a resort shall not, on this account be had to reprisals, aggression, or hostility of any kind, by the one republic against the other, until the Government of that which deems itself aggrieved shall have maturely considered, in the spirit of peace and good neighborship, whether it would not be better that such difference should be settled by the arbitration of commissioners appointed on each side, or by that of a friendly nation. An should such a course be proposed by either part, it shall be acceded to by the other, unless deemed by it altogether incompatible with the nature of the difference, or the circumstances of the case.[19]

This provision was one that the Mexican negotiators of 1848 had insisted upon. Their original language was to bind both countries to compulsory arbitration, but Trist refused to accept it and instead compromise language allowed some leeway to avoid it. Thus the Treaty of Guadalupe Hidalgo established a permanent precedent for the arbitration of future disputes between the two countries.[20]

The Pious Fund and Chamizal controversies were both submitted to arbitration with Mexico demonstrating more good faith in abiding by the spirit of the treaty than the United States. Other major efforts to arbitrate disputes between the two countries included the establishment of the Mixed Arbitration Commission of 1868 and the Bucareli Conferences in 1923. Both arbitration efforts dealt with damages suffered by nationals of both countries. The Claims Convention, signed on July 4, 1864, established a commission composed of U.S. and Mexican representatives appointed by the presidents of each country. Together they examined claims to determine legitimate liability and the amount of award. In case of disagreement they were to select an umpire by lot who would cast the deciding vote.[21] The commissioners considered more than 2,000 claims, 1,017 from the United States and 988 from Mexico. Most of the Mexican claims that were eventually approved were those arising from the 1855 raid led by Callahan's Texas Volunteers that burned the town of Piedras Negras to the ground. Mexico was awarded US $15,498.41 while the U.S. citizens were awarded US $4,125,622.20, including an award of US $1,420,682.67 for the interest on the Pious Fund since 1848. All claims for Indian depredations were disallowed by the commissioners as stipulated in the Gadsden Treaty. Mexico's obligation to the United States was to pay US $300,000 a year in gold. This was dutifully paid by Porfirio Díaz's government until the debt was extinguished.[22]

Mexican politicians continued to believe that arbitration was an important instrument of its relationship with the United States. In 1904 the United States suggested that Mexico enter into an arbitration treaty similar to the one that France and Britain had concluded. The next year the Mexican foreign minister formally accepted the proposal with the following caveat: "Since 1848, in the Treaty of Peace and Amnesty with our neighbor to the north, Article XXI has established the principle of obligatory arbitration for all questions that are not 'absolutely incompatible with nature and the circumstances of the case.' "[23] In subsequent discussions regarding the proposed arbitration treaty the Mexican government reiterated its concern that it not be interpreted as superseding the Treaty of Guadalupe Hidalgo and thus specific language to that effect was inserted in the final convention. Four years later, when the arbitration convention was renewed, the same concerns resurfaced and again the primacy of the Treaty of Guadalupe Hidalgo's Article XXI was recognized.[24]

Many Mexican historians tend to view the history of international arbitration between Mexico and the United States as a Machiavellian saga, with the domination of the stronger power over the weaker one a foregone conclusion.[25] The United States tended to appeal to arbitration when it served its national interest as in 1868 and again in 1923 with the Bucareli Conferences, and it chose to ignore arbitration findings in 1902 in the Chamizal case and rejected a peaceful settlement in 1914 when the U.S. Navy occupied the city of Vera Cruz.

The threat of U.S. military intervention in Mexico during the 1910 revolution precipitated a meeting between General Victoriano Huerta, president of Mexico, and Nelson O'Shaughnessy, chargé d'affaires to the U.S. secretary of state. Unknown to Huerta, the Wilson government was anxious to find a pretext to support General Venustanio Carranza, leader of what the United States thought was a more progressive revolutionary faction. To do this the United States needed a precipitating incident. When a Huertista general arrested some U.S. officers at Tampico, this seemed to be an opportunity to justify U.S. military action. At a meeting with O'Shaughnessy on April 14, 1914, Huerta strongly urged that the issue be submitted to the Hague Tribunal for arbitration and he supported this avenue by referring to Article XXI of the

Treaty of Guadalupe Hidalgo.[26] This appeal for arbitration ran counter to the interests of the Wilson government, so the conflict soon escalated into the bombardment and occupation of the port city of Vera Cruz.

An important episode in the history of U.S.-Mexican arbitration since 1848 was the agreement reached during a series of meetings known as the Bucareli conference. Early in the 1920s the U.S. government was anxious that settlement be made on the damages that its nationals had suffered during the Mexican revolution. The U.S. government was also interested in clarifying, to its advantage, the status of U.S. land and oil ownership in Mexico. For three months in 1923, representatives from both countries met to discuss the problems. The resulting agreements were later adhered to by both governments and are sometimes referred to by Mexicans as the Bucareli Treaty. The main points of the agreements were: (1) the United States accepted the expropriation of lands under Article 27 of the Mexican Constitution; (2) all claims for damages since 1868 would be settled by a joint commission and claims arising from revolutionary violence would be treated separately by another special commission; and (3) Mexico would not apply its expropriation laws retroactively to U.S.-owned oil properties providing that some "positive act" had been made to tap the oil prior to 1917. These agreements paved the way for U.S. recognition of the Obregon government, which took place soon after the conference on August 31, 1923.[27]

Later that same year a Special Claims Commission was established to begin working on the revolutionary claims, but its operation was so unsatisfactory to the United States that in 1934 the country signed a convention to settle the revolutionary claims using a complex formula. Mexico eventually paid US $5,448,000 under this convention. Similarly a General Claims Commission was established with the United States presenting 2,781 claims against Mexico amounting to US $513,694,267.17 and Mexico presenting 836 claims worth US $245,158,395.32. Included in the Mexican claims were the damages suffered by Tejanos whose lands had been expropriated in violation of the Treaty of Guadalupe Hidalgo (Asociación de Reclamantes), the bombardment of Vera Cruz in 1914, and the Pershing expedition. In 1941 all these claims were settled, with Mexico agreeing to pay the United States 40 million dollars in full payment for all damages incurred since 1868.[28]

Since 1848, Mexico and the United States have, in the spirit of Article XXI of the Treaty of Guadalupe Hidalgo, entered into arbitration, conventions, and discussions to resolve mutual problems. On balance the United States has gained more monetarily even though it has not fully complied with the spirit of the treaty. The Mexican government has avoided further conflicts with the United States and gained some prestige both at home and abroad by its willingness to arbitrate disputes.

The Treaty of Guadalupe Hidalgo was one of the first steps in establishing a permanent means to reach peaceful solutions to conflicts between the two countries. Always in the background was the reality of U.S. military power and the fear that the United States would enforce its will on Mexico as it had in 1848. These fears were realized in 1914 during the Mexican Revolution, when the U.S. military occupied Veracruz, and again in 1917, when the United States invaded northern Mexico to search for Pancho Villa's army. Bellicose statements made by spokesmen for private businesses whose investments were threatened by Mexican governments during the 1920s and 1930s continued to fan distrust between the two countries. Treaties, conventions, and other agreements have always been temporal expressions of slippery political realities. Although the specific conditions that gave rise to the Treaty of Guadalupe Hidalgo have long since passed, the disparity in military and economic power between the United States and Mexico has remained, making the treaty both a landmark of the past and a warning for the future.

CHAPTER 10

Conclusion

The current condition of the world, including the state of the relationship between the United States and the countries south of the Rio Grande, suggests that many lessons from the past have not been learned and that much remains to be done to achieve an acceptable international climate.

OSCAR MARTINEZ
TROUBLESOME BORDER

In 1848, U.S. and Mexican negotiators entered into an agreement with the understanding that the civil and property rights of the Mexican citizens who were being transferred to the United States would be respected. This understanding was not a gift of the U.S. Congress or the president but an international agreement that emerged out of a complex negotiation that was subject to shifting political and military contingencies. In contrast to those historians who believe that the acquisition of the Mexican territories was inevitable, the final agreement between the two countries was more the result of a series of fortuitous events than it was the result of a U.S. military victory. Twenty years after the Mexican War, the French, led by Archduke Maximillian, conquered Mexico, only to be swallowed up by its vast geography and its people's resistance. The United States was lucky to conclude the war when it did.

The spirit of the Treaty of Guadalupe Hidalgo, embodied within Articles VIII and IX and the Protocol of Querétaro, has survived through the years. The promises the U.S. government made with respect to the conquered Mexican populations, however, have remained largely unfulfilled. Enforcement of the treaty depended entirely on the good will of the American people and their governmental institutions. That good will was not always forthcoming in the years after 1848, which resulted in repeated violations of the treaty. It joined the ranks of hundreds of other treaties that the United States made with Native American tribes in the nineteenth century that have been almost totally ignored since then.

Today the Treaty of Guadalupe Hidalgo gives Mexican Americans a special relationship to the majority society. As a conquered people, Mexicans within the United States have been given special considerations under an international treaty. Although these considerations proved to be illusory when the U.S. government undermined the intention of the original document, Mexican Americans continue to have a historical claim on the collective moral conscience of America.

The Treaty of Guadalupe Hidalgo has been interpreted in various ways by different constituencies, and has influenced the course of both U.S. and Mexican history. Courts and civil governments have changed their interpretations according to shifts in political and economic fortunes. Intellectuals in both countries have not given a high priority to an analysis of the treaty; and it has not been until very recently that the rights of those of Mexican descent north of the Rio Grande have become an item for serious discussion within both the United States and Mexico. In the 1960s, the Indians and Mexican Americans, those people whose ancestors were most directly affected by the treaty, began to make a larger audience aware of the Treaty of Guadalupe Hidalgo. For them the treaty still had the power to coerce "the establishment" into making restitution, if not in land, then in human dignity and recognition for past injustices.

On the international front, Mexican diplomats have invoked provisions of the treaty in their attempts to retain territory and sovereignty in the face of an overwhelming U.S. presence. On a few occasions the power of the treaty has been effective; for example, in the Bucareli Conferences in the 1920s and in the Chamizal controversy. Within the past few years Indians and Chicanos have begun to realize that the treaty may be important in organizing on the international front. They have formed a coalition to seek the support of international organizations for the recognition of the justice of their complaints, invoking the treaty as the basis for their argument.

Constituents of the Treaty of Guadalupe Hidalgo have not allowed it to become an antiquarian artifact. The contemporary issues of Mexican immigration, the Mexican debt, drug smuggling, and foreign economic competition are all affected indirectly by the treaty. The growing Hispanic minority within the United States will compel us to consider, again and again, the meaning of the Treaty of Guadalupe Hidalgo within American history. Our diplomats and politicians need to consider the treaty as our country begins to forge new policies with the Pacific Rim countries and the Soviet Bloc. It is hoped that one of the lessons that can be learned from this record is that agreements between nations must allow for the imperfections of national self-interest and provide for an institutionalized means for rectifying inevitable violations. The enforcement and interpretation of treaty provisions has been a periodic source of controversy both between the two countries and between Indian and Mexican-American populations and the U.S. authorities. The recent negotiation of a disarmament treaty with the Soviet Union demonstrates the importance of having mutually verified compliance with the terms of international treaties. Unfortunately there was no provision for the Mexican government to verify compliance by the United States with the terms of the Treaty of Guadalupe Hidalgo. One of the major differences between Mexico and the Soviet Union is that of military power, and this difference counts for a good deal in explaining the degree of mutuality in the treaties signed between the two superpowers. Lacking the threat of military power, Mexico and other Latin American countries, as well as minorities in the United States, have attempted to present their position by appealing to the rule of international law, or by appealing to the American people's sense of justice. The latter sometimes has been quite effective, as in the case of Nicaragua's appeal to the American people to stop funding the Contras. But many issues lack the dramatic appeal that violence always lends, so the American public has not been easy to rouse when the issue has been one concerning the peaceful resolution of problems such as poverty and civil rights.

The past twenty years have taught another lesson: minorities cannot always depend on the passive fairness of the system to defend their rights. The idea that an international treaty dealing with minority groups in the United States can protect rights and be used as an instrument for social and economic survival may appear to be naïve. The record of treaty compliance between the United States and Mexico since 1848 is not a good one: the United States not only has repeatedly violated the

Treaty of Guadalupe Hidalgo's provision for the peaceful settlement of future disputes (Article XXI) but also has either ignored or violated international laws during military and political interventions in the twentieth century. During the period of easing tensions in the Cold War and with the increased political importance of Third World countries, the United States may develop a new regard for international treaties, especially when those treaties advance a just national interest and insure a more peaceful world. If this is the case, then the Treaty of Guadalupe Hidalgo's most lasting significance may be that it can provide inspiration and hope for minority peoples everywhere.

Appendices

The Original Text of Articles IX and X of the Treaty of Guadalupe Hidalgo and the Protocol of Querétaro

citizens?
Property proctection?
Civil rights?

ARTICLE IX[1]

The Mexicans who, in the territories aforesaid, shall not preserve the character of citizens of the Mexican Republic, conformably with what is stipulated in the preceding Article, shall be incorporated into the Union of the United States, and admitted as soon as possible, according to the principles of the Federal Constitution, to the enjoyment of all the rights of citizens of the United States. In the mean time, they shall be maintained and protected in the enjoyment of their liberty, their property, and the civil rights now vested in them according to the Mexican laws. With respect to political rights, their condition shall be on an equality with that of the inhabitants of the other territories of the United States; and at least equally

Text excerpted from David Hunter Miller, *Treaties and Other International Acts of the United States of America*, vol. 5 (Washington, D.C.: Government Printing Office, 1937).

good as that of the inhabitants of Louisiana and the Floridas, when these provinces, by transfer from the French Republic and the Crown of Spain, became territories of the United States. The same most ample guaranty shall be enjoyed by all ecclesiastics and religious corporations or communities, as well in the discharge of the offices of their ministry, as in the enjoyment of their property of every kind, whether individual or corporate. This guaranty shall embrace all temples, houses and edifices dedicated to the Roman Catholic worship; as well as all property destined to it's [sic] support, or to that of schools, hospitals and other foundations for charitable or beneficent purposes. No property of this nature shall be considered as having become the property of the American Government, or as subject to be, by it, disposed of or diverted to other uses.

Finally, the relations and communication between the Catholics living in the territories aforesaid, and their respective ecclesiastical authorities, shall be open, free and exempt from all hindrance whatever, even although such authorities should reside within the limits of the Mexican Republic, as defined by this treaty; and this freedom shall continue, so long as a new demarcation of ecclesiastical districts shall not have been made, conformably with the laws of the Roman Catholic Church.

ARTICLE X[2]

All grants of land made by the Mexican Government or by the competent authorities, in territories previously appertaining to Mexico, and remaining for the future within the limits of the United States, shall be respected as valid, to the same extent that the same grants would be valid, if the said territories had remained within the limits of Mexico. But the grantees of lands in Texas, put in possession thereof, who, by reason of the circumstances of the country since the beginning of the troubles between Texas and the Mexican Government, may have been prevented from fulfilling all the conditions of their grants, shall be under the obligation to fulfill the said conditions within the periods limited in the same respectively; such periods to be now counted from the date of the exchange of ratifications of this treaty: in default of which the said grants shall not be obligatory upon the State of Texas, in virtue of the stipulations contained in this Article.

The foregoing stipulation in regard to grantees of land in Texas, is extended to all grantees of land in the territories aforesaid, elsewhere than in Texas, put in possession under such grants; and, in default of the fulfillment of the conditions of any such grant, within the new period, which, as is above stipulated, begins with the day of the exchange of ratifications of this treaty, the same shall be null and void.

THE PROTOCOL OF QUERÉTARO

In the city of Querétaro on the twenty sixth of the month of May eighteen hundred and forty-eight at a conference between Their Excellencies Nathan Clifford and Ambrose H. Sevier Commissioners of the United States of America, with full powers from their Government to make to the Mexican Republic suitable explanations in regard to the amendments which the Senate and Government of the said United States have made in the treaty of peace, friendship, limits and definitive settlement between the two Republics, signed in Guadalupe Hidalgo, on the second day of February of the present year, and His Excellency Don Luis de la Rosa, Minister of Foreign Affairs of the Republic of Mexico, it was agreed, after adequate conversation respecting the changes alluded to, to record in the present protocol the following explanations which Their aforesaid Excellencies the Commissioners gave in the name of their Government and in fulfillment of the Commission conferred upon them near the Mexican Republic.

First.

The american Government by suppressing the IXth article of the Treaty of Guadalupe and substituting the III article of the Treaty of Louisiana did not intend to diminish in any way what was agreed upon by the aforesaid article IXth in favor of the inhabitants of the territories ceded by Mexico. Its understanding that all of that agreement is contained in the IIId article of the Treaty of Louisiana. In consequence, all the privileges and guarantees, civil, political and religious, which would have been possessed by the inhabitants of the ceded territories, if the IXth article of the Treaty had been retained, will be enjoyed by them without any difference under the article which has been substituted.

Second.

The American Government, by suppressing the Xth article of the Treaty of Guadalupe did not in any way intend to annul the grants of lands made by Mexico in the ceded territories. These grants, notwithstanding the suppression of the article of the Treaty, preserve the legal value which they may possess; and the grantees may cause their legitimate titles to be acknowledged before the american tribunals.

Conformably to the law of the United States, legitimate titles to every description of property personal and real, existing in the ceded territories, are those which were legitimate titles under the Mexican law in California and New Mexico up to the 13th of May 1846, and in Texas up to the 2d March 1836.

Third.

The Government of the United States by suppressing the concluding paragraph of article XIIth of the Treaty, did not intend to deprive the Mexican Republic of the free and unrestrained faculty of ceding, conveying or transferring at any time (as it may judge best) the sum of the twelfe [sic] millions of dollars which the same Government of the United States is to deliver in the places designated by the amended article.

And these explanations having been accepted by the Minister of Foreign Affairs of the Mexican Republic, he declared in name of his Government that with the understanding conveyed by them, the same Government would proceed to ratify the Treaty of Guadalupe as modified by the Senate and Government of the United States. In testimony of which their Excellencies the aforesaid Commissioners and the Minister have signed and sealed in quintuplicate the present protocol.

[Seal] A. H. Sevier
[Seal] Nathan Clifford
[Seal] Luis de la Rosa

The Treaty of Guadalupe Hidalgo, as Ratified by the United States and Mexican Governments, 1848

Treaty signed at Guadalupe Hidalgo February 2, 1848

Senate advice and consent to ratification, with amendments, March 10, 1848

Ratified by the President of the United States, with amendments, March 16, 1848

Ratified by Mexico May 30, 1848

Ratifications exchanged at Querétaro May 30, 1848

Entered into force May 30, 1848

Proclaimed by the President of the United States July 4, 1848

Articles V, VI, and VII amended and article XI abrogated by treaty of December 30, 1853

Article XXI continued in effect by convention of March 24, 1908

Articles II–IV, XII–XV, and XVII–XX terminated upon fulfillment of terms

9 STAT. 922; TREATY SERIES 207

In the name of Almighty God:

The United States of America, and the United Mexican States, animated by a sincere desire to put an end to the calamities of the war which unhappily exists between the two Republics, and to establish upon a solid basis relations of peace and friendship, which shall confer reciprocal benefits upon the

Text reprinted from Charles I. Bevans, ed., *Treaties and Other International Agreements of the United States of America, 1776–1949,* vol. 9 (Washington, D.C.: Department of State, 1972), pp. 791–806.

citizens of both, and assure the concord, harmony and mutual confidence, wherin the two Peoples should live, as good Neighbours, have for that purpose appointed their respective Plenipotentiaries: that is to say, the President of the United States has appointed Nicholas P. Trist, a citizen of the United States, and the President of the Mexican Republic has appointed Don Luis Gonzaga Cuevas, Don Bernardo Couto, and Don Miguel Atristain, citizens of the said Republic; who, after a reciprocal communication of their respective full powers, have, under the protection of Almighty God, the author of Peace, arranged, agreed upon, and signed the following

TREATY OF PEACE, FRIENDSHIP, LIMITS AND SETTLEMENT BETWEEN THE UNITED STATES OF AMERICA AND THE MEXICAN REPUBLIC

Article I

There shall be firm and universal peace between the United States of America and the Mexican Republic, and between their respective Countries, territories, cities, towns and people, without exception of places or persons.

Article II

Immediately upon the signature of this Treaty, a convention shall be entered into between a Commissioner or Commissioners appointed by the General in Chief of the forces of the United States, and such as may be appointed by the Mexican Government, to the end that a provisional suspension of hostilities shall take place, and that, in the places occupied by the said forces, constitutional order may be reestablished, as regards the political, administrative and judicial branches, so far as this shall be permitted by the circumstances of military occupation.

Article III

Immediately upon the ratification of the present treaty by the Government of the United States, orders shall be transmitted to the Commanders of their land and naval forces, requiring the latter, (provided this Treaty shall then have been ratified by the Government of the Mexican Republic and the ratifications exchanged) immediately to desist from blockading any Mexican ports; and requiring the former (under the same condition) to commence, at the earliest moment practicable, withdrawing all troops of the United States then in the interior of the Mexican Republic, to points, that shall be selected by common agreement, at a distance from the sea-ports, not exceeding thirty leagues; and such evacuation of the interior of the Republic shall be completed with the least possible delay: the Mexican Government hereby binding itself to afford every facility in it's power for rendering the same convenient to the troops, on their march and in their new positions, and for promoting a good understanding between them and the inhabitants. In like manner, orders shall be dispatched to the persons in charge of the custom houses at all ports occupied by the forces of the United States, requiring them (under the same condition) immediately to deliver possession of the same to the persons authorized by the Mexican Government to receive it, together with all bonds and evidences of debt for duties on importations and on exportations, not yet fallen due. Moreover, a faithful and exact account shall be made out, showing the entire amount of all duties on imports and on exports, collected at such Custom Houses, or elsewhere in Mexico, by authority of the United States, from and after the day of ratification of this Treaty by the Government of the Mexican Republic; and also an account of the cost of collection; and such entire amount, deducting only the cost of collection, shall be delivered to the Mexican Government, at the City of Mexico, within three months after the exchange of ratifications.

The evacuation of the Capital of the Mexican Republic by the Troops of the United States, in virtue of the above stipulation, shall be completed in one month after the orders there stipulated for shall have been received by the commander of said troops, or sooner if possible.

Article IV

Immediately after the exchange of ratifications of the present treaty, all castles, forts, territories, places and possessions, which have been taken or occupied by the forces of the United States during the present war, within the limits of the Mexican Republic, as about to be established by the following Article, shall be definitively restored to the said Republic, together with all the artillery, arms, apparatus of war, munitions, and other public property, which were in the said castles and forts when captured, and which shall remain there at the time when this treaty shall be duly ratified by the Government of the Mexican Republic. To this end, immediately upon the signature of this treaty, orders shall be despatched to the American officers commanding such castles and forts, securing against the removal or destruction of any such artillery, arms, apparatus of war, munitions, or other public property. The city of Mexico, within the inner line of intrenchments surrounding the said city, is comprehended in the above stipulations, as regards the restoration of artillery, apparatus of war, &c.

The final evacuation of the territory of the Mexican Republic, by the forces of the United States, shall be completed in three months from the said exchange of ratifications, or sooner, if possible: the Mexican Government hereby engaging, as in the foregoing Article, to use all means in it's power for facilitating such evacuation, and rendering it convenient to the troops, and for promoting a good understanding between them and the inhabitants.

If, however, the ratification of this treaty by both parties should not take place in time to allow the embarkation of the troops of the United States to be completed before the commencement of the sickly season, at the Mexican ports on the Gulf of Mexico; in such a case a friendly arrangement shall be entered into between the General in Chief of the said troops and the Mexican Government, whereby healthy and otherwise suitable places at a distance from the ports not exceeding thirty leagues shall be designated for the residence of such troops as may not yet have embarked, until the return of the healthy season. And the space of time here referred to, as comprehending the sickly season, shall be understood to extend from the first day of May to the first of November.

All prisoners of war taken on either side, on land or on sea, shall be restored as soon as practicable after the exchange of ratifications of this treaty. It is also agreed that if any Mexicans should now be held as captives by any savage tribe within the limits of the United States, as about to be established by the following Article, the Government of the said United States will exact the release of such captives, and cause them to be restored to their country.

Article V

The Boundary line between the two Republics shall commence in the Gulf of Mexico, three leagues from land, opposite the mouth of the Rio Grande, otherwise called Rio Bravo del Norte, or opposite the mouth of it's deepest branch, if it should have more than one branch emptying directly into the sea; from thence, up the middle of that river, following the deepest channel, where it has more than one to the point where it strikes the Southern boundary of New Mexico; thence, westwardly along the whole Southern Boundary of New Mexico (which runs north of the town called *Paso*) to it's western termination; thence, northward, along the western line of New Mexico, until it intersects the first branch of the river Gila; (or if it should not intersect any branch of that river, then, to the point on the said line nearest to such branch, and thence in a direct line to the same;) thence down the middle of the said branch and of the said river, until it empties into the Rio Colorado; thence, across the Rio Colorado, following the division line between Upper and Lower California, to the Pacific Ocean.

The southern and western limits of New Mexico, mentioned in this Article, are those laid down in the Map, entitled *"Map of the United Mexican States, as organized and defined by various acts of the Congress of said Republic, and constructed according to the best authorities, Revised edition, Published at New York in 1847 by J. Disturnell:"* Of which Map a Copy is added to this Treaty, bearing the signatures and seals of the Undersigned Plenipotentiaries. And, in order to preclude all difficulty in tracing upon the ground the limit separating Upper from Lower California, it is agreed that the said limit shall consist of a straight line, drawn from the middle of the Rio Gila, where it unites with the Colorado, to a point on the Coast of the Pacific Ocean, distant one marine league due south of the southernmost point of the Port of San Diego, according to the plan of said port, made in the year 1782, by Don Juan Pantoja, second sailing-Master of the Spanish fleet, and published at Madrid in the year 1802, in the Atlas to the voyage of the schooners *Sutil* and *Mexicana:* of which plan a

Copy is hereunto added, signed and sealed by the respective Plenipotentiaries.

In order to designate the Boundary line with due precision, upon authoritative maps, and to establish upon the ground landmarks which shall show the limits of both Republics, as described in the present Article, the two Governments shall each appoint a Commissioner and a Surveyor, who, before the expiration of one year from the date of the exchange of ratifications of this treaty, shall meet at the Port of San Diego, and proceed to run and mark the said Boundary in it's whole course to the mouth of the Rio Bravo del Norte. They shall keep journals and make out plans of their operations; and the result, agreed upon by them, shall be deemed a part of this treaty, and shall have the same force as if it were inserted therein. The two Governments will amicably agree regarding what may be necessary to these persons, and also as to their repsective escorts, should such be necessary.

The Boundary line established by this Article shall be religiously respected by each of the two Republics, and no change shall ever be made therein, except by the express and free consent of both nations, lawfully given by the General Government of each, in conformity with it's own constitution.

Article VI

The vessels and citizens of the United States shall, in all time, have a free and uninterrupted passage by the Gulf of California, and by the river Colorado below it's confluence with the Gila, to and from their possessions situated north of the Boundary line defined in the preceding Article: it being understood that this passage is to be by navigating the Gulf of California and the river Colorado, and not by land, without the express consent of the Mexican Government.

If, by the examinations which may be made, it should be ascertained to be practicable and advantageous to construct a road, canal or railway, which should, in whole or in part, run upon the river Gila, or upon it's right or it's left bank, within the space of one marine league from either margin of the river, the Governments of both Republics will form an agreement regarding its construction, in order that it may serve equally for the use and advantage of both countries.

Article VII

The river Gila, and the part of the Rio Bravo del Norte lying below the southern boundary of New Mexico, being, agreeably to the fifth Article, divided in the middle between the two Republics, the navigation of the Gila and of the Bravo below said boundary shall be free and common to the vessels and citizens of both countries; and neither shall, without the consent of the other, construct any work that may impede or interrupt, in whole or in part, the exercise of this right: not even for the purpose of favoring new methods of navigation. Nor shall any tax or contribution, under any denomination or title, be levied upon vessels or persons navigating the same, or upon merchandise or effects transported thereon, except in the case of landing upon one of their shores. If, for the purpose of making the said rivers navigable, or for maintaining them in such state, it should be necessary or advantageous to establish any tax or contribution, this shall not be done without the consent of both Governments.

The stipulations contained in the present Article shall not impair the territorial rights of either Republic, within it's established limits.

Article VIII

Mexicans now established in territories previously belonging to Mexico, and which remain for the future within the limits of the United States, as defined by the present Treaty, shall be free to continue where they now reside, or to remove at any time to the Mexican Republic, retaining the property which they possess in the said territories, or disposing thereof and removing the proceeds wherever they please; without their being subjected, on this account, to any contribution, tax or charge whatever.

Those who shall prefer to remain in the said territories, may either retain the title and rights of Mexican citizens, or acquire those of citizens of the United States. But, they shall be under the obligation to make their election within one year from the date of the exchange of ratifications of this treaty: and those who shall remain in the said territories, after the expiration of that year, without having declared their intention to retain the character of Mexicans, shall be considered to have elected to become citizens of the United States.

In the said territories, property of every kind, now belonging to Mexicans not established there, shall be inviolably respected. The present owners, the heirs of these, and all Mexicans who may hereafter acquire said property by contract, shall enjoy with respect to it, guaranties equally ample as if the same belonged to citizens of the United States.

Article IX [1]

The Mexicans who, in the territories aforesaid, shall not preserve the character of citizens of the Mexican Republic, conformably with what is stipulated in the preceding article, shall be incorporated into the Union of the United States and be admitted, at the proper time (to be judged of by the Congress of the United States) to the enjoyment of all the rights of citizens of the United States according to the principles of the Constitution; and in the mean time shall be maintained and protected in the free enjoyment of their liberty and property, and secured in the free exercise of their religion without restriction.

Article X [2]

Stricken out by U.S. Senate.

Article XI

Considering that a great part of the territories which, by the present treaty, are to be comprehended for the future within the limits of the United States, is now occupied by savage tribes, who will hereafter be under the exclusive control of the Government of the United States, and whose incursions within the territory of Mexico would be prejudicial in the extreme; it is solemnly agreed that all such incursions shall be forcibly restrained by the Government of the United States, whensoever this may be necessary; and that when they cannot be prevented, they shall be punished by the said Government, and satisfaction for the same shall be exacted: all in the same way, and with equal diligence and energy, as if same incursions were meditated or committed within it's own territory against it's own citizens.

It shall not be lawful, under any pretext whatever, for any

inhabitant of the United States, to purchase or acquire any Mexican or any foreigner residing in Mexico, who may have been captured by Indians inhabiting the territory of either of the two Republics; nor to purchase or acquire horses, mules, cattle or property of any kind, stolen within Mexican territory by such Indians;

And, in the event of any person or persons, captured within Mexican territory by Indians, being carried into the territory of the United States, the Government of the latter engages and binds itself, in the most solemn manner, so soon as it shall know of such captives being within it's territory, and shall be able so to do, through the faithful exercise of it's influence and power, to rescue them, and return them to their country, or deliver them to the agent or representative of the Mexican Government. The Mexican Authorities will, as far as practicable, give to the Government of the United States notice of such captures; and it's agent shall pay the expenses incurred in the maintenance and transmission of the rescued captives; who, in the mean time, shall be treated with the utmost hospitality by the American Authorities at the place where they may be. But if the Government of the United States, before receiving such notice from Mexico, should obtain intelligence through any other channel, of the existence of Mexican captives within it's territory, it will proceed forthwith to effect their release and delivery to the Mexican agent, as above stipulated.

For the purpose of giving to these stipulations the fullest possible efficacy, thereby affording the security and redress demanded by their true spirit and intent, the Government of the United States will now and hereafter pass, without unnecessary delay, and always vigilantly enforce, such laws as the nature of the subject may require. And finally, the sacredness of this obligation shall never be lost sight of by the said Government, when providing for the removal of the Indians from any portion of the said territories, or for it's being settled by citizens of the United States; but on the contrary, special care shall then be taken not to place it's Indian occupants under the necessity of seeking new homes, by committing those invasions which the United States have solemnly obliged themselves to restrain.

Article XII

In consideration of the extension acquired by the boundaries of the United States, as defined in the fifth Article of the present treaty, the Government of the United States engages to pay to that of the Mexican Republic the sum of fifteen Millions of Dollars.

Immediately after this Treaty shall have been duly ratified by the Government of the Mexican Republic, the sum of three Millions of Dollars shall be paid to the said Government by that of the United States at the city of Mexico, in the gold or silver coin of Mexico. The remaining twelve Millions of Dollars shall be paid at the same place, and in the same coin, in annual instalments of three Millions of Dollars each, together with interest on the same at the rate of six per centum per annum. This interest shall begin to run upon the whole sum of twelve millions, from the day of ratification of the present treaty by the Mexican Government, and the first of the instalments shall be paid at the expiration of one year from the same day. Together with each annual instalment, as it falls due, the whole interest accruing on such instalment from the beginning shall also be paid.

Article XIII

The United States engage moreover, to assume and pay to the claimants all the amounts now due them, and those hereafter to become due, by reason of the claims already liquidated and decided against the Mexican Republic, under the conventions between the two Republics, severally concluded on the eleventh day of April eighteen hundred and thirty-nine, and on the thirtieth day of January eighteen hundred and forty three: so that the Mexican Republic shall be absolutely exempt for the future, from all expense whatever on account of the said claims.

Article XIV

The United States do furthermore discharge the Mexican Republic from all claims of citizens of the United States, not heretofore decided against the Mexican Government, which may have arisen previously to the date of the signature of this treaty: which discharge shall be final and perpetual, whether the said claims be rejected or be allowed by the Board of Commissioners provided for in the following Article, and whatever shall be the total amount of those allowed.

Article XV

The United States, exonerating Mexico from all demands on account of the claims of their citizens mentioned in the preceding Article, and considering them entirely and forever cancelled, whatever their amount may be, undertake to make satisfaction for the same, to an amount not exceeding three and one quarter millions of dollars. To ascertain the validity and amount of those claims, a Board of Commissioners shall be established by the Government of the United States, whose awards shall be final and conclusive: provided that in deciding upon the validity of each claim, the board shall be guided and governed by the principles and rules of decision described by the first and fifth Articles of the unratified convention, concluded at the city of Mexico on the twentieth day of November one thousand eight hundred and forty-three; and in no case shall an award be made in favor of any claim not embraced by these principles and rules.

If, in the opinion of the said Board of Commissioners, or of the claimants, any books, records or documents in the possession or power of the Government of the Mexican Republic, shall be deemed necessary to the just decision of any claim, the Commissioners or the claimants, through them, shall, within such period as Congress may designate, make an application in writing for the same, addressed to the Mexican Minister for Foreign Affairs, to be transmitted by the Secretary of State of the United States; and the Mexican Government engages, at the earliest possible moment after the receipt of such demand, to cause any of the books, records or documents, so specified, which shall be in their possession or power, (or authenticated copies or extracts of the same) to be transmitted to the said Secretary of State, who shall immediately deliver them over to the said Board of Commissioners: *Provided* That no such application shall be made, by, or at the instance of, any claimant, until the facts which it is expected to prove by such books, records or documents, shall have been stated under oath or affirmation.

Article XVI

Each of the contracting parties reserves to itself the entire right to fortify whatever point within it's territory, it may judge proper so to fortify, for it's security.

Article XVII

The Treaty of Amity, Commerce and Navigation, concluded at the City of Mexico on the fifth day of April A.D. 1831, between the United States of America and the United Mexican States, except the additional Article, and except so far as the stipulations of the said treaty may be incompatible with any stipulation contained in the present treaty, is hereby revived for the period of eight years from the day of the exchange of ratifications of this treaty, with the same force and virtue as if incorporated therein; it being understood that each of the contracting parties reserves to itself the right, at any time after the said period of eight years shall have expired, to terminate the same by giving one year's notice of such intention to the other party.

Article XVIII

All supplies whatever for troops of the United States in Mexico, arriving at ports in the occupation of such troops, previous to the final evacuation thereof, although subsequently to the restoration of the Custom Houses at such ports, shall be entirely exempt from duties and charges of any kind: the Government of the United States hereby engaging and pledging it's faith to establish and vigilantly to enforce, all possible guards for securing the revenue of Mexico, by preventing the importation, under cover of this stipulation, of any articles, other than such, both in kind and in quantity, as shall really be wanted for the use and consumption of the forces of the United States during the time they may remain in Mexico. To this end, it shall be the duty of all officers and agents of the United States to denounce to the Mexican Authorities at the respective ports, any attempts at a fraudulent abuse of this stipulation, which they may know of or may have reason to suspect, and to give to such authorities all the aid in their power with regard thereto: and every such attempt, when duly proved and established by sentence of a competent tribunal, shall be punished by the confiscation of the property so attempted to be fraudulently introduced.

Article XIX

With respect to all merchandise, effects and property whatsoever, imported into ports of Mexico, whilst in the occupation of the forces of the United States, whether by citizens of either republic, or by citizens or subjects of any neutral nation, the following rules shall be observed:

I. All such merchandise, effects and property, if imported previously to the restoration of the Custom Houses to the Mexican Authorities, as stipulated for in the third Article of this treaty, shall be exempt from confiscation, although the importation of the same be prohibited by the Mexican tariff.

II. The same perfect exemption shall be enjoyed by all such merchandise, effects and property, imported subsequently to the restoration of the Custom Houses, and previously to the sixty days fixed in the following Article for the coming into force of the Mexican tariff at such ports respectively: the said merchandise, effects and property being, however, at the time of their importation, subject to the payment of duties as provided for in the said following Article.

III. All merchandise, effects and property, described in the two rules foregoing, shall, during their continuance at the place of importation, and upon their leaving such place for the interior, be exempt from all duty, tax or impost of every kind, under whatsoever title or denomination. Nor shall they be there subjected to any charge whatsoever upon the sale thereof.

IV. All merchandise, effects and property, described in the first and second rules, which shall have been removed to any place in the interior, whilst such place was in the occupation of the forces of the United States, shall, during their continuance therein, be exempt from all tax upon the sale or consumption thereof, and from every kind of impost or contribution, under whatsoever title of denomination.

V. But if any merchandise, effects or property, described in the first and second rules, shall be removed to any place not occupied at the time by the forces of the United States, they shall, upon their introduction into such place, or upon their sale or consumption there, be subject to the same duties which, under the Mexican laws, they would be required to pay in such cases, if they had been imported in time of peace through the Maritime Custom Houses, and had there paid the duties, conformably with the Mexican tariff.

VI. The owners of all merchandise, effects or property, described in the first and second rules, and existing in any port of Mexico, shall have the right to reship the same, exempt from all tax, impost or contribution whatever.

With respect to the metals, or other property, exported from any Mexican port, whilst in the occupation of the forces of the United States, and previously to the restoration of the Custom House at such port, no person shall be required by the Mexican Authorities, whether General or State, to pay any tax, duty or contribution upon any such exportation, or in any manner to account for the same to the said Authorities.

Article XX

Through consideration for the interest of commerce generally, it is agreed, that if less than sixty days should elapse between the date of signature of this treaty and the restoration of the Custom Houses, conformably with the stipulation in the third Article, in such case, all merchandise, effects and property whatsoever, arriving at the Mexican ports after the restoration of the said Custom Houses, and previously to the expiration of sixty days after the day of the signature of this treaty, shall be admitted to entry; and no other duties shall be levied thereon than the duties established by the tariff found in force at such Custom Houses at the time of the restoration of the same. And to all such merchandise, effects and property, the rules established by the preceding Article shall apply.

Article XXI

If unhappily any disagreement should hereafter arise between the Governments of the two Republics, whether with respect to the interpretation of any stipulation in this treaty, or with respect to any other particular concerning the political or commercial relations of the two Nations, the said Governments, in the name of those Nations, do promise to each other, that they will endeavour, in the most sincere and earnest manner, to settle the differences so arising, and to preserve the state of peace and friendship, in which the two countries are now placing themselves: using, for this end, mutual representations and pacific negotiations. And if, by these means, they should not be enabled to come to an agreement, a resort shall not, on this account, be had to reprisals, aggression or hostility of any kind, by the one Republic against the other, until the Government of that which deems itself aggrieved, shall have maturely considered, in the spirit of peace and good neighbourship, whether it would not be better that such difference should be settled by the arbitration of Commissioners appointed on each side, or by that of a friendly nation. And should such course be proposed by either party, it shall be acceded to by the other, unless deemed by it altogether incompatible with the nature of the difference, or the circumstances of the case.

Article XXII

If (which is not to be expected, and which God forbid!) war should unhappily break out between the two Republics, they do now, with a view to such calamity, solemnly pledge themselves to each other and to the world, to observe the following rules: absolutely, where the nature of the subject permits, and as closely as possible in all cases where such absolute observance shall be impossible.

I. The merchants of either Republic, then residing in the other, shall be allowed to remain twelve months (for those dwelling in the interior) and six months (for those dwelling at the sea-ports) to collect their debts and settle their affairs; during which periods they shall enjoy the same protection, and be on the same footing, in all respects, as the citizens or subjects of the most friendly nations; and, at the expiration thereof, or at any time before, they shall have full liberty to depart, carrying off all their effects, without molestation or hinderance: conforming therein to the same laws, which the citizens or subjects of the most friendly nations are required to conform to. Upon the entrance of the armies of either nation into the territories of the other, women and children, ecclesiastics, scholars of every faculty, cultivators of the earth, merchants, artisans, manufacturers, and fisherman, unarmed and inhabiting unfortified towns, villages or places, and in general all persons whose occupations are for the common subsistence and benefit of mankind, shall be allowed to continue their respective employments, unmolested in their persons. Nor shall their houses or goods be burnt, or otherwise destroyed; nor their cattle taken, nor their fields wasted, by the armed force, into whose power, by the events of war, they may happen to fall; but if the necessity arise to take anything from them for the use of such armed force, the same shall be paid for at an equitable price. All churches, hospitals, schools, colleges, libraries, and other establishments for charitable and beneficent purposes, shall be respected, and all persons connected with the same protected in the discharge of their duties and the pursuit of their vocations.

II. In order that the fate of prisoners of war may be alleviated, all such practices as those of sending them into distant, inclement or unwholesome districts, or crowding them into close and noxious places, shall be studiously avoided. They shall not be confined to dungeons, prison-ships, or prisons; nor be put in irons, or bound, or otherwise restrained in the use of their limbs. The officers shall enjoy liberty on their paroles, within convenient districts, and have comfortable quarters; and the common soldier shall be disposed in cantonments, open and extensive enough for air and exercise, and lodged in barracks as roomy and good as are provided by the party in whose power they are for it's own troops. But, if any officer shall break his parole by leaving the district so assigned him, or any other prisoner shall escape from the limits of his cantonment, after they shall have been designated to him, such individual, officer or other prisoner, shall forfeit so much of the benefit of this article as provides for his liberty on parole or in cantonment. And if any officer so breaking his parole, or any common soldier so escaping from the limits assigned him, shall afterwards be found in arms, previously to his being regularly exchanged, the person so offending shall be dealt with according to the established laws of war. The officers shall be daily furnished by the party in whose power they are, with as many rations, and of the same articles as are allowed either in kind or by commutation, to officers of equal rank in it's own army; and all others shall be daily furnished with such ration as is allowed to a common soldier in it's own service: the value of all which supplies shall, at the close of the war, or at periods to be agreed upon between the respective commanders, be paid by the other party on a mutual adjustment of accounts for the subsistence of prisoners; and such accounts shall not be mingled with or set off against any others, nor the balance due on them be withheld, as a compensation or reprisal for any cause whatever, real or pretended. Each party shall be allowed to keep a commissary of prisoners, appointed by itself, with every cantonment of prisoners, in possession of the other: which commissary shall see the prisoners as often as he pleases; shall be allowed to receive, exempt from all duties or taxes, and to distribute whatever comforts may be sent to them by their friends; and shall be free to transmit his reports in open letters to the party by whom he is employed.

And it is declared that neither the pretence that war dissolves all treaties, nor any other whatever shall be considered as annulling or suspending the solemn covenant contained in this article. On the contrary, the state of war is precisely that for which it is provided; and during which it's stipulations are to be as sacredly observed as the most acknowledged obligations under the law of nature of nations.

Article XXIII

This treaty shall be ratified by the President of the United States of America, by and with the advice and consent of the Senate thereof; and by the President of the Mexican Republic, with the previous approbation of it's General Congress: and the ratifications shall be exchanged in the City of Washington, or at the seat of government of Mexico, in four months from the date of the signature herof, or sooner if practicable.

In faith whereof, we, the respective Plenipotentiaries, have signed this Treaty of Peace, Friendship, Limits and Settlement, and have hereunto affixed our seals respectively. Done in Quintuplicate, at the City of Guadalupe Hidalgo, on the second day of February in the year of Our Lord one thousand eight hundred and forty eight.

N. P. TRIST [SEAL]
LUIS G. CUEVAS [SEAL]
BERNARDO COUTO [SEAL]
MIG[1] ATRISTAIN [SEAL]

U.S. Court Cases Interpreting the Treaty of Guadalupe Hidalgo

Amaya et al. v. Stanoline Oil and Gas Co. et al. 158 F.2d 554 (1947).

Anisa v. New Mexico and Arizona Rail Road 175 U.S. 76 (1899).

Apapos et al. v. United States 233 U.S. 587 (1914).

Application of Robert Galvan for Writ of Habeus Corpus 127 F. Supp. 392 (1954).

Asociación de Reclamantes v. The United Mexican States 735 F.2d 1517 (1984).

Astiazaran et al. v. Santa Rita Land and Mining Co. et al. 148 U.S. 80 (1984).

Baker et al. v. Harvey 181 U.S. 481 (1901).

Baldwin v. Goldrank 88 Tex. 249 (1896).

Basse v. Brownsville 154 U.S. 168 (1875).

Borax Consolidated Ltd. et al. v. City of Los Angeles 296 U.S. 10 (1935).

Botiller et al. v. Dominguez 130 U.S. 238 (1889).

California Power Works v. Davis 151 U.S. 389 (1894).

Carpentier v. Montgomery et al. 80 U.S. 460 (1891).

Cartwright v. Public Service of New Mexico 66 N.M. 64 (1858).
Cessna v. United States et al. 169 U.S. 165 (1898).
Chadwick v. Campbell 115 F.2d 401 (1940).
City and County of San Francisco v. Scott 111 U.S. 768 (1884).
City of Los Angeles v. Venice Peninsula Properties et al. 31 Cal. 3d 288 (1913).
City of San Diego v. Cuyamaca Water Co. 209 Cal. 105 (1930).
Grant v. Jaramillo 6 N.M. 313 (1892).
Horner v. United States 143 U.S. 570 (1892).
Interstate Land Co. v. Maxwell Land Co. 139 U.S. 569 (1891).
Lockhart v. Johnson 181 U.S. 481 (1901).
Lockhart v. Wills et al. 54 S.W. 336 (1898).
Lopez Tijerina v. Henry 48 F.R.D. 274 (1969).
Lopez Tijerina et al. v. United States 396 U.S. 990 (1969).
McKinney v. Saviego 59 U.S. 365 (1856).
Merrion v. Jicarilla Apache Tribe 617 F. 2d 537 (1980).
Minturn v. Brower et al. 24 Cal. 644 (1864).
Northwestern Bands of Shoshone Indians v. United States 324 U.S. 335 (1945).
Palmer v. United States 65 U.S. 125 (1857).
Phillips et al. v. Mound City 124 U.S. 605 (1888).
Pitt River Tribe v. United States 485 F.2d 660 (1973).
Pueblo of Zia v. United States et al. 168 U.S. 198 (1897).
Reynolds v. West 1 Cal. 322 (1850).
State of Texas v. Balli et al. 144 Tex. 195 (1945).
State of Texas v. Gallardo 135 S.W. 644 (1911).
Summa Corporation v. State of California 80 L.Ed. 2d 237 (1984).
Tameling v. United States Freehold land and Emigration Co. 2 Colo. 411 (1874).
Tee-Hit-Ton Indians v. United States 348 U.S. 272 (1955).
Tenorio v. Tenorio 44 N.M. 89 (1940).
Texas Mexican Railroad v. Locke 74 Tex. 340 (1889).
Townsend et al. v. Greeley 72 U.S. 326 (1866).
United States v. Abeyta 632 F.Supp. 1301 (1986).
United States v. Aguisola 68 U.S. 352 (1863).
United States ex rel. Chunie v. Ringrose 788 F.2d 638 (1986).
United States v. Green et al. 185 U.S. 256 256 (1901).
United States v. Lucero 1 N.M. 422 (1869).
United States v. Moreno 68 U.S. 400 (1863).
United States v. Naglee 1 Cal. 232 (1850).

United States v. O'Donnell 303 U.S. 501 (1938).

United States v. Reading 59 U.S. 1 (1855).

United States v. Rio Grande Dam and Irrigation Co. et al. 175 U.S. 690 (1899).

United States v. Rio Grande Dam and Irrigation Co. et al. 184 U.S. 416 (1901).

United States v. Sandoval et al. 167 U.S. 278 (1897).

United States v. Sandoval et al. 231 U.S. 28 (1913).

United States v. Santistevan 1 N.M. 583 (1874).

United States v. State of Louisiana et al. 363 U.S. 1 (1960).

United States v. Title Insurance and Trust Co. et al. 265 U.S. 472 (1924).

United States v. Utah 238 U.S. 64 (1931).

Ward v. Broadwell 1 N.M. 75 (1854).

Notes

PREFACE

1. See especially Alan Riding, *Distant Neighbors: A Portrait of the Mexicans* (New York: Alfred A. Knopf, 1985); Robert H. McBride, ed., *Mexico and the United States* (Englewood Cliffs, N.J.: Prentice Hall, 1981); and Robert J. Shafer and Donald Mabry, *Neighbors: Mexico and the United States* (Chicago: Nelson Hall, 1981).

2. Donald C. Cutter, "The Legacy of the Treaty of Guadalupe Hidalgo," *New Mexico Historical Review* vol. 53, no. 4 (October 1978): 305–315.

3. Two authoritative and exhaustive works on the treaty are David M. Pletcher, *The Diplomacy of Annexation: Texas, Oregon, and the Mexican War* (Columbia: University of Missouri Press, 1973) and David Hunter Miller, *Treaties and Other International Acts of the United States of America*, vol. 5 (Washington, D.C.: Government Printing Office, 1937).

CHAPTER 1. BACKGROUND ISSUES

1. For a classic analysis of the ideas of Manifest Destiny in American life, see Albert K. Weinberg, *Manifest Destiny: A Study of Nationalist Expansion in American History* (1935; Reprint, Chicago: Quadrangle Books, 1963). See also Frederick Merk, *Manifest Destiny and Mission in American History: A Reinterpretation* (New York: Alfred A. Knopf, 1963).

2. *New York Morning News*, December 27, 1845, in Weinberg, p. 194.

3. *New York Herald*, September 25, 1845, in Merk, p. 46.

4. See quotes in Weinberg by these and other notable figures.

5. John D. P. Fuller, "Slaveholder Opposed Conquest of Mexico," in Ramon Ruiz, ed., *The Mexican War: Was it Manifest Destiny?* (New York: Holt, Rhinehart and Winston, 1963), pp. 29–38.

6. During his inaugural parade, Polk supposedly told George Bancroft, his secretary of navy and ambassador to England, of the four goals of his administration: the acquisition of California, settlement of the Oregon boundary dispute, lowering of the tariff, and the establishment of an independent treasury. See George Bancroft, "James K. Polk," in *Appleton's Cyclopedia of American Biography*, vol. 5, p. 55, cited in Charles A. McCoy, *Polk and the Presidency* (Austin: University of Texas Press, 1960), p. 50.

7. See James T. Horn, "Trends in Historical Interpretation: James K. Polk," *North Carolina Historical Review*, vol. 42 (October 1965):454–465; Richard R. Stenberg, "The Failure of Polk's Mexican War Intrigue of 1845," *Pacific Historical Review*, vol. 4 (1935), in Ruiz, 65–76; Glenn Price, *Origins of the War with Mexico: The Polk-Stockton Intrigue* (Austin: University of Texas Press, 1967); Hubert Howe Bancroft, *History of Mexico, 1824–1861*, vol. 15 (San Francisco: A. L. Bancroft and Company, 1885), pp. 545–547, who argues that Polk was primarily responsible for causing the war.

8. See Samuel F. Bemis, *A Diplomatic History of the U.S.*, quoted in Ruiz, "Defense of Polk," pp. 77–84; see also Justin H. Smith, *The War with Mexico*, 2 vols. (1919; Reprint, Gloucester, Mass.: Peter Smith, 1963).

9. Justin Smith, "Mexico Wanted War," in Ruiz, pp. 95–105.

10. William R. Manning, *Early Diplomatic Relations Between the U.S. and Mexico* (Baltimore: John Hopkins Press, 1916), pp. 205–251; Mexico refused to sign the Treaty of Amity and Commerce prior to the signing of a treaty of limits regarding Texas. For a detailed discussion of this dispute see Cesar Sepulveda, *La frontera norte de Mexico: historia, conflictos 1762–1975* (Mexico, D.F.: Editorial Porrua, 1983).

11. William Campbell Binkley, *The Expansionist Movement in Texas, 1836–1850*, University of California Publications in History, vol. 13 (Berkeley: University of California Press, 1925) pp. 1–12.

12. Thomas M. Marshall, *A History of the Western Boundary of the Louisiana Purchase, 1819–1841*, University of California Publications in History, vol. 2 (Berkeley: University of California Press, 1914) pp. 17–45. The Adams-Onis Treaty provided that each country would prevent Indians on its side of the boundary from raiding the other's territory. Later, this same provision was included in the Treaty of Guadalupe Hidalgo and was a source of conflict between the two countries. See Justin H. Smith, 2:64–73.

13. Accompanying this proposal was one to purchase San Francisco Bay. It appears that a later Mexican proposal, to cede San Francisco and create a no-man's land between the Nueces River and the Rio Grande was based on this earlier offer by the Jackson government.

14. Binkley, p. 18.

15. Binkley, pp. 13–18.

16. Binkley, pp. 127–129.

17. Binkley, p. 134. In 1843, the Mexican minister to the United States told the U.S. government that "the Mexican Government will consider equivalent to a declaration of war against the Mexican Republic the passage of an act for the incorporation of Texas with the territory of the United States; the certainty of the fact being sufficient for the immediate declaration of war." Justin Smith, 1:84.

CHAPTER 2. THE WAR AND SECRET DIPLOMACY

1. Paul R. Pillar, *Negotiating Peace: War Termination as a Bargaining Process* (Princeton, N.J.: Princeton University Press, 1983). Pillar analyzes the negotiation process using the 142

wars fought since 1800 and finds that in most modern wars, negotiations have preceded the armistice that ended the hostilities. The Mexican War was one of these modern conflicts. See also Thomas C. Schelling, *The Strategy of Conflict* (Cambridge: Harvard University Press, 1963).

2. For an analysis, see Charles A. Lofgren, "Force and Diplomacy, 1846–1848: The View from Washington," *Military Affairs*, vol. 31, no. 2 (Summer 1967): 57–64. During the Vietnam War, Secretary of State Henry Kissinger openly discussed his strategy of using military force to force a negotiated settlement.

3. Schelling, p. 5. See also Rifa Howard, *The Art and Science of Negotiation* (Cambridge: Harvard University Press, 1982).

4. Pillar, pp. 37–38.

5. Charles E. Hill, *Leading American Treaties* (New York: Macmillan Co., 1922), p. 201; David M. Pletcher, *The Diplomacy of Annexation: Texas, Oregon, and the Mexican War* (Columbia: University of Missouri Press, 1973) pp. 366–367. Pletcher characterized Atocha's offer as "an ingenious mixture of half-truths and plausible lies," but subsequent relations with Santa Anna give credence to Atocha's offer in 1846.

6. Milton Quaife, ed., *The Diary of James K. Polk: During his Presidency, 1845 to 1849*, 4 vols. (Chicago: A. C. McClurg and Co., 1910), 2: 325–326 (January 14, 1847).

7. This seems to have been the origin of the unusual powers given Trist by the Department of State when he was appointed.

8. Quaife, pp. 236–240.

9. Dennis Berge, "Mexican Response to U.S. Expansion: 1841–1848" (Ph.D. diss., University of California, Berkeley, 1965), p. 214.

10. Pletcher, pp. 299–307; Hill, p. 205.

11. Moses S. Beach, "A Secret Mission to Mexico," *Scribner's Monthly*, vol. 18, no. 1 (1879): 137. The article is by Moses Y. Beach's son.

12. Ibid., pp. 136–137.

13. Alan Nevins, ed. *Polk: The Diary of a President, 1845–1849* (London, New York, and Toronto: Longman, Green and Co., 1929), pp. 217–218.

14. William R. Manning, ed., *Diplomatic Correspondence*

of the U.S.: Inter American Affairs, 1831−1860, Mexico 1831−1848 (midyear) (Washington, D.C.: Government Printing Office, 1937), p. 201.

15. No published biography of Trist exists, but there are a number of dissertations and articles. See Arthur Brent, "Nicholas Trist: A Biography" (Ph.D. dissertation, University of Virginia, 1950). Trist's reputation as a diplomat has been subject to debate. Those favorable to him include the eulogistic Louis Martin Sears, "Nicholas Trist: A Diplomat with Ideals," *Mississippi Valley Historical Review*, vol. 11, no. 1 (1924):85−98, who portrays him as an impoverished aristocrat who remained committed to ideals bordering on utopianism. Those who consider Trist less than competent include Eugene K. Chamberlin, "Nicholas Trist and Baja California," *Pacific Historical Review*, vol. 32, no. 1 (February 1963):63.

16. For Polk's recollection of the cabinet meeting that drafted the draft treaty see Quaife, pp. 472−473; for a complete copy of the original treaty and instructions given to Trist, see Manning, pp. 201−207.

17. Manning, p. 206. This section of the Louisiana Purchase Treaty, with some revision later, became part of the Treaty of Guadalupe Hidalgo (Article IX).

18. Luis Zorrilla, *Historia entre Mexico y los Estados Unidos de America, 1800−1958*, 2 vols. (Mexico, D.F.: Editorial Porrua, 1977), 2:203.

19. J. D. Whipley, "The Late Negotiations for Peace," *American Review*, vol. 6, no. 5 (November 1847):444.

20. Ibid., p. 453.

21. John Bassett Moore, ed. *The Works of James Buchanan*, 8 vols. (New York: Antiquarian Press, 1960), 8:275.

22. See Fletcher, pp. 504−507, for a detailed account of this period.

23. Carlos Castaneda, "Relations of General Scott with Santa Anna," *Hispanic American Historical Review*, vol. 29, no. 4 (November 1949):460−461. Thornton had suggested a bribe two weeks earlier, but Trist had rejected the idea. José Fernando Ramírez, Minister of Foreign Relations under Gómez Farias wrote that the members of the Mexican Congress were well aware that Trist brought with him a draft on the U.S. Treasury for three million dollars for expenses in concluding a treaty. It was considered common knowledge that this money

was essentially for bribes—an understandable misinterpretation of the American motives. See José Fernando Ramírez, *Mexico During the War with the United States*, Walter Scholes, ed., University of Missouri Studies, vol. 23, no. 1 (Columbia: University of Missouri, 1950), p. 122. The documentary evidence concerning this episode and subsequent investigation into its propriety is to be found in Senate Document 34, Cong. 3rd Session, February 2, 1857, and in Department of War, Office of Judge Advocate General (Record Group 153), General Court Martials, 1812–1938, Box FFF-300, "Proceedings of a Court of Inquiry Held in Mexico and the Secretary of War, 17th March 1848 in regard to the use of Secret Service Money for the Purchase of Peace." Notes based on this collection, compiled by Justin Smith and used by Castaneda in his article, are to be found in the Justin H. Smith Papers, University of Texas, Austin.

24. W. A. Corffert, ed., *Fifty Years in Camp and Field: The Diary of Major General Ethan Allen Hitchcock, U.S.A.* (1909; Reprint, Freeport, New York: Books for Libraries Press, 1971), p. 268.

25. Castaneda, p. 466.

26. Ibid., p. 468.

27. Scott explained his actions to the satisfaction of Polk. "At the time it appeared that peace was possible and that entering the city in hot pursuit might 'scatter the elements of peace.'" For a less-charitable view of Santa Anna's motives in this episode, see Francisco Castillo Najera, "El Tratado de Guadalupe," Ponencia al Congreso Mexicano de Historia, VII Reunion, Durango, Septiembre 17–26, 1947 (Mexico, D.F.: n.p., 1948).

CHAPTER 3. STRIKING THE BARGAIN: FROM ARMISTICE TO TREATY

1. Paul R. Pillar, *Negotiating Peace: War Termination as a Bargaining Process* (Princeton, N.J.: Princeton University Press, 1983), pp. 92–119.

2. David M. Pletcher, *The Diplomacy of Annexation: Texas, Oregon, and the Mexican War* (Columbia: University of Missouri Press, 1973), p. 516.

3. George Lockhart Rives, *The United States and Mexico, 1821–1848* (New York: Charles Scribner's & Sons, 1913), vol. 2, pp. 513–516.

4. Pillar, p. 142.

5. Salvador Bermudez de Castro, July 27, 1847, Despacho no. 530 in *Relaciones diplomaticos hispano-mexicanas (1839–1898): Documentos procedentes del Archivo de la Embajada de Espana en Mexico,* Serie I, Despachos generales (Mexico, D.F.: El Colegio de Mexico, 1968), vol. 4, pp. 126–127.

6. Trist to Buchanan, September 27, 1847, in William R. Manning, ed., *Diplomatic Correspondence of the United States, Inter-American Affairs, 1812–1860,* vol. 8, "Mexico 1831–1848 (midyear)" (Washington D.C.: Government Printing Office, 1937), pp. 956, 964. According to Zorrilla, Santa Anna began preparing in earnest for renewal of the war when he first received news of the "exorbitant and pretentious" territorial demands of the United States on August 27, however, Santa Anna undoubtedly knew of the U.S. proposals long before August. See Luis Zorrilla, *Historia entre Mexico y los Estados Unidos de America, 1800–1958* (Mexico, D.F.: Editorial Porrua, 1977), vol. 1, pp. 206–207.

7. *Diario del Gobierno,* August 21, 1847 quoted in Jack Northrup, "The Trist Mission," *Journal of Mexican American History,* vol. 3 (1973); 19.

8. Raiffa Howard, *The Art and Science of Negotiation* (Cambridge, Mass.: Harvard University Press, 1982), p. 166; quote is by John Dunlop, former U.S. Secretary of Labor.

9. Zorrilla, vol. 1, p. 208. Actually there were fifteen counterproposals made by Santa Anna. They are reproduced and translated in Manning, "Mexican Commissioners to Nicholas Trist," September 6, 1847, No. 3729. Ironically several of these rejected counterproposals found their way into the final treaty. Article 10 of Santa Anna's proposal became Article 8, and Articles 3 and 13 of the counterproposal became parts of the final treaty.

10. C. Mariano Otero, "Comunicación que sobre las negociaciones diplomáticos habidos en la casa de Alfaro," in *Algunos Documentos sobre el tratado de Guadalupe,* Archivo historico diplomatico Mexicano, no. 31 (Mexico, D.F.: Editorial Porrua, 1970), pp. 92–103.

11. Buchanan to Trist, 6 October 1847, in John Bassett Moore, ed., *The Works of James Buchanan*, vol. 7, 1846–1848 (New York: Antiquarian Press, 1960), p. 427.

12. Pletcher, pp. 533–537.

13. Rives, vol. 2, p. 595.

14. Thomas J. Farnham, "Nicholas Trist and James Freaner and the Mission to Mexico," *Arizona and the West*, vol. 11, no. 3 (Autumn 1969): 253–256.

15. Norman A. Graebner, "Party Politics and the Trist Mission," *Journal of Southern History*, vol. 19, no. 2 (May 1953): 154–155. In his diary, Polk confided his belief that Scott was behind Trist's insubordination. Initially the president's decision to recall his ambassador was based on the failure of the armistice talks and a desire to pressure the Mexican government into negotiating in earnest. See Polk's entry for October 5, 1847, in Alan Nevins, ed., *Polk: Diary of a President, 1845–1849* (New York: Longman, Green and Co.), p. 267. Later, as Polk learned the details of the armistice talks and of Trist's willingness to submit the Nueces boundary proposal to Washington, he grew more angry. See the entry for October 21, 1847, in Nevins, p. 271.

16. Rives, vol. 2, p. 597; *Algunos documentos sobre el tratado de Guadalupe y la situacion de Mexico durante la invasión Americana* (Mexico, D.F.: Editorial Porrua, 1971), pp. 107–108.

17. Quoted in Norman Graebner, *Empire on the Pacific: A Study in American Continental Expansion* (1955; Reprint, Santa Barbara: ABC-CLIO, 1983), p. 207.

18. Ibid, pp. 207–208. At one point in the discussions, Trist offered to give half the harbor of San Diego to Mexico in exchange for a piece of land on the Mexican side of the Colorado River (since the international boundary cut the Colorado twice after its intersection with the Gila River). See *Siglo XIX*, June 6, 1848, p. 3, col. 2.

19. Trist to Buchanan, January 25, 1848, in Manning, p. 1043.

20. Ibid., p. 1051.

21. Barbara Tenenbaum suggests that the *agiotistas* played an important role in the negotiations between the United States and Mexico during the war. Ewen MacKintosh, the British consul, represented the most powerful creditors in Mexico. He was appointed as a government representative in the armi-

stice and treaty negotiations. Barbara Tenenbaum, *Mexico en la época de los agiotistas, 1821–1857* (Mexico, D.F.: Fondo de cultural económico, 1985), pp. 98–99.

22. Barbara Tenenbaum, "'Neither a borrower nor a lender be': Financial Constraints on the Treaty of Guadalupe Hidalgo," in Jaime Rodriquez O., ed., *The Mexican and Mexican American Experience in the Nineteenth Century* (Tempe, Arizona: Bilingual Press, 1988).

CHAPTER 4. FINALIZING THE TREATY, 1848–1854

1. David Pletcher, *The Diplomacy of Annexation: Texas, Oregon, and the Mexican War* (Columbia: University of Missouri Press, 1973), p. 558.

2. Senate Executive Documents No. 52, 30th Congress, 1st session, 4–5.

3. Ibid., 9.

4. Robert Selph Henry, *The Story of the Mexican War* (New York: Frederick Unger, 1950), pp. 386–388. The most complete documentary collection regarding the treaty and its ratification is assembled in David Hunter Miller, *Treaties and Other International Acts of the United States of America*, vol. 5, *Mexico, 1848* (Washington, D.C.: Government Printing Office, 1937), pp. 207–428. The best account of the Senate's ratification debates is Ralph A. Rowley, "Precedents and Influences Affecting the Treaty of Guadalupe-Hidalgo," (Master's thesis, University of New Mexico, 1970), pp. 78–96.

5. Miller, 5:241.

6. Matt S. Meier and Feliciano Rivera, *Dictionary of Mexican American History* (Westport, Conn.: Greenwood Press, 1979), p. 409.

7. Miller, 5:255.

8. See François Xavier Martin, *The History of Louisiana From the Earliest Periods*, (New Orleans: James A. Gresham, 1882), pp. 322–323.

9. Miller, 5:242.

10. Conditions required by the federal government usually included five actions: (1) presentation of a petition describing the parcel along with a map (*diseño*) to the local government official; (2) examination of the land to ascertain its availability and the filing of a report (*informe*); (3) the issuance of formal

grant by the local government (*expediente*); (4) approval of the grant by the territorial or state Assembly or Deputation; and (5) approval by the central government. See William W. Robinson, *Land in California*, (Berkeley: University of California Press, 1948).

11. Miller, 5:255.

12. Later these broadsides were published as *Pensamiento Politico* (Mexico, D.F.: UNAM, 1968). See "Observations on the Treaty of Guadalupe Hidalgo," in that work, pp. 93–145.

13. Ibid., pp. 119–20.

14. Ibid., pp. 122, 123.

15. Ibid., pp. 127–33.

16. Ibid., pp. 127, 133.

17. The news of the discovery of gold in Alta California did not reach Mexico City until after the ratification of the treaty. Although gold was discovered on January 24, 1848, John Marshall and John Sutter tried to keep the discovery secret. It was not until the middle of May that news reached San Francisco. See J. S. Holliday, *The World Rushed In: The California Gold Rush Experience* (New York: Simon & Schuster, 1981).

18. *Siglo XIX*, June 2, 1848, 3:2.

19. Ibid., June 7, 1848, 3:4.

20. Ibid., June 10, 1848, 3:3.

21. Ibid., June 2, 1848, 1:5.

22. José María Roa Bárcena, *Recuerdos de la invasión norteamericana (1846–1848)*, vol. 3 (1883; Reprint, Mexico, D.F.: Editorial Porrua, 1947), 3:323.

23. Francisco de Paula de Arrangoiz, *Mexico desde 1808 hasta 1867* (1872; Reprint, Mexico, D.F.: Editorial Porrua, 1969), p. 401.

24. *Siglo XIX*, May 19, 1848, 3:6.

25. *Algunos documentos sobre el tratado de Guadalupe y la situación de Mexico durante la invasión Americana*, (Mexico, D.F.: Editorial Porrua, 1970), p. 380.

26. Roa Bárcena, p. 304.

27. *Algunos documentos*, pp. 51–65, 168–92.

28. Dennis E. Berge, "Mexican Response to United States Expansionism, 1841–1848" (Ph.D. diss., Berkeley, 1965), pp. 304–306.

29. *Siglo XIX*, June 2, 1848, 3:2.

30. The Protocol of Querétaro also dealt with the modified

Article XII, which did not specify the timing of the final 12 million dollar U.S. payment to Mexico.

31. Miller, 5:381.

32. Geofry Mawn, "A Land Grant-Guarantee: The Treaty of Guadalupe Hidalgo or the Protocol of Querétaro?" *Journal of the West*, vol. 14, no. 4 (October 1975):57–58. This article is a detailed study of the protocol issue.

33. Mawn, p. 59.

34. Mawn (p. 61) believes that the protocol did not guarantee land grants any more than the treaty.

35. Meier and Rivera, p. 403.

36. For the primary reports of the boundary survey from the American point of view, see John Russell Bartlett, "Report on the United States and Mexican Boundary Commission," *House Executive Documents*, 34th Cong., 1st sess. (Serial no. 861). Recent researchers using the Mexican Archives, have begun to tell the Mexican side of the story. See Joseph Richard Werne, "Mexico's Interpretation of the Guadalupe Hidalgo Line," (a paper presented for the American Historical Association, Washington, D.C., 1987); and Harry P. Hewitt, "The Treaty of Guadalupe Hidalgo Revisited: Myths and Realities of the Mexican Boundary Survey," (paper presented for the American Historical Association, Washington, D.C., 1987).

37. Luis Zorrilla, *Historia de las relaciones entre Mexico y los Estados Unidos de America, 1800–1958*, vol. 1 (Mexico, D.F.: Editorial Porrua, 1977), pp. 338–339.

38. Angela Moyano Pahissa, *México y Estados Unidos: Orígenes de una relación, 1819–1861* (Mexico, D.F.: Secretaría de Educación Pública, 1985), pp. 175–177. Pahissa believes that the transfer of these three communities after 1848 was a violation of Article V of the treaty specifying boundaries.

39. Paul Garber, *The Gadsden Treaty* (Gloucester, Mass.: Peter Smith, 1959), pp. 29–30. This is the best study of the origins of this treaty.

40. For the best detailed study of the complicated boundary disputes arising between 1848 and 1853, see W. H. Goetzmann, "The United States—Mexico Boundary Survey, 1848–1853," *Southwestern Historical Quarterly*, vol. 62, no. 2 (October 1958):164–190. See also Jack D. Rittenhouse, *The Story of Disturnell's Treaty Map* (Santa Fe: Stage Coach Press, 1965).

41. See Robert D. Gregg, *The Influence of Border Troubles*

on *Relations Between the United States and Mexico, 1876–1910*, (Baltimore: Johns Hopkins Press, 1937).

CHAPTER 5. CITIZENSHIP AND PROPERTY RIGHTS

1. Oscar Martinez, "On the Size of the Chicano Population" *Aztlan*, 4, no. 1 (Spring 1975):43–67.

2. Francisco F. de la Maza, ed., *Codigo de Colonización y Terrenos Baldios de la Republica Mexicana* (Mexico, D.F.: Secretaria de Fomento, 1873), pp. 402–427.

3. Hubert Howe Bancroft, *History of Arizona and New Mexico* (San Francisco: The History Book Co., 1889), p. 473. The Mexican government made only 25,000 dollars available for the recruitment drive; the funds were to be drawn from those paid by the United States under the terms of the Treaty of Guadalupe Hidalgo. By 1851 eighteen frontier outposts were established, with 1,093 Mexican soldiers including people from the northern provinces and repatriated Mexicans from the United States. The Mexican government also recruited Seminole and Muskogee Indians to establish settlements. See Angela Moyano Pahissa, *México y Estados Unidos: Orígenes de una relación, 1819–1861* (Mexico, D.F.: Secretaría de Educación Pública, 1985), pp. 206–207.

4. Richard Griswold del Castillo, *The Los Angeles Barrio: 1850–1890: A Social History* (Los Angeles: University of California Press, 1980), pp. 123–124.

5. Bancroft, p. 472; Ralph Emerson Twitchell, *The Leading Facts of New Mexican History*, vol. 1, (1911–1912; Reprint, Albuquerque: Horn and Wallace, 1963), p. 102.

6. The most detailed account of the activities of the commissioners in New Mexico is Mary Childers Mangusso, "A Study of the Citizenship Provisions of the Treaty of Guadalupe Hidalgo," (Masters thesis, University of New Mexico, 1966). For later protests see Manuel Marrimar to the Minister of Relaciones Exteriores, June 2, 1852, Archivo de la Secretaria de Relaciones Exteriores (ASRE), Mexico City, no. 2-12-2904. See Also Angela Moyano Pahissa, *México y Estados Unidos: Orígenes de una relación, 1819–1861* (Mexico, D.F.: Secretaría de Educación Pública, 1985), pp. 182–184.

7. Official correspondence, ASRE, nos. 2-13-2976 and 2-13-2975.

8. Twitchell, p. 241. Later problems with non-citizens serving on juries in New Mexico led the territorial legislature to pass a law to allow persons who had declared their intention of becoming naturalized citizens to serve; see Mangusso, pp. 67–68.

9. J. Ross Browne, ed., *Report of the Debates on the Convention of California on the Formation of the State Constitution in September and October 1849* (Washington, D.C.: John Towers, 1850), p. 62.

10. Leonard Pitt, *Decline of the Californios: A Social History of the Spanish-Speaking Californians, 1846–1890* (Berkeley: University of California Press, 1970), p. 50.

11. The history of the Mexican government's protests regarding the treatment of Mexicans in the United States in the period immediately after the Mexican war can be found in a number of published works: William R. Manning, ed., *Diplomatic Correspondence of the United States, Interamerican Affairs*, vol. 9 (Washington, D.C., 1937), pp. 129–130, 133–134, 568–570; Maria de Los Angeles, "La anexación de Texas a los Estados Unidos," (Thésis, U.N.A.M, 1959), pp. 192–195; and Toribio Esquivel Obregon, *Apuntes para la historia del derecho en Mexico*, 4 vols. (Mexico, D.F.: Porrua e hijos, 1948), 3:426–427.

12. 1 Cal 232; Cal Stats 1850, Ch. 97; Pitt, pp. 66–67. The legal history of the Foreign Miner's Tax Law is given in Carl I. Wheat, ed., "California's Bantam Cock: The Journals of Charles E. De Long, 1854–1863," *California Historical Quarterly* 8 (1929):353–355.

13. Pitt, pp. 48–57.

14. The argument against de la Guerra's full citizenship is a revealing comment on the status of Mexican Americans after 1848. "In conclusion we insist that the respondent was an alien enemy up to the ratification of the Treaty of Guadalupe Hidalgo; that between that time and the date of the admission of California into the Union, he joined, by virtue of his silence, that class of Mexicans who are deemed to have elected to become citizens of the United States, but he is not and never was a citizen." *People v. de la Guerra* 40 Cal 311 (1870).

15. Van Hastings Garner, "The Treaty of Guadalupe Hidalgo and the California Indians," *The Indian Historian* 9, no. 1 (Winter, 1976):10–13.

16. Robert W. Larson, *New Mexico's Quest for Statehood, 1846–1912* (Albuquerque: University of New Mexico Press, 1968), p. 19.

17. See U.S. Congress, House of Representatives, *New Mexico-Convention of Delegates: Journal and Proceedings*, 31st Cong. 1st sess., 1850, House Misc. Doc. 39, pp. 1–13.

18. Quoted in Walter La Feber, "The Constitutions and United States Foreign Policy: An Interpretation," *Journal of American History*, vol. 74, no. 3 (December 1987): 705. See *Downs v. Bidwell*, 182 US 244 and *Balzac v. Puerto Rico* 258 US 309; Also Whitney Perkins, *Denial of Empire: the United States and Its Dependencies* (The Netherlands: A. W. Sythoff-Lyden, 1962), pp. 13, 28. The question of citizenship for residents of the territories was a thorny one for jurists. The net effect of the Spanish-American War was to restrict the rights of citizenship to those residing within the borders of continental United States. By 1901 the people of Puerto Rico and the Philippines were made citizens of those places, not of the United States.

19. *U.S. v. Lucero*, 1 NM 422 (1869); *U.S. v Santistevan* 1 N.M. 583 (1874).

20. For a complete discussion of Pueblo Indian citizenship after 1848 see Mary Childers Mangusso, "A Study of the Citizenship Provisions of the Treaty of Guadalupe Hidalgo," (Master's thesis, University of New Mexico, 1966), pp. 77–99. Ralph Rowley, "The Acquisition of the Spanish Borderlands: Problems and Legacy" (Ph.D. diss., University of New Mexico, 1975), p. 168.

21. See *Teschmacher v. Thompson* 8 Cal 23.

22. See Griswold del Castillo, pp. 41–49; "Speech of Hon. Pablo de la Guerra of Santa Barbara," April 17, 1855 (Sacramento: State Tribune Office, 1855), p. 7.

23. Jan Bazant, "Joseph Yves Limantour (1812–1885) y su aventura californiana–I," *Historia Mexicana*, 28, no. 1 (julio–septiembre, 1978): 1–23; "Joseph Yves Limantour (1812–1885) y su aventura californiana–II," *Historia Mexicana*, 29, no. 3 (enero–marzo, 1980): 353–374. Bazant uncovered new evidence at the University of Texas archives that seems to support Limantour's case.

24. 130 U.S. 238 (1889); for a citation of cases that challenged the 1851 land law citing the Treaty of Guadalupe Hi-

dalgo see *Mintern v. Brower* 24 Cal 644 (1864). An excellent discussion of the court cases affecting Mexican land grants is Richard Powell, *Compromises of Conflicting Claims: A Century of California Law, 1760 to 1860* (Dobbs Ferry, New York: Oceana Publications, 1977), pp. 170–171.

25. U.S. Supreme Court, *Brigido Botiller et al. v. Dominga Dominguez,* File Copies of the Briefs, October Term, 1888, vol. 15, pp. 1–23; others who opposed Dominga's claim were Pedro Sepulveda, Manuel Felix, Manuel Sanchez, Pablo Bojorquez, Gregorio Tapia, and Ramon Tapia.

26. Willard B. Cowels, *Treaties and Constitutional Law: Property Interferences and Due Process of Law* (Washington, D.C.: American Council of Public Affairs, 1941), p. 240. 74 Cal 457 (1887).

27. 130 US 238; 9 S.Ct. 525, 527.

28. John Currey, *The Treaty of Guadalupe Hidalgo and Private Land Claims and Titles Existing in California at the Date of the Treaty* (San Francisco: Bancroft Whitney, 1891), p. 22.

29. Ralph Emerson Twitchell, *The Leading Facts of New Mexico's History* (Albuquerque: Horn and Wallace, 1963), 2: 458. New Mexican land-grant litigation, a complex subject, can be treated only superficially in a survey such as this. For a more detailed analysis of the legal and historical aspects involved, see: Victor Westphall, *The Public Domain in New Mexico: 1854–1891* (Albuquerque: University of New Mexico Press, 1965); and J. J. Bowden, *Spanish and Mexican Land Grants in the Chihuahuan Acquisition* (El Paso: Texas Westernlore Press, 1971).

30. Howard Robert Lamar, *The Far Southwest, 1846–1912: A Territorial History* (New York: W. W. Norton, 1966), pp. 141–146.

31. Twitchell, 2:462.

32. Commercial Club of Las Vegas, New Mexico, to Matias Romero, Minister Plenipotentiary, December 27, 1890, ASRE, no. 11-5-1.

33. Matias Romero to Secretaría de Relaciones Exteriores, April 20, 1891, ASRE, no. 11-5-1.

34. *Analysis of the Act to Establish a Court of Private Land Claims,* ASRE, no. 11-5-1, p. 309.

35. Rowley, p. 210.

36. Ibid., pp. 213–214.

37. *McKinney v. Saviego,* S.C. 18 Howard 235.

38. Miller, Doc. 129, p. 381.

39. R. S. Sanchez to the Secretaría de Relaciones Exteriores, June 10, 1895, *Boletin oficial,* tomo I, num. 1 (1895), p. 135. This volume also contains correspondence regarding the applicability of the treaty to Texas.

40. *State v. Gallardo et al,* 135 S.W. 664; "Juridical Decisions Involving Questions of International Law," *American Journal of International Law,* vol. 6 (1912), p. 227.

41. Rudolfo O. de la Garza, and Karl Schmitt, "Texas Land Grants and Chicano-Mexican Relations: A Case Study," *Latin American Research Review* 21, No. 1 (1986): 123–138.

42. Florence Johnson Scott, *Royal Land Grants North of the Rio Grande, 1771–1821* (Rio Grande City: La Retama Press, 1969). This book studies the histories of the grants in the area of Reynosa, Texas: Llano Grande, La Feria, Las Mestenas, San Salvador de Tule, Santa Anita, and Padre Island.

43. Arnoldo de Leon and Kenneth L. Stewart, "Lost Dreams and Found Fortunes: Mexican and Anglo Immigrants into South Texas, 1850–1900," *Western Historical Quarterly,* vol. 14, no. 3 (July 1983): 296.

44. Gilberto Miguel Hinojosa, *A Borderlands Town in Transition: Laredo, 1775–1850* (College Station: Texas A & M University Press, 1983), pp. 58–59.

45. Arnoldo de Leon, *They Called Them Greasers* (Austin: University of Texas Press, 1983).

46. Scott, p. 38.

47. Andrew A. Tijerina, "Tejanos and Texans: The Native Mexicans of Texas, 1820–1850" (Ph.D. diss., University of Texas Austin, 1977), pp. 319–320.

48. David Montejano, *Anglos and Mexicans in the Making of Texas, 1836–1986* (Austin: University of Texas Press, 1987), pp. 63–70. This discussion of the Tejano lands is the best summary of a complex process.

49. *Message of the Governor Transmitting the Report of the Commissioners to Investigate Land Titles West of the Nueces* (Austin: Cushney and Hampton, 1851). The commissioners reported on Webb, Kinney, and Cameron counties, recommending the vast majority of the land grants; See Scott, pp. 105–106.

50. *State of Texas v. Gallardo et al.,* 135 SW 664 (1911); *State of Texas v. Bali,* 173 SW2nd 522.

51. Robert Salazar, "Texas Land Grant Heirs Seek Compensation," *Ajenda: A Journal of Hispanic Issues*, vol. 9, no. 2 (March/April, 1979): pp. 14–16. *Asociación de reclamantes et al. v. The United Mexican States*, no. 81–2299, U.S. Court of Appeals for the District of Columbia Circuit, 561 F. 2d. 1190 (June 20, 1983); *Asociación de reclamantes et al. v. The United Mexican States*, no. 83–1596, U.S. Court of Appeals for the District of Columbia Circuit, 735 F. 2d. 1517 (June 5, 1984).

CHAPTER 6. U.S. COURTS AND THE TREATY

1. The procedure followed to analyze United States court cases dealing with the Treaty of Guadalupe Hidalgo was to utilize the on-line computerized reference system called Lexis-Nexis. This system enables a user to access all court cases mentioning a specific treaty or law and to generate paragraphs where the treaty was referenced in the court conclusions. Shephard's Citations were also used to access references to the treaty that did not appear in the Lexis-Nexis system. In this way more than 200 court cases were singled out, along with some detail on the treaty interpretation given by the court. My study was focused on how the court interpreted the treaty, not on how defendants and plaintiffs argued using the treaty. Only direct references to the treaty were the subject of this study, not the hundreds of cases flowing from land-grant litigation where the treaty was not a substantive concern. Of the 200 cases sampled, only 64 were found to be substantial interpretations of the treaty. My judgment as to what constituted an important interpretation depended both on the length to which the court went in discussing the treaty as well as the importance ascribed to the treaty by the court. Most references to the treaty were minor, where the document was used as a point of reference to make some larger legal argument.

2. Robert McCloskey, *The American Supreme Court* (Chicago and London: University of Chicago Press, 1960), pp. 103–105.

3. *Reynolds v. West* 1 Cal. 322 (1850).

4. *Mintern v. Bowers et al.* 24 Cal. 644 (1864) at 672.

5. *United States v. Reading* 59 U.S. 1 (1855); *Palmer v. United States* 65 U.S. 125 (1857); *Townsend et al. v. Greeley* 72 U.S. 326 (1866).

6. *United States v. Moreno* 68 U.S. 400 (1863); *City and County of San Francisco v. Scott* 111 U.S. 768 (1884); *Phillips v. Mound City* 124 U.S. 605 (1888).

7. *United States v. Lucero* 1 N.M. 422 (1869) at 441. For California's interpretation see *People v. de la Guerra* 40 CAL 311 (1870).

8. *Tenorio v. Tenorio* 44 N.M. 89 (1940) reversed the *Lucero* decision and ruled that the treaty had not made the Pueblo Indians citizens of the United States and that they were not entitled to the protections of Article VIII and IX.

9. *McKinney v. Saviego* 59 U.S. 365 (1856) at 263. This decision was affirmed at the state level in *The State of Texas v. Gallardo* 135 S.W. 644 (1911).

10. *Botiller v. Dominguez* 130 U.S. 238 (1889).

11. *Horner v. United States* 143 U.S. 570 (1892; *Grant v. Jaramillo* 6 N.M. 313 (1892); *Lockhart v. Wills et al.* 54 S.W. 366 (1898).

12. *Baker et al. v. Harvey* 181 U.S. 481 (1901); *United States v. Title Insurance Co. et al.* 265 U.S. 472 (1924).

13. *California Powderworks v. Davis* 151 US 389 (1894); *United States v. Sandoval et al.* 167 US 278 (1897); *Arisa v. New Mexico and Arizona Railroad* 175 US 76 (1899).

14. *United States v. Green et al.* 185 US 256 (1901).

15. *Lockhart v. Johnson* 181 US 516 (1901) at 528.

16. Ibid. at 523.

17. *City of Los Angeles v Venice Peninsula Properties et al.* 31 Cal. 3d 288 (1913); *City of San Diego v. Cuyamaca Water Co.* 209 Cal. 105 (1930).

18. *Interstate Land Company v. Maxwell Land Co.* 80 US 460 (1891) at 588.

19. *Cessna v. United States et al.* 169 US 165 (1898) at 186.

20. *Pueblo of Zia v. United States et al.* 168 US 198 (1897); *United States v. Lucero* 1 NM 422 (1869); *United States v. Sandoval* 231 US 28 (1913) at 39, 48.

21. *Apapos et al. v. United States* 233 US 587 (1914); *Tenorio v. Tenorio* 44 NM 89 (1940).

22. *McKinney v. Saviego* 59 US 365 (1856); *Texas Mexican Rail Road v. Locke* 74 Tex. 370 (1889); *State of Texas v. Gallardo et al.* 106 Tex. 274 (1914); *State of Texas v. Sais* 47 Tex. 307 and *Clark v. Hills* 67 Tex. 141.

23. *United States v. Rio Grande Dam and Irrigation Co. et al.* 175 US 690 (1899), at 699, 700.

24. *United States v. Rio Grande Dam and Irrigation Co. et al.* 184 US 416 (1901).

25. *United States v. State of Utah* 238 U.S. 64 (1931); *United States v. O'Donnell* 303 U.S. 501 (1938).

26. *United States v. States of Louisiana et al.* 363 U.S. 1 (1960); For a discussion of the diplomacy surrounding the negotiation of Mexico's off shore limit see 99 *Cong. Rec.* 3623–3624, June 3, 1936.

27. *Chadwick et al. v. Campbell* 115 F. 2d 401 (1940).

28. *Summa Corporation v. State of California ex rel. State Lands Commission et al.* 104 S.Ct. 1751 (1984), at 1754.

29. *Tenorio v. Tenorio* 44 N.M. 89 (1940); *Pitt River Tribe et al. v. United States* 485 F. 2d 660 (1973).

30. *United States v. Abeyta* 632 F. Supp. 1301 (1986); at 1301.

31. *United States ex rel. Chunie v. Ringrose* 788 F. 2d 638 (1986).

32. *State of Texas v. Balli* 173 S.W.2d 522 (1943).

33. *Amaya et al. v. Stanolind Oil and Gas Co. et al.* 158 F.2d 554 (1946).

34. Ibid., at 559.

35. *Application of Robert Galvan for Writ of Habeus Corpus* 127 F. Supp. 392 (1954).

36. *López Tijerina v. Henry* 48 F.R.D. 274 (1969).

37. *Tijerina et al. v. United States* 398 U.S. 922 (1970)

38. See *Treaty on Final Settlement of Certain Claims, United States and Mexico,* 56 Stat. 1347, T.S. No. 980 (Nov. 19, 1941).

39. *Asociación de Reclamantes et al. v. United Mexican States* 735 F.2d 1517 (1984); See *Treaty on Final Settlement of Certain Claims, United States and Mexico,* 56 Stat. 1347, T.S. No. 980 (Nov. 19, 1941).

CHAPTER 7. HISTORICAL INTERPRETATIONS OF 1848

1. Since 1848, 36 articles and 19 books have appeared in English and Spanish dealing principally with the Treaty of Guadalupe Hidalgo. The overwhelming majority of the English

language works have been analyses of the negotiation process and its immediate aftermath, or, in the case of most of the books, reprints and analysis of the treaty itself.

2. Norman E. Tutorow, comp. and ed., *The Mexican-American War: An Annotated Bibliography* (Westport, Conn.: Greenwood Press, 1981).

3. Roswell W. Ripley, *The War With Mexico*, 2 vols. (New York: privately printed, 1849). For a detailed discussion of the historiography of the Mexican War during the immediate postwar years—1848–1860—see Robert W. Johannsen, *To the Halls of the Montezumas: The Mexican War in the American Imagination* (New York: Oxford University Press, 1985), ch. 9, "The Historian's War."

4. Ripley believed that as a result of the war, Mexico might be able to follow the example of the United States. "But before that time the superstition of her people must be eradicated. . . . Otherwise the temporary benefits which she may have derived will soon be overshadowed by the clouds of superstition, and domestic difficulties and foreign wars will continue until the last of the Spanish-Mexican race shall have passed away." Ripley, 2:646.

This same point of view, with some variation, was reflected in Nathan C. Brooks, *A Complete History of the Mexican War: Its Causes and Consequences*, (1849, Chicago: Rio Grande Press, 1965).

5. William Jay, *A Review of the Causes and Consequences of the Mexican War* (Boston: Benjamin B. Mussey and Co., 1849). This book went through four editions and was translated into Spanish.

6. Ibid., p. 270.

7. Justin Smith, *The War with Mexico*, 2 vols. (New York: Macmillan, 1919). Although highly regarded for exhaustive research, Smith's methodology and scholarship has been suspect, mainly due to his consistently inaccurate citations and interpretations. See Tutorow, p. 241.

8. Smith 2:240–241; Ch. 32, *passim*. A modern interpretation of the Mexican War that follows Smith's is William H. Goetzmann's editorial introduction to George Ballentine's, *Autobiography of an English Soldier in the United States Army* (Chicago: R.R. Donnelley and Sons Co., 1986). Goetzmann presents a panoramic view of the military and diplomatic ma-

neuvers during the war, criticizing the Whig and neo-Whig interpretations as "clouded by guilt and moral justification." He characterizes the war as provoked by Mexican bellicosity upon a reasonable and peace-loving American presidential administration (pp. lv.–lvi.). Goetzmann sees the treaty as a huge success because it rescued the American army from being bogged down in the Mexican highlands indefinitely and it allowed the United States to acquire everything that could be desired.

9. David Hunter Miller, *Treaties and Other International Acts of the United States,* 5 vols. (Washington, D.C.: Government Printing Office, 1937), vol. 5, "Mexico: 1848." David M. Pletcher, *The Diplomacy of Annexation: Texas, Oregon and the Mexican War* (Colombia: University of Missouri Press, 1973).

10. *Ibid.,* pp. 610–611, 549.

11. James A. Henretta, W. Elliot Brownlee, David Brody, and Susan Ware, *America's History* (Chicago: The Dorsey Press, 1987), pp. 345–346.

12. Glyndon G. Van Deusen, *The Jacksonian Era, 1828–1848* (New York: Harper & Row, 1963), ch. 12 "The Dose of Arsenic".

13. Gary B. Nash, Julie Roy Jeffrey, et. al., *The American People: Creating a Nation and a Society* (New York: Harper & Row, 1986), pp. 448.

14. Jack Ray Thomas, *Biographical Dictionary of Latin American History and Historiography* (Westport, Conn.: Greenwood Press, 1984), pp. 68–69.

15. The other collaborators were Alejo Barriero, José María Castillo, Feliz María Escalante, José María Iglesias, Manuel Muñoz, Ramón Ortiz, Manuel Payno, Guillermo Prieto, Ignacio Ramírez, Napoleon Sabario, Francisco Siafino, Francisco Segura, Pablo María Torescano, and Francisco Urguidi.

16. Ramón Alcaraz et al., *The Other Side or Notes for the History of the War Between Mexico and the United States,* translated by Albert C. Ramsey (New York and London: Wiley, 1850; reprint, New York: Burt Franklin, 1970).

17. *Ibid.,* pp. 3, 32, 450.

18. In Genaro García, *Documentos ineditos o muy raros para la historia de México* (Mexico: n.p., 1905) edited by Walter V. Scholes and translated by Elliot B. Scherr as *Mexico*

During the War with the United States, The University of Missouri Studies, vol. 23, No. 1 (Columbia: University of Missouri Press, 1950), p. 51.

19. Carlos María de Bustamante, *El nuevo Bernal Díaz del Castillo o sea historia de la invasión de los Anglo-Americanos en Mexico . . . ,* 2 vols. (Mexico, D.F.: Imprente de Vicente Garcia Torres, 1847).

20. Francisco de Paula de Arrangoiz y Berzábal, *México desde 1808 hasta 1867,* 2d ed. (Madrid: A. Perez Dubrull, 1871–1872; Reprint, Mexico, D.F.: Editorial Porrua, 1969).

21. Italics in original; ibid., p. 398. For an in-depth study of the Mexico City *ayuntamiento* during the war, see Dennis E. Berge, "A Mexican Dilemma: The Mexico City Ayuntamiento and the Question of Loyalty, 1846–1848," *Hispanic American Historical Review* vol. 50, no. 2 (May 1970): 229–256.

22. Arrangoiz, pp. 401–406.

23. *Recuerdos de la invasión norteamericana (1846–1848),* 2 vols. (1887; Reprint, Mexico, D.F.: Editorial Porrua, 1947). Roa Bárcena's work first appeared as a series of articles in the Mexico City newspapers, published between 1876 and 1877.

24. Ibid., vol. 2; pp. 240, 299–300, 341, 347.

25. Justo Sierra, *Evolución política del pueblo Mexicano,* ed. Edmundo O'Gorman, *Obras completas del maestro Justo Sierra,* vol. 13 (Mexico, D.F.: J. Ballesca y Cía, 1900–1902; reprint, Mexico: UNAM, 1948).

26. Ibid., pp. 231, 249.

27. Lazaro Gutierrez de Lara, *El pueblo mexicana y sus luchas por la libertad* (Los Angeles, 191?); Mariano Cuevas, *Historia de la iglesia en México,* vol. 5 (Mexico, D.F., 1928); Alberto María Cuevas, *Historia de los Estados Unidos de America . . .* (Mexico, D.F., 1922).

28. Jose Vasconcelos, *Breve historia de México* (Mexico, D.F., 1936); Rafael Ramos Pedrueza, *La lucha de clases a traves de la historia de México* (Mexico, D.F., 1936).

29. Mariano Cuevas, *Historia de la nación Mexicana,* 3d ed. (Mexico, D.F.: Editorial Porrua, 1967).

30. Ibid., pp. 676, 678, 680.

31. Vicente Fuentes Díaz, *La intervención Norteamericana en México* (Mexico, D.F.: Imprente Nuevo Mundo, 1947), pp. 11, 179–282.

32. Francisco Castillo Najera, "El Tratado de Guadalupe," Presented before El Congreso Mexicano de Historia, September 17–26, 1947 (Mexico, D.F.: n.p., 1947).

33. José Bravo Ugarte, "Guerra a México de Estados Unidos, 1846–1848," *Historia Mexicana*, vol. 1, no. 2 (October–December, 1951), pp. 180–226.

34. Ibid., p. 225.

35. Carlos Bosch García, *Historia de las relaciones entre México y los Estados Unidos, 1819–1848* (Mexico, D.F.: Escuela Nacional de Cíencias Políticas y Sociales, 1961).

36. Carlos Pereyra, *Breve historia de America*, 4th ed. (Mexico, D.F.: Aguilar, 1958), pp. 555–557; José C. Valadés, *Breve historia de la guerra con los Estados Unidos* (Mexico, D.F.: Editorial Patria, 1947), p. 556.

37. Augustín Cue Cánovas, *Los Estados Unidos y el México olvidado* (Mexico, D.F.: B. Costa Amic, 1970).

38. Ibid., pp. 28, 23. Matt Meier and Feliciano Rivera, eds., *Dictionary of Mexican American History* (Westport, Conn.: Greenwood Press, 1981), p. 428.

39. Gastón García Cantú, *Las invasiones Norteamericanas en México* (Mexico, D.F.: Ediciones Era, 1971).

40. Ibid., p. 120.

41. Luis G. Zorrilla, *Historia de las relaciones entre México y los Estados Unidos de America, 1800–1958*, 2 vols. (Mexico, D.F.: Editorial Porrua, 1977).

42. Ibid., 1:218.

43. César Sepúlveda, *La frontera norte de México, historia, conflictos, 1762–1975* (Mexico, D.F.: Editorial Porrua, 1980).

44. Ibid., p. 65. Of course, this statement ignores both the Taos rebellion and the Mexican recapture of Los Angeles and much of Southern California in 1847.

45. Ibid., p. 67.

46. Daniel Cosío Villegas, coord., *Historia general de México*, 3 Vols. (Mexico, D.F.: Colegio de Mexico, 1976), 2:84. The section discussing the war and the treaty was written by Josefina Zoraida Vásaquez reflects the best current Mexican scholarship with a heavy emphasis on facts and chronology. Other college-level texts of high quality are Martín Quirarte, *Visión panoramica de la historia de México* (Mexico, D.F.: Liberia Porrua, 1967) and Vicente Riva Palacio, coord., *Resumen*

integral de México a través de los siglos, vol. 4, *Mexico independiente, 1821–1855* (Mexico, D.F.: Compañía General de ediciones, S.A., 1952).

47. W. Jímenez Mareno and A. García Ruíz, *Historia de México: Un síntesis* (Mexico, D.F.: Antropologia e Historia, 1970), pp. 49–62.

48. Benjaime Arrendando Munozledo, *Historia universal moderna y contemporanea* (Mexico, D.F.: n.p., 1977).

49. Homer Campbell Chaney, Jr., "The Mexican-United States War as Seen by Mexican Intellectuals, 1846–1959 (Ph.D. diss., Stanford University, 1959), pp. 302–313. Chaney agrees with the ascendancy of the conservative interpretation, which he terms "revisionist."

CHAPTER 8. THE CHICANO MOVEMENT AND THE TREATY

1. Patricia Bell Blawis, *Tijerina and the Land Grants* (New York: International Publishers, 1970), p. 37; see also Richard Gardner, *Grito!: Reies Tijerina and the New Mexican Land Grant Wars of 1967* (New York: Harper & Row, 1970), and Peter Nabokov, *Tijerina and the Courthouse Raid* (Albuquerque: University of New Mexico Press, 1969). For Tijerina's own account of the trip and the Alianza, see Reies Tijerina, *Mi lucha por tierra* (Mexico: Fondo de Cultura y Economia, 1978).

2. Richard Gardner, p. 96.

3. Reies Tijerina, *The Spanish Land Grant Question Examined* (Albuquerque: Alianza Federal, 1966).

4. See *Tijerina et al. vs. U.S.* 396 U.S. 843; 396 U.S. 990; and 396 U.S. 922.

5. Tijerina, *Mi Lucha,* p. 106.

6. Ibid., pp. 104–110.

7. See Senate Bill 68 and House Resolution 3595 (need exact citation); *Congressional Record,* vol. 21, pt. 1, January 15, 1975, pp. 321–22.

8. The summaries of these bills were provided by the Library of Congress as follows: HR2207, 94th Congress 1/28/75; HRES 585, 95th Congress 5/18/77; HRES 16, 96th Congress 1/15/79; *Albuquerque Journal,* March 16, 1979, 8:6.

9. "We Demand," in Luis Valdez and Stan Steiner, eds., *Aztlan: An Anthology of Mexican American Literature* (New York: Alfred A. Knopf, 1972), p. 220.

10. Armando Rendon, *Chicano Manifesto* (New York: Macmillan Publishing Co., 1972), p. 81.

11. Ibid., pp. 84–85.

12. María Blanco, "A Brief History About the Brown Beret National Organization," unpublished ms., November 10, 1975, San Diego State University, Love Library, pp. 4–6.

13. Adelaide Lefert Daron, *The Ranch That Was Robbins': Santa Catalina Island, California* (Los Angeles: Arthur Clark Co., 1963), ch. 6.

14. See J. N. Bowman, "California's Off-Shore Islands," *Pacific Historical Review* 31, No. 3 (August 1962):291–300.

15. In Mexico, J. Antonio Rosete Murgia, produced a master's thesis arguing that the islands were still part of Mexico. It is entitled "El Tratado de Guadalupe y el problema de las islas Catalina" (Master's thesis, UNAM, 1957). Rosete Murgía recommended that Mexico reopen negotiations over the status of the Catalina islands under Article 21 of the Treaty of Guadalupe Hidalgo. See *Los Angeles Times*, August 31, 1972, for details of the initial occupation.

16. Luis Zorrilla, *Historia de la relaciones entre Mexico y los Estados Unidos de America, 1800–1958*, vol. 2. (Mexico: Editorial Porrua, 1977), p. 85.

17. David Sanchez, *Expedition Through Aztlan* (La Puente: Perspectiva Publications, 1978), p. 174. Sanchez provides a detailed account of the invasion in this book.

18. *Los Angeles Times*, August 31, 1972, I, 1:2.

19. Sanchez, pp. 180–81; *Los Angeles Times*, September 2, I, 1:5; *Los Angeles Times*, August 31, 1972, loc. cit.

20. *Los Angeles Times*, September 23, 1972, II, 1:2.

21. Fernando Chacon Gómez, "The Intended and Actual Effects of Article VIII of the Treaty of Guadalupe Hidalgo: Mexican Treaty Rights Under International and Domestic Law," (Ph.D. diss., University of Michigan, 1977), p. 197.

22. For a history of the American Committee for the Protection of the Foreign Born, see Louise Pettibone Smith, *Torch of Liberty: Twenty-Five Years in the Life of the Foreign Born in the U.S.A.* (New York: Dwight-King Publishers, 1959); American Committee for the Protection of the Foreign Born, "Our Badge of Infamy: A Petition to the United Nations on the Treatment of Mexican Immigrants," (New York: American Committee for Protection of Foreign Born, 1959).

23. Ibid., p. 5.
24. Ibid., p. 10.
25. International Indian Treaty Council, "Plans for Treaty of Gudalupe Hidalgo Conference," 1986, Mimeograph.
26. IITC, "General Working Paper," 1986, Hopi Nation, "The Treaty of Guadalupe Hidalgo: A Native American Perspective," 1981, Mimeograph. The Indians were being relocated following an agreement that the Bureau of Indian Affairs had arranged with opposing factions with the two tribes.
27. Ibid., p. 2.
28. "Aztlan vs. the United States," 198?, Mimeograph.
29. Armando B. Rendon, "The Treaty of Guadalupe Hidalgo and its Modern Implications for the Protection of the Human Rights of Mexican Americans," 1982, p. 27, Mimeograph.
30. Roberto E. Barragan, "The Treaty of Guadalupe Hidalgo and the American Convention on Human Rights: A Political Analysis for Chicano Self Determination," Senior thesis, Politics Department, Princeton University, 1984. Barragan's thesis and Rendon's essays have been circulated by the Tonantzin Land Institute in New Mexico as part of the Treaty of Guadalupe Hidalgo Project.
31. Ibid. , p. 44.
32. International Indian Treaty Council, "Question of Violation of Human Rights or Fundamental Freedoms in Any Part of the World," Agenda Item 12, Commission on Human Rights, 43 Session, Geneva, Switzerland.
33. Ron Sandoval, "Diary," 1987, Mimeograph. Most of the xerox materials relating to the IITC and the treaty are available through the Tonatzin Land Institute, 1504 Bridge Blvd., Albuquerque, New Mexico.

CHAPTER 9. THE TREATY AND INTERNATIONAL RELATIONS

1. The count of treaties in force as of 1986 was 104, not counting extensions and amendments. See U.S. Department of State, *Treaties in Force 1986* (Washington, D.C.: Government Printing Office, 1986).
2. Kenneth M. Johnson, *The Pious Fund* (Los Angeles: Dawson's Book Shop, 1963), pp. 20–21.
3. Ibid., p. 38.
4. The Hague, Permanent Court of Arbitration, *Transcript*

of *Record of Proceedings Before the Mexican and American Mixed Claim Commission . . . Thaddeus Amat, Bishop of Monterey and Joseph S. Alemany, Archbishop of San Francisco vs. Mexico* (Washington, D.C.: Government Printing Office, 1902), pp. 90–95, passim.

5. Johnson, p. 55.

6. Fulton Freeman to Antonio Carrillo Flores, August 1, 1967, U.S. Secretary of State, *United States Treaties and Other International Agreements, 1967*, vol. 18, pt. 3 (Washington, D.C.: Government Printing Office, 1969).

7. J. J. Bowden, *The Ponce de Leon Land Grant*, Southwestern Studies Monograph, no. 24 (El Paso: Texas Western Press, 1969), pp. 31–33.

8. Lic. Joaquín D. Casasus, *El Chamizal: demanda, réplica, alegato é informes* (Mexico, D.F.: Eusebio Gómez de la Puente, 1911), pp. 4, 568–569, 583. Those who served on the Tribunal were Eugene Lafleur (France), Anson Mills (United States), and F. B. Pulga (Mexico).

9. Ibid., p. 616; see also Berta Ulloa, *La revolución intervenida: relaciones diplomáticas entre México y los Estados Unidos (1910–1914)* (Mexico, D.F.: Colegio de Mexico, 1971), pp. 260–262.

10. J. J. Bowden, pp. 38–39.

11. Sheldon B. Liss, *A Century of Disagreement: The Chamizal Conflict 1864–1964* (Washington, D.C.: University Press of Washington, 1965), Appendices A and B for texts of Conventions and Statistics. Antonio Gómez Roblodo, *Mexico y el arbitraje international* (Mexico, D.F.: Editorial Porrua, 1965).

12. Antonio Luna Arroyo, ed., *Mexico recibe El Chamizal* (Mexico, D.F.: Editorial Justa, 1964) for an account of the media reaction to the Chamizal ceremonies.

13. Ibid.; *Novedades* 29 September 1964.

14. "Notes and Comments," *American Journal of International Law* Vol. 55, No. 3 (July 1961): 669–679.

15. Ibid.: 670–671.

16. Karl M. Schmitt, "The Problem of Maritime Boundaries in U.S.—Mexican Relations," *Natural Resources Journal* vol. 22 (January 1982): 138–153.

17. For a summary of the Robles-Dean debate see Alberto Szekey, *Mexico y el derecho internacional del mar* (Mexico D.F.: U.N.A.M, 1979), pp. 85–87.

18. U.S. Department of State, *Treaty with Mexico Resolving Boundary Differences . . . November 23, 1970* (Washington, D.C.: Government Printing Office, 1971).

19. John Bassett Moore, "The United States and International Arbitration," *American Historical Association, Annual Report* (1891), pp. 65–78.

20. Merele Curti, "Pacifist Propaganda and the Treaty of Guadalupe Hidalgo," *American Historical Review*, 33, no. 3 (1928): 596–598. For text of Article XXI see Appendix XXX.

21. Charles I. Bevans, ed., *Treaties and Other International Agreements of the United States of America, 1776–1949*, 13 vols. (Washington, D.C.: Department of State Publications, 1972), 9:827–28.

22. Joseph Hubley Ashton, Esq., *Report to the Secretary of State: The United States and Mexican Claims Commission 1869–1876, October 28, 1874* (Washington, D.C.: Government Printing Office, 1874).

23. Ignacio Mariscal, Minister for Foreign Relations to Powell Clayton, U.S. Ambassador to Mexico, 11 November 1904, "Tratado de arbitraje entre Mexico y Estados Unidos." Mexico, Archivo de Secretaría de Relaciones Exteriores, 7-8-6.

24. Article III of the 1904 Arbitration Convention read: "The foregoing stipulation in no wise annuls, but on the contrary defines, confirms and continues in effect the declaration and rules contained in Article XXI of the Treaty of Peace, Friendship, and Boundaries between the United States and Mexico signed at the city of Guadalupe Hidalgo." *Treaty of Arbitration*, January 18, 1904, Mexico, Archivo de La Secretaría de Relaciones Exteriores, 7-8-6; Also *Tratado de arbitraje*, 24 Marzo 1908, SRE 7-8-8. See *Convention between the United States and Mexico: Arbitration*, March 24, 1908.

25. César Sepúlveda, *Las Reclamaciones fraudulentas contra Mexico* (Mexico, D.F.: Secretaría de Relaciones Exteriores, 1965) and Antonio Gómez Robledo, *The Bucareli Agreements and International Law* transl. by Salomón de la Selva (Mexico, D.F.: The National University Press of Mexico, 1940).

26. U.S. Department of State, *Papers Relating to the Foreign Relations of the United States, 1914* (Washington, D.C.: Government Printing Office, 1922), pp. 460–461.

27. Daniel Cosio Villegas, ed., *Historia General de Mexico*, 4 vols. (Mexico, D.F.: Colegio de Mexico, 1976), 4:150–151.

28. Gómez Robledo, p. 136; *Convention between the United States of America and Mexico Respecting Claims* 56 Stat. 1347 (November 19, 1941).

APPENDIX 1. THE ORIGINAL TEXT OF ARTICLES IX AND X

1. Text, as modified by the U.S. Senate, can be found in Appendix 2.
2. Article X was omitted by the U.S. Senate and did not appear in the final treaty.

APPENDIX 2. THE TRATY OF GUADALUPE HIDALGO

1. For original text of Article IX, see Appendix 1.
2. Article X was stricken from the treaty. See Appendix 1 for text of Article X.

Bibliography

UNPUBLISHED MATERIAL

Blanco, María. "A Brief History About the Brown Seret National Organization." Manuscript on file at San Diego State University, Love Library, San Diego, November 10, 1975.

Castillo Nájera, Francisco. "El Tratado de Guadalupe." Presented before El Congreso Mexicano de Historia. Mexico, D.F.: n.p., September 17–26, 1947.

Mariscal, Ignacio, Minister for Foreign Relations, to Powell Clayton, U.S. Ambassador to Mexico. "Tratado de arbitraje entre Mexico y Estados Unidos." No. 7-8-6. Archivos de la Secretaría de Relaciones Exteriores, Mexico City, November 11, 1904.

Marrimar, Manuel, to the Minister of Relaciones. No. 2-12-2904. Archivos de la Secretaría de Relaciones Exteriores, Mexico City, June 2, 1852.

DISSERTATIONS AND THESES

Berge, Dennis. "Mexican Response to United States Expansion: 1841–1848." Ph.D. dissertation, University of California, Berkeley, 1965.

Brent, Arthur. "Nicholas Trist: A Biography." Ph.D. dissertation, University of Virginia, Charlottesville, 1950.

Chacon Gómez, Fernando. "The Intended and Actual Effects of Article VIII of the Treaty of Guadalupe Hidalgo: Mexican Treaty Rights Under International and Domestic Law." Ph.D. dissertation, University of Michigan, Ann Arbor, 1966.

Chaney, Homer Campbell, Jr. "The Mexican-United States War as seen by Mexican Intellectuals, 1846–1959." Ph.D. dissertation, Department of History, Stanford University, Stanford, 1959.

Mangusso, Mary Childers. "A Study of the Citizenship Provisions of the Treaty of Guadalupe Hidalgo." Master's thesis, University of New Mexico, Albuquerque, 1966.

Rosete, Murgia, J. Antonio. "El Tratado de Guadalupe y el problema de las islas Catalina." Master's thesis, Universidad Nacional Autónoma de México, Mexico, D.F.

Rowley, Ralph A. "Precedents and Influences Affecting the Treaty of Guadalupe Hidalgo." Master's thesis, University of New Mexico, Albuquerque, 1970.

———. "The Acquisition of the Spanish Borderlands: Problems and Legacy." Ph.D. dissertation, University of New Mexico, Albuquerque, 1975.

Tijerina, Andrew A., "Tejanos and Texans: The Native Mexicans of Texas, 1820–1850." Ph.D. dissertation, University of Texas, Austin, 1977.

GOVERNMENT PUBLICATIONS

Ashton, Joseph Hubley, Esq. *Report to the Secretary of State: The United States and Mexican Claims Commission 1869–1876, October 28, 1874.* Washington D.C.: Government Printing Office, 1874.

Algunos Documentos sobre el tratado de Guadalupe. Archivo historico diplomatico Mexicano, no. 31. Mexico, D.F.: Editorial Porrua, 1970.

Bevans, Charles I., ed. *Treaties and Other International Agree-*

ments of the United States of America, 1776–1949. 13 vols. Washington D.C.: Department of State Publications, 1972.

Boletin oficial, tomo I, num 1. 1895.

Browne, J. Ross, ed. *Report of the Debates on the Convention of California on the Formation of the State Constitution in September and October 1849*. Washington, D.C.: John Towers, 1850.

Convention between the United States of America and Mexico Respecting Claims 56 Stat. 1347 (November 19, 1941).

The Hague. Permanent Court of Arbitration. *Transcript of Record of Proceedings Before the Mexican and American Mixed Claim Commission . . . Thaddeus Amat, Bishop of Monterey and Joseph S. Alemany, Archbishop of San Francisco vs. Mexico*. Washington D.C.: Government Printing Office, 1902.

Maza, Francisco F. de la, ed. *Codigo de Colonizacion y Terrenos Baldios de la Republica Mexicana*. Mexico, D.F.: Secretaría de Fomento, 1873.

Message of the Governor Transmitting the Report of the Commissioners to Investigate Land Titles West of the Nueces. Austin: Cushney and Hampton, 1851.

Relaciones diplomaticos hispano-mexicanas. 1839–1898: Documentos procedentes del Archivo de la Embajada de España en Mexico. Serie I. Despachos generales. Mexico, D.F.: El Colegio de Mexico, 1968.

U.S. Congress. House of Representatives. *New Mexico-Convention of Delgates: Journal and Proceedings*. 31st Cong. 1st sess., 1850. House Misc. Doc. 39, 1850.

U.S. Congress. House of Representatives. *Congressional Record*, vol. 21, pt. 1. January 15, 1975.

U.S. Department of State. *Convention Between the United States and Mexico: Arbitration*, March 24, 1908.

U.S. Department of State. *Papers Relating to the Foreign Relations of the United States, 1914*. Washington, D.C.: Government Printing Office, 1922.

U.S. Department of State. *Treaties in Force, 1986*. Washington, D.C.: Government Printing Office, 1986.

U.S. Department of State. *Treaty with Mexico Resolving Boundary Differences . . . November 23, 1970*. Washington, D.C.: Government Printing Office, 1971.

U.S. Department of State. *United States Treaties and Other*

International Agreements, 1967. vol. 18, Pt. 3. Washington D.C.: Government Printing Office, 1969. U.S. Senate. *Senate Executive Documents.* No. 52. 30th Congress. 1st session.

ARTICLES

Bazant, Jan. "Joseph Yves Limantour (1812–1885) y su aventura californiana–I." *Historia Mexicana.* 28, no. 1 (julio–septiembre, 1978): 1–23.

————. "Joseph Yves Limantour (1812–1885) y su aventura californiana–II." *Historia Mexicana.* 29, no. 3 (enero–marzo, 1980): 353–374.

Beach, Moses S. "A Secret Mission to Mexico." *Scribner's Monthly.* 18, no. 1 (1879): 136–140.

Berge, Dennis E. "A Mexican Dilemma: The Mexico City Ayuntamiento and the Question of Loyalty, 1846–1848." *Hispanic American Historical Review.* 50, no. 2 (May 1970): 229–256.

Bowman, J. N. "California's Off-Shore Islands," *Pacific Historical Review,* 31, no. 3 (August 1962): 291–300.

Bravo Ugarte, José. "Guerra a México de Estados Unidos, 1846–1848." *Historia Mexicana.* 1, no. 2 (October–December, 1951): 180–226.

Castaneda, Carlos E. "Relations of General Scott with Santa Anna." *Hispanic American Historical Review.* 29, no. 4 (November 1949): 456–473.

Chamberlin, Eugene K. "Nicholas Trist and Baja California." *Pacific Historical Review.* 32, no. 1 (February 1963): 49–63.

Curti, Merele. "Pacifist Propaganda and the Treaty of Guadalupe Hidalgo." *American Historical Review.* 33, no. 3 (1928): 596–598.

De Leon, Arnoldo and Stewart, Kenneth L. "Lost Dreams and Found Fortunes; Mexican and Anglo Immigrants into South Texas, 1850–1900." *Western Historical Quarterly.* 14, no. 3 (July 1983): 291–310.

Farnham, Thomas J. "Nicholas Trist and James Freaner and the Mission to Mexico." *Arizona and the West.* 11, no. 3 (Autumn 1969): 247–260.

Garza, Rudolfo O. de la, and Schmitt, Karl. "'Texas Land Grants and Chicano-Mexican Relations: A Case Study," *Latin American Research Review* 21, no. 1 (1986): 123–138.

Goetzmann, W.H. "The United States-Mexico Boundary Survey, 1848–1853." *Southwestern Historical Quarterly.* 62, no. 2 (October 1958): 164–190.

Graebner, Norman A. "Party Politics and the Trist Mission." *Journal of Southern History.* 19, no. 2 (May 1953): 137–156.

Hale, Charles. "The War with the United States and the Crises in Mexican Thought." *The Americas.* 14, no. 2 (October 1957): 153–174.

Horn, James T. "Trends in Historical Interpretation: James K. Polk." *North Carolina Historical Review*, 42 (October 1965): 454–465.

Lofgren, Charles A. "Force and Diplomacy, 1846–1848: The View from Washington." *Military Affairs.* 31, no. 2 (Summer 1967): 57–64.

Martinez, Oscar. "On the Size of the Chicano Population." *Aztlan.* 4, no. 1 (Spring 1975): 43–67.

Mawn, Geofry. "A Land Grant-Guarantee: The Treaty of Guadalupe Hidalgo or the Protocol of Querétaro?" *Journal of the West.* 14, no. 4 (October 1975): 49–63.

Northrup, Jack. "The Trist Mission." *Journal of Mexican American History.* 3 (1973): 13–31.

"Notes and Comments." *American Journal of International Law.* 55, no. 3 (July 1961): 669–679.

Salazar, Robert. "Texas Land Grant Heirs Seek Compensation." *Ajenda: A Journal of Hispanic Issues.* 9, no. 2 (March/April, 1979): 14–16.

Schmitt, Karl M. "The Problem of Maritime Boundaries in U.S.–Mexican Relations." *Natural Resources Journal.* 22 (January 1982): 138–153.

Van Hastings, Garner. "The Treaty of Guadalupe Hidalgo and the California Indians." *The Indian Historian.* 9, no. 1 (Winter, 1976): 10–13.

Wheat, Carl I. ed. "California's Bantam Cock: The Journals of Charles E. De Long, 1854–1863." *California Historical Quarterly.* 8 (1929): 353–355.

Whipley, J. D. "The Late Negotiations for Peace." *American Review.* 6, no. 5 (November 1847): 441–453.

NEWSPAPERS

Albuquerque Journal.
Diario del Gobierno. Mexico City.
Los Angeles Times.
New York Daily News.
New York Herald.
Novedades. Mexico City.
Siglo XIX. Mexico City.

BOOKS AND MONOGRAPHS

Acuña, Rudolfo. *Occupied America: The Chicano's Struggle Toward Liberation.* San Francisco: Canfield Press, 1972.

Alcaraz, Ramón. *The Other Side, or Notes for the History of the War Between Mexico and the United States.* Translated by Albert C. Ramsey. 1850. Reprint, New York: Burt Franklin, 1970.

Arrendando Munozledo, Benjaime. *Historia universal moderna y contemporanea.* Mexico, D.F.: N.p, 1977.

Bancroft, Hubert Howe. *History of Arizona and New Mexico.* San Francisco: The History Book Co., 1889.

————. *History of Mexico, 1824–1861.* 17 vols. San Francisco: A. L. Bancroft and Company, 1885.

Barcena, José Maria Roa. *Recuerdos de la invasión norteamericana. 1846–1848.* 3 vols. 1883. Reprint, Mexico, D.F.: Editorial Porrua, 1947.

Binkley, William Campbell. *The Expansionist Movement in Texas, 1836–1850.* University of California Publications in History. vol. 13. Berkeley: University of California Press, 1925.

Blawis, Patricia Bell. *Tijerina and the Land Grants.* New York: International Publishers, 1970.

Bosch Garcia, Carlos. *Historia de las relaciones entre México y los Estados Unidos, 1819–1848.* Mexico, D.F.: Escuela Nacional de Cíencias Políticas y Sociales, 1961.

Bowden, J. J. *The Ponce de Leon Land Grant.* Southwestern Studies Monograph, no. 24. El Paso: Texas Western Press, 1969.

————. *Spanish and Mexican Land Grants in the Chihuahuan Acquisition.* El Paso: Texas Westernlore Press, 1971.

Casasus, Lic. Joaquín D. *El Chamizal: demanda, réplica, alegato é informes*. Mexico D.F.: Eusebio Gomez de la Puente, 1911.

Chávez, John R. *The Lost Land: The Chicano Image of the Southwest*. Albuquerque: University of New Mexico Press, 1984.

Coffert, W. A. ed. *Fifty Years in Camp and Field: The Diary of Major General Ethan Allen Hitchcock, U.S.A.* 1909. Reprint, Freeport, New York: Books for Libraries Press, 1971.

Cosío Villegas, Daniel, coord. *Historia general de México.* 3 vols. Mexico, D.F.: Colegio de Mexico, 1976. 2:84.

Cowels, Willard B. *Treaties and Constitutional Law: Property Interferences and Due Process of Law.* Washington, D.C.: American Council of Public Affairs, 1941.

Cue Cánovas, Augustín. *Los Estados Unidos y el México olvidado.* Mexico, D.F.: B. Costa Amic, 1970.

Cuevas, Mariano. *Historia de la iglesia en México.* vol. 5. Mexico, D.F., 1928.

———. *Historia de la nación Mexicana.* 3d ed. Mexico, D.F.: Editorial Porrua, 1967.

Currey, John. *The Treaty of Guadalupe Hidalgo and Private Land Claims and Titles Existing in California at the Date of the Treaty.* San Francisco: Bancroft Whitney, 1891.

Daron, Adelaide Lefert. *The Ranch That Was Robbins': Santa Catalina Island, California.* Los Angeles: Arthur Clark Company, 1963.

De Leon, Arnoldo. *They Called them Greasers.* Austin: University of Texas, 1983.

Fuentes Díaz, Vicente. *La intervención Norteamericana en México.* Mexico, D.F.: Imprente Nuevo Mundo, 1947.

Garber, Paul. *The Gadsden Treaty.* Gloucester, Mass.: Peter Smith, 1959.

García Cantú, Gastón. *Las invasiones Norteamericanas en México.* Mexico, D.F.: Ediciones Era, 1971.

Gomez Quinones, Juan, and Camarillo, Albert, eds. *Selected Bibliography in Chicano Studies.* Los Angeles: Chicano Studies Research Center, 1975.

Gómez Robledo, Antonio. *Mexico y el arbitraje international.* Mexico, D.F.: Editorial Porrua, 1965.

Graebner, Norman. *Empire on the Pacific: A Study in Ameri-*

can Continental Expansion. 1955. Reprint, Santa Barbara: ABC-CLIO, 1983.

Gregg, Robert D. *The Influence of Border Troubles on Relations Between the United States and Mexico, 1876–1910.* Baltimore: John Hopkins Press, 1937.

Griswold del Castillo, Richard. *The Los Angeles Barrio: 1850–1890: A Social History.* Los Angeles: University of California Press, 1980.

Gutierrez de Lara, Lazaro. *El pueblo mexicana y sus luchas por la libertad.* Los Angeles: N.p., 191?.

Henry, Robert Selph. *The Story of the Mexican War.* New York: Frederick Unger Publishing Co., 1950.

Hill, Charles E. *Leading American Treaties.* New York: Macmillan, 1922.

Hinojosa, Gilberto Miguel. *A Borderlands Town in Transition: Laredo, 1775–1850.* College Station: Texas A&M University Press, 1983.

Holliday, J. S. *The World Rushed In: The California Gold Rush Experience.* New York: Simon & Schuster, 1981.

Holmes Jr., Oliver Wendel. *The Common Law.* Boston: Little, Brown and Co., 1881.

Howard, Riaffa. *The Art and Science of Negotiation.* Cambridge: Harvard University Press, 1982.

Jímenez Moreno, W., and A. García Ruíz. *Historia de México: Un síntesis.* Mexico, D.F.: Antropología e Historia, 1970.

Johnson, Kenneth M. *The Pious Fund.* Los Angeles: Dawson's Book Shop, 1963.

Lamar, Howard Robert. *The Far Southwest, 1846–1912: A Territorial History.* New York: W. W. Norton, 1966.

Larson, Robert W. *New Mexico's Quest for Statehood, 1846–1912.* Albuquerque: University of New Mexico Press, 1968.

Liss, Sheldon B. *A Century of Disagreement: The Chamizal Conflict 1864–1964.* Washington, D.C.: University Press of Washington, 1965.

Luna Arroyo, Antonio. ed. *Mexico recibe El Chamizal.* Mexico D.F.: Editorial Justa, 1964.

McCloskey, Robert. *The American Supreme Court.* Chicago and London: University of Chicago Press, 1960.

Manning, William R. *Early Diplomatic Relations Between the United States and Mexico.* Baltimore: John Hopkins Press, 1916.

———, ed., *Diplomatic Correspondence of the United States, Interamerican Affairs*. vol. 9. Washington, D.C., 1937.

María Cuevas, Alberto. *Historia de los Estados Unidos de America*. Mexico City, 1922.

María de Bustamante, Carlos. *El nuevo Bernal Díaz del Castillo o sea historia de la invasión de los Anglo-Americanos en Mexico* . . . 2 vols. Mexico, D.F.: Imprente de Vicente Garcia Torres, 1847.

Marshall, Thomas M. *A History of the Western Boundary of the Louisiana Purchase, 1819–1841*. University of California Publications in History. vol. 2. Berkeley: University of California Press, 1914.

Martin, François Xavier. *The History of Louisiana From the Earliest Periods*. New Orleans: James A. Gresham, 1882.

Martínez, Oscar J. *Troublesome Border*. Tucson: University of Arizona Press, 1988.

Meier, Matt S., and Rivera, Feliciano. *Dictionary of Mexican American History*. Westport, Conn.: Greenwood Press, 1981.

Merk, Frederick. *Manifest Destiny and Mission in American History: A Reinterpretation*. New York: Alfred A. Knopf, 1963.

Miller, David Hunter. *Treaties and Other International Acts of the United States of America*. 5 vols. Washington, D.C.: Government Printing Office, 1937.

Montejano, David. *Anglos and Mexicans in the Making of Texas, 1836–1986*. Austin: University of Texas Press,1987.

Moore, John Bassett, ed. *The Works of James Buchanan*. 8 vols. New York: Antiquarian Press, 1960.

Moyano Pahissa, Angela. *México y Estados Unidos: Orígenes de una relación 1819–1961*. Mexico, D.F.: Secretaría de Educación Pública, 1985.

Nevins, Allan, ed. *Polk: The Diary of a President, 1845–1849*. New York: Longman, Green and Co., 1929.

Paula de Arrangoiz y Berzábal, Francisco. *México desde 1808 hasta 1867*. 2d ed. 1872. Reprint, Mexico, D.F.: Editorial Porrua, 1969.

Pereya, Carlos. *Breve historia de America*. 4th ed. Mexico: Aguilar, 1958.

Perkins, Whitney. *Denial of Empire: the United States and Its Dependencies*. The Netherlands: A. W. Sythoff-Lyden, 1962.

Pillar, Paul R. *Negotiating Peace: War Termination as a Bargaining Process.* Princeton, N.J.: Princeton University Press, 1983.

Pitt, *Decline of the Californios: A Social History of the Spanish-Speaking Californians, 1846–1890.* Berkeley: University of California Press, 1970.

Pletcher, David M. *The Diplomacy of Annexation: Texas, Oregon, and the Mexican War.* Columbia: University of Missouri Press, 1973.

Powell, Richard. *Compromises of Conflicting Claims: A Century of California Law, 1760 to 1860.* Dobbs Ferry, New York: Oceana Pubications Inc., 1977.

Price, Glenn. *Origins of the War Against Mexico: The Polk-Stockton Intrigue.* Austin: University of Texas Press, 1963.

Quiafe, Milton, ed. *The Diary of James K. Polk: During his Presidency, 1845 to 1849,* 4 vols. Chicago: A. C. McClurg and Co., 1910.

Ramirez, José Fernando. *Mexico During the War with the United States.* Ed. and trans. Walter Scholes. University of Missouri Studies, vol. 23. no. 1. Columbia: University of Missouri, 1950.

Ramos Pedrueza, Rafael. *La lucha de clases a traves de la historia de México.* Mexico, D.F.: "Revista Lux," 1934.

Rendon, Armando. *Chicano Manifesto.* New York: Macmillan, 1972.

Rittenhouse, Jack D. *The Story of Disturnell's Treaty Map.* Santa Fe: Stage Coach Press, 1965.

Rives, George Lockhart. *The United States and Mexico, 1821–1848.* 2 vols. New York: Charles Scribner's & Sons, 1913.

Ruiz, Ramon, ed. *The Mexican War: Was it Manifest Destiny?* New York: Holt, Rhinehart and Winston, 1963.

Sanchez, David. *Expedition Through Aztlan.* La Puente: Perspectiva Publications, 1978.

Schelling, Thomas C. *The Strategy of Conflict.* Cambridge, Mass.: Harvard University Press, 1963.

Scholes, Walter V., ed., and Elliot B. Scherr, trans. *Mexico During the War with the United States; Documentos ineditos o muy raros para la historia de México,* by Genaro Garcia. Mexico, D.F.: Genaro García y Carlos Pereyra, 1905. The University of Missouri Studies. vol. 23. no. 1. Columbia: University of Missouri, 1950.

Scott, Florence Johnson. *Royal Land Grants North of the Rio Grande, 1771–1821*. Rio Grande City, Texas: La Retaña Press, 1969.

Selva, Salamón de la, trans. *The Bucareli Agreements and International Law*. By Antonio Gómez Robledo. Mexico, D.F.: The National University Press of Mexico, 1940.

Sepulveda, Cesar. *Las Reclamaciones fraudulentes contra Mexico*. Mexico, D.F.: Secretaria de Relaciones Exteriores, 1965.

———. *La frontera norte de Mexico: historia, conflictos 1762–1975*. Mexico, D.F.: Editorial Porrua, 1983.

Sierra, Justo. *Evolución política del pueblo Mexicano*. Ed. Edmundo O'Gorman. *Obras completas del maestro Justo Sierra*. Vol. XIII. 1910. Reprint. Mexico, UNAM, 1948.

Smith, Justin H. *The War with Mexico*. 2 vols. 1919; reprint ed., Gloucester, Mass.: Peter Smith, 1963.

Szekey, Alberto. *Mexico y el derecho internacional del mar*. Mexico, D.F.: UNAM, 1979.

Tennebaum, Barbara A. "Neither a borrower nor a lender be": Financial Constraints and the Treaty of Guadalupe Hidalgo." *The Mexican and Mexican American Experience in the 19th Century*. Ed. Jaime E. Rodríguez O. Tempe, Arizona: Bilingual Review Press, 1989.

Thomas, Jack Ray. *Biographical Dictionary of Latin American History and Historiography*. Westport, Conn.: Greenwood Press, 1984.

Tijerina, Reies. *The Spanish Land Grant Question Examined*. Albuquerque: Alianza Federal, 1966.

Twitchel, Ralph Emerson. *The Leading Facts of New Mexican History*. 2 vols. Reprint, 1911–12; Albuquerque: Horn and Wallace, 1963.

Ulloa, Berta. *La revolución intravenida: Relaciones diplomáticas entre México y los Estados Unidos (1910–1914)*. Mexico, D.F.: Colegio de Mexico, 1971.

Valadés, José C. *Breve historia de la guerra con los Estados Unidos*. Mexico, D.F.: Editorial Patria, 1947.

Valdez, Luis and Stan Steiner, eds., *Aztlan: An Anthology of Mexican American Literature*. New York: Alfred A. Knopf, 1972.

Vasconcelos, Jose. *Breve historia de México*. Mexico, D.F.: Ediciones Botas, 1936.

Sierra, Justo. *The Political Evolution of the Mexican People.* Translated by Charles Ramsdell. Austin: University of Texas Press, 1969.

Weinberg, Albert K. *Manifest Destiny: A Study of Nationalist Expansion in American History.* 1935. Reprint, Chicago: Quadrangle Books, 1963.

Westphall, Victor. *The Public Domain in New Mexico: 1854–1891.* Albuquerque: University of New Mexico Press, 1965.

Zorrilla, Luis G. *Historia de las relaciones entre Mexico y los Estados Unidos de America, 1800–1958.* 2 vols. Mexico, D.F.: Editorial Porrua, 1977.

Index

245